Paul Simpson has been writing

A BRIEF GUIDE TO

C.S. LEWIS

PAUL SIMPSON

ROBINSON

RUNNING PRESS
PHILADELPHIA • LONDON

Constable & Robinson Ltd.
55–56 Russell Square
London WC1B 4HP
www.constablerobinson.com

First published in the UK by Robinson,
an imprint of Constable & Robinson Ltd, 2013

A copy of the British Library Cataloguing in Publication Data is available
from the British Library

UK ISBN: 978-1-47210-066-5 (paperback)
UK ISBN: 978-1-47210-067-2

1 3 5 7 9 10 8 6 4 2
First published in the United States in 2013 by
Running Press Book Publishers,
A Member of the Perseus Books Group

Books published by Running Press are available at special discounts for bulk
purchases in the United States by corporations, institutions and other organi-
zations. For more information, please contact the Special Markets Department
at the Perseus Books Group, 2300 Chestnut Street, Suite 200, Philadelphia, PA
19103, or call (800) 810-4145, ext. 5000, or e-mail
special.markets@perseusbooks.com.

US ISBN: 978-0-7624-5076-3
US Library of Congress Control Number: 2013931825

9 8 7 6 5 4 3 2 1
Digit on the right indicates the number of this printing

Running Press Book Publishers
2300 Chestnut Street
Philadelphia, PA 19103-4371

Visit us on the web!
www.runningpress.com

Typeset by TW Typesetting, Plymouth, Devon

Printed and bound in the UK

This one is for my father, Ian Howden-Simpson,
who I have no doubt is delighted
that I've moved away from spaceships and spies
to deal with far more important topics!

CONTENTS

3 The Religious Writings

'I think there's an alchemy to life. Call it what you will – circumstance, fate, magic – but it's always felt to me like there's an underlying pattern that brings together certain people in the same place at the right time. You can't force it. It just has to happen. And when it does, when those pieces come together . . . sometimes they make something really special. But part of what makes those mixtures special is that they never last.'

Storming Heaven, David Mack

INTRODUCTION

As with so many people across the years, my first introduction to the writings of C. S. Lewis came through the Chronicles of Narnia. On the bookshelf downstairs I still have the original set of seven books which I was given aged around eight, which I read and reread over the years (and which my daughter is now starting to delve into). I was just a little too young for the first televised version of them in 1967 but I remember the broadcast of the animated version at Easter 1980 – with Leo McKern's rendition of Professor Kirke and Sheila Hancock's terrifying White Witch remaining firmly in my memory to this day.

My parents were Christians, and I went to church weekly – as a member of the choir, rather than out of any particular devoutness – but although the parallels of Aslan's sacrifice in *The Lion, the Witch and the Wardrobe* with the events of Christ's Passion were clear, even to a youngster, I never felt that these books were being used as any form of religious instruction. Indeed, until I began researching this guide, I hadn't really seen the connection between *The Horse and His Boy* and the stories of Esther or Moses – it felt as if Lewis had decided simply to write an adventurous story within the Narnia universe. I was never that keen on *The Last Battle*, although it's a story that I've come to appreciate far more as an adult.

An interest in science fiction – more specifically, *Doctor Who* and *Star Trek* – led me to the first readings of Lewis's science-fiction trilogy. *Out of the Silent Planet* was a revelation when I first encountered it, and I eagerly devoured the other Ransom novels, although it did occasionally feel as if I was being preached at in the latter two, far more than I ever felt with the Narnia stories. Around the same time, my father introduced me to *The Screwtape Letters*, which I enjoyed (and listening to them again, as read by John Cleese, I was delighted to find that the tone of voice I had ascribed to them was spot on). I was also reading Giovanni Guareschi's terrific tales of Don Camillo, a little priest by the river Po, who is also caught between a devil and Christ, and the resonance of the two has never left me.

But it was only in later life that I started to learn more about Clive Staples Lewis himself – his journey from religion to atheism and then through theism to Christianity. It wasn't something that was *necessary* to enjoy his fiction writings, but that information has helped me to understand and enjoy them even more. Lewis himself was not a great believer in the idea of making a spectacle of the author; he thought it more important to look at the work. The example of *The Horse and His Boy* mentioned above is a case in point: to a ten-year-old, it was a great excursion into Arabian Nights territory, and I don't think that I lost out by not seeing the other elements at play.

The angle which *The Brief Guide to C. S. Lewis* takes is different from most companions to Lewis's work. Whereas most such books (and biographies of him) are written from a Christian perspective – or, in the case of some of them, an almost deliberately anti-Christian stance – this book isn't going to assume great swathes of biblical scholarship on the part of the reader. Chances are, you've seen one of the big-screen versions of the Chronicles released over the past decade, and want to know more; the fact that Jack Lewis (as he was known) wrote about the problems of praying is important – the specific texts that he discusses and dissects to come to his answers, not so much. We won't get bogged down in large chunks of detailed analysis, but if one of the topics catches your attention, there's hopefully enough to whet your appetite to seek out Lewis's original writing. Many of his key religious pieces were written as talks for radio, and are, sometimes surprisingly, very accessible.

During his lifetime, Lewis received a great deal of praise for his work; it was unfortunate that he wasn't recognized as fully on his death as he might have been. The same day that he passed through the door into Aslan's kingdom, 22 November 1963, the writer Aldous Huxley, creator of *Brave New World*, also died; more importantly, as far as the world's media were concerned, US President John F. Kennedy was assassinated in Dallas, Texas. Both these deaths overshadowed that of an Oxbridge don and broadcaster who had written an enjoyable series of children's stories, but now, on the fiftieth anniversary of his passing, C. S. Lewis is being properly honoured with a memorial in Poets' Corner in Westminster Abbey.

We begin with a biography of Jack Lewis's life, followed by a discussion of his fictional works, and an overview of his religious writings. There are references within the biography to his key works of literary criticism, but these have not received separate entries – those interested in that side of Lewis's work are recommended to read Walter Hooper's *C. S. Lewis: A Companion & Guide*, which summarises these volumes in great detail. The final part of this book looks at the many different versions of his stories that have been created – from radio adaptations and audio recordings to the stage and screen renditions, with new interviews with some of the creative forces behind them.

In *The Lion, the Witch and the Wardrobe*, Lucy, followed by her siblings, enter Narnia through a wardrobe. Hopefully this *Brief Guide to C. S. Lewis* will act as a similar portal to the works of a great writer.

Paul Simpson
March 2013

1. THE LIFE OF JACK LEWIS

I

THE BOXEN YEARS

Much of literature – both fiction and non-fiction – stands up by itself without the reader needing to understand where it came from. The travails of the author do not necessarily communicate themselves in his or her output. However, in the case of Clive Staples Lewis, his life story provides vital clues to comprehending his work. Born into the Protestant branch of Christianity, he renounced his faith, as so many do, during the questioning years of adolescence, but found himself dragged, almost reluctantly, back to the precepts of religion in his early thirties. From thereon it became the prism through which he viewed the world – not just this world, but the many different worlds that he re-imagined or created in his fiction.

Although he was christened Clive Staples following his birth on 29 November 1898, the creator of the Chronicles of Narnia, *The Screwtape Letters* and *The Silent Planet* was known for the vast majority of his life as Jack – a decision he announced to his family at the tender age of four, apparently following the death of a neighbourhood dog known as Jack-sie. He was the second of two boys born to Albert and Flora Lewis at their home, Dundela Villas, in Belfast. His brother Warren Hamilton was three years older, but despite the disparity in age, they were firm friends, referring to each other as 'the Archpigiebotham' and 'the Smallpigiebotham', after a phrase used by their nursemaid Lizzie Endicott.

The Lewis boys had a very happy early childhood in Dundela Villas with their parents. Their father's grandfather had been a Welsh farmer, whose son had emigrated to Ireland, becoming a partner in a shipbuilding firm. Albert James Lewis, Jack's father, was a clever lad, who was educated at Lurgan College, County Armagh, before studying law in Dublin. After qualifying in 1885, he returned to Belfast and started up his own law firm – at this point, the whole of Ireland was still part of Great Britain (the Irish Free State was eventually established in 1922). He became a well-respected solicitor working in the Belfast police courts, although his dreams of entering politics never came to anything.

Jack's mother Flora was the daughter of a Church of Ireland clergyman, who came from a long line of clerics – while her husband's great-grandfather was tending sheep, hers had been the Bishop of Ossory. Flora was well educated and spent part of her childhood in Rome when her father, the Reverend Thomas Hamilton, was chaplain of Holy Trinity Church there, before returning to Ireland in 1874. She read Mathematics at the Royal University of Ireland (now Queen's University) in Belfast, initially gaining First Class Honours in Geometry and Algebra in 1881, then First Class Honours in Logic and Second Class Honours in Mathematics in 1885.

The Lewis and Hamilton families knew each other – Flora's father was the Rector of St Mark's, Dundela, at which the Lewises worshipped – and in 1886, Albert began to court Flora. She, however, was not interested in him as anything more than a friend, but he was not put off. It took seven years before she consented to marry him, even then freely wondering if she really loved him, or was simply very fond of him. They wed in 1894, and Warren arrived a year later.

Jack Lewis's autobiography, *Surprised by Joy*, paints a rosy picture of the decade before his mother's death from cancer in 1908. He describes his blessings as 'good parents, good food and a garden (which then seemed large) to play in' as well as his nurse Lizzie and brother Warren (or 'Warnie', as Jack referred to him). The pair would spend hours drawing and telling stories: Warren was inclined towards pictures of ships, trains or battles, while Jack began a lifelong interest in anthropomorphizing animals. He created 'Animal-Land' in which dressed animals roamed, the precursors of the Talking Beasts of Narnia, after reading the books of Beatrix Potter, whose second animal tale, *Squirrel Nutkin*, was published three months before Jack's fifth birthday.

Books were everywhere in the Lewis household: both his parents were avid readers, and one of Jack's lasting impressions of his childhood was when the family moved in April 1905 to a new, bigger house, overlooking the Belfast Lough, and every room seemed filled with piles of volumes. The young Lewis boys were encouraged to dive into this treasure trove of writing, particularly as they spent a lot of time indoors since their parents were petrified in case they fell ill. The older Lewises may not have been great admirers of fantasy, but young Jack had been brought up with Irish folk tales and legends told to him by his nursemaid Lizzie: stories about the Daoine Sidhe, the Tuatha Da Danaan and the Milesians. Albert and Flora may have disapproved of this encouragement but it led him to love the romance of Coleridge, and Mark Twain's *A Connecticut Yankee in King Arthur's Court*. He went on to lap up E. Nesbit's stories when they were printed in the *Strand* magazine during the first few years of the twentieth century, as well as Sir Arthur Conan Doyle's chivalrous tale *Sir Nigel*.

The new house, Little Lea, would become 'almost a major character in my story', Lewis admitted. There were huge spaces in its eaves, through which the two boys could crawl

and make up adventures when Warren wasn't away at boarding school, and where Jack would listen to the 'distant noises
of gurgling cisterns and pipes and the noise of wind under
the tiles'. He made a study for himself in one of the attics,
decorating the walls with pictures cut out from magazines or
drawn himself, and, seated at a special desk that his parents
arranged to be made for him, wrote tales of chivalrous mice
and rabbits who rode out in full chainmail to do battle with
cats. Together with Warnie, he developed Animal-Land, a
decidedly modern fantasy world, which was linked by trains
and steamships with India (Warnie's preferred locale) to eventually become the land of Boxen (see part 2, chapter 1, for a
detailed look at these stories, which Lewis described as his
training to be a novelist).

During that period, Lewis had three experiences which he
talked about as critical to the development of his imagination.
The first was a 'memory of a memory': Lewis recalled being
at Little Lea and remembering a moment at their old house
when Warnie had brought a toy garden that he had made
inside the lid of a biscuit tin into the nursery. It was the first
time that Jack really appreciated nature, and the memory of
that incident incited a desire for something which he couldn't,
as yet, quantify.

The second came through re-readings of *Squirrel Nutkin*,
which led to Lewis becoming enamoured of 'the Idea of Autumn',
as odd as he himself admitted that sounded. Once again, he
knew he was feeling a desire which he could not explain.

The final experience derived from his reading of American
author Henry Wadsworth Longfellow's poem *The Saga of
King Olaf*, which tells the story of a Norwegian king who is
encouraged by the Norse god Thor to reclaim his throne. The
section entitled 'Tegner's Drapa' relates the death of Balder
the Beautiful, and when Lewis read that he once again had
this same desire. In all three instances, Lewis felt 'an unsatisfied desire which is itself more desirable than any other satisfaction', a feeling he came to describe as 'Joy'.

Jack missed his brother, who had been sent to school at Wynyard House, near Watford, in May 1905. While he waited for Warnie's presence during the holidays, he was taught maths, French and Latin by his mother and otherwise educated by a governess, Miss Hooper. Jack, Warnie and their mother travelled to France in September 1907 – one of the very few occasions in his life that Lewis would take a foreign holiday – and that Christmas, Jack began a diary, describing the way of life at Little Lea, with his grandfather now staying with them because of his gradually deteriorating health.

Everything was to change for the Lewis boys in 1908. In February, his mother, who had been feeling ill for some time, was operated on at the house, and the surgeon discovered she had cancer. Despite constant nursing care and some respite, she died on 23 August, Albert's birthday. Her father-in-law, who had been asked to leave Little Lea during Flora's illness, had suffered a stroke on 24 March, and died eight days later. To compound Albert's grief, his older brother Joe died two weeks after Flora.

It is clear from *Surprised by Joy* that Jack felt his father was not able to cope with his wife's impending death and give his sons the love they needed. Indeed, he talks about the alienation which the two boys felt, and that, as a result, his father was not just losing his wife, but also his sons. Certainly the brothers clung together more in the weeks following their mother's death, and were to be united at school, since the decision had already been taken to send Jack to join Warnie at Wynyard that September.

To get a barometer of Jack Lewis's feelings towards his first school, the chapter of his autobiography which covers this period is called 'Concentration Camp', and he refers to it as Belsen, the name of one of the first Nazi concentration camps relieved by Allied forces, which became synonymous with the evils of that regime. Wynyard was run by a sadistic headmaster, the Reverend Richard Capron, who flogged boys for the slightest offence, but despite desperate pleas from his boys, Albert Lewis didn't remove them. On Capron's recommendation, Warnie progressed to Malvern College in the autumn of 1909, leaving Jack at Wynyard, but following a court case against Capron brought by one of the parents, the school was shut at the end of the summer term, and in autumn 1910, Jack was sent to Campbell College, the local public boarding school in Belfast.

Wynyard and Capron – the latter Lewis never names in *Surprised by Joy* but refers to by the man's schoolroom nickname of 'Oldie' – both had a lasting effect on Lewis. He learned the benefits of the friendship of a group of close friends, as the five remaining boarders at Wynyard banded together. He also became a believer in Christianity; although his grandfather had spent much of his time muttering from the Book of Psalms during his time living with them, and his father was a very pious man, this appears not to have had that much influence on Jack. It was at Wynyard that he heard Christian doctrine explained by men who clearly believed it. It wasn't the Protestantism of his maternal grandfather – who was known to preach against the evils of Catholicism, in a city that was already riven by religious hatred – but a 'High Church' variant of Anglicanism, known as 'Anglo-Catholicism'. This version of the faith adopts many of the trappings of Catholicism – the use of incense, and bells for example – but within a Protestant framework, where the authority of the Pope is not accepted as God's right hand on Earth.

Although he claimed that his reading deteriorated during his time at Wynyard, it's clear that some of Lewis's tastes were formed during this period: in particular, he recalled reading the scientific romances of H. G. Wells, whose novels *The Time Machine* and *The War of the Worlds* excited the young man. He also dived into historical dramas such as *Ben-Hur* and *The Last Days of Pompeii*, perhaps, as some have suggested, because of their scenes of cruelty which matched the life he was being forced to live. Another influence became felt around this time: one of his mother's second cousins, Hope Ewart, accompanied Jack to a performance of J. M. Barrie's *Peter Pan* in London. From the references to this visit in his various letters, it obviously had a great effect on him, far more so than the musical comedies and vaudeville acts which his father would take him and his brother to see at the theatre in Belfast.

Jack's period at Campbell College was extremely short-lived: in November he came back from the school for his usual Sunday afternoon visit with a very bad chesty cough, and his father decided to find an alternate place for him, hopefully near Malvern College, where Warnie was studying. Although Jack suffered from the rough-and-tumble life that characterized some public schools of the period, he gained some benefit from his meagre time in the Belfast establishment: he was introduced to Matthew Arnold's poem *Sohrab and Rustum*, which tells how a great warrior unknowingly kills his son in single combat. This opened his eyes to the wonders of poetry, even if he didn't necessarily appreciate the ways in which it worked at the time.

The two Lewis brothers made their way from Belfast to Malvern in January 1911, beginning a routine that saw them catch the last possible train south from Liverpool so they could enjoy some free time there, reading and smoking (Jack began his lifelong nicotine habit aged twelve). While Warnie headed for the main college, Jack was ensconced at Cherbourg preparatory school, where he stayed until July 1913. During this time, he would lose his nascent Christian faith, blaming it on the lax religious views of the matron, Miss Cowrie, and her dismissal from the school; the influence of, and Jack's infatuation, with an apparently sophisticated young master known as Pogo; and an adolescent questioning as to why Christianity should dare to call itself the one true faith, when it was clear that there were many other religious ideas and faiths in the world. What replaced it to a large extent was a growing interest and devotion to the Norse myths, which was magnified when Jack was exposed to the music of Richard Wagner, as well as a normal teenage interest in the opposite sex.

Lewis's love of what he called 'pure Northernness' was incited by seeing Arthur Rackham's illustrations for a version of *Siegfried* and *Twilight of the Gods* which was printed in the Christmas edition of the *Bookman* magazine in December 1911, depicting Siegfried gazing in wonder at the sleeping, half-naked Brünhilde. It brought back that feeling of Joy that he had experienced when reading the Longfellow poem a few years earlier. Over the following six months, Jack read synopses of Wagner's Ring cycle in the magazine *Soundbox*, enabling him to taste the full story of the great Germanic operas. As well as penning his own poem based on Wagner's vision of the Nibelung story, he began to collect records of the operas. In later life, he would claim that this period marked his return from exile and desert lands to his own country.

Jack did well at Cherbourg, receiving acclaim for his writing, with two essays appearing in the school magazine; the opposite was true of his brother at Malvern. Although Warnie would later write a glowing account of his time at the college for an edition of the college paper (mainly to try to counter the very negative image that Jack gave of the place in *Surprised by Joy*), he was by no means a star pupil. Despite his being a prefect, his rule-breaking was so considerable that when he was caught smoking once too often, he was asked to leave at the end of the spring term 1913, a few weeks before his brother was due to sit the entrance exam (during which Jack was ill, and only achieved a second-class scholarship, rather than the higher level which his studies would seem to have merited).

As Jack headed to Malvern in September 1913 to begin his short time there, Warnie was travelling to Great Bookham in Surrey to begin preparations for the entrance examination for the officers' training college at Sandhurst with his father's old headmaster, William T. Kirkpatrick. Known as 'The Great Knock', Kirkpatrick would have a great effect on Jack himself when he too was sent for private education at Great Bookham the following September.

2

MALVERN COLLEGE AND GREAT BOOKHAM

Jack Lewis had high expectations of Malvern College, but, if you believe the account that he gives in *Surprised by Joy*, these were dashed pretty quickly. It's important to note that many of his contemporaries, in particular his brother Warnie, did not agree with Lewis's assessment of the college in the period leading up to the Great War, in particular his insistence that the primary topic of conversation among the pupils was the homosexual relationships that existed between some – or, according to Lewis, many – of them.

Lewis also didn't like the 'fagging' system that existed at Malvern College: junior boys were expected to be at the beck and call of their seniors, irrespective of what they might have to do otherwise themselves. Since he wasn't particularly good at games, partly because of a congenital defect in his thumbs (like his father's, Jack's joints didn't bend), and he wasn't physically attractive enough to be one of the 'Tarts' (the younger boys adopted by their seniors), he didn't fit into the college way of life as easily as he had at Cherbourg. When Warnie visited the college at the end of the autumn term, he noticed that Jack was gloomy and bored, and when Jack's pleadings to be allowed to leave Malvern seemed to be gaining ground with their father in the spring term, Warnie wrote to Albert noting that many of Jack's problems were of his own making. With the benefit of hindsight, though, Warnie did accept that public school wasn't right for Jack: even aged fourteen, he would have fitted more easily into an undergraduate environment than what he called 'the collective-minded and standardizing Public School system'.

Jack didn't dislike everything about Malvern, and was prone to exaggerate the elements he hated – in fact, he admits as much in *Surprised by Joy*. The school library, known as the Grundy, was a place of sanctuary for him, as well as the source of more material to feed his Northern obsession. He found a copy of the *Corpus Poeticum Boreale*, a translation and reworking of Norse mythological poems from the Elder Edda, which he used to help with the play he was writing, *Loki Bound*. This took the form of a Greek tragedy dealing with Norse subjects, contrasting the sad wisdom of Loki with the 'brutal orthodoxy' of his half-brother Thor (a not particularly subtle dig at those he disliked at Malvern, since Thor was their symbol), and Lewis was self-aware enough to realize that he was imbuing Loki with his own sense of 'priggish superiority'.

He also felt blessed to have Harry Wakelyn Smith – or Smewgy, as Lewis calls him in *Surprised by Joy* – as his form master. Smith introduced him to Greek drama with Euripides' *Bacchae*, as well as Latin and English poetry, and took great pleasure in reading poems aloud to the class showing Lewis the 'right sensuality of poetry, how it should be savoured and mouthed in solitude'. From there Lewis began to discover the joys of John Milton's poetry and became so enamoured of the Irish poet W. B. Yeats that he asked his father for a copy of his own. That led to an interest in Celtic mythology in addition to Norse, an addiction which he discovered that he shared with a new friend that he made when he returned home during the Easter vacation.

Arthur Greeves wasn't, strictly speaking, a new friend for Jack. The Greeves family had been neighbours at Little Lea for many years, and when a telephone was installed at the house in 1907, Jack had made the first call to Arthur, who was Warnie's contemporary in age. However, the strong bond between Jack and Warnie meant that few others were able to break into their private world. Now, with Warnie away at the Royal Military College at Sandhurst, Jack was told that Greeves was convalescing from an illness and would appreciate a visit from his neighbour. When he went over, he was astounded to find that Greeves was reading H. M. A. Guerber's *Myths of the Norsemen*, the very book Jack adored. As they discovered a shared love of Northernness, a great friendship sprang up between the two, which would last throughout Jack's life; the letters which they exchanged, published in 1979, give great insight into Jack's development and state of mind across the decades.

Jack's dislike, bordering on hatred, of Malvern led him to write home threatening to take his own life if he wasn't removed from the school, and eventually Albert agreed to take him out, and send him to Kirkpatrick's school in Great Bookham. Lewis didn't let his schoolmates know that he wasn't returning in September, although he did pen a poem praising Smewgy which may have acted as a hint to some.

Instead of a college filled with people with whom he felt he had little or nothing in common, Jack Lewis was to spend the next two and a half years having a thoroughly enjoyable time. Kirkpatrick's methods were unorthodox, to say the least, but they were exactly what the young Lewis needed to stretch his mind and intellect. A casual comment when he first met his tutor, that Surrey seemed 'wilder' than he had anticipated, led to the demolition of his comment by the application of logic, with Jack eventually admitting that he had nothing on which to base his comment. Greek epic poems became a race between tutor and pupil: Kirkpatrick would read aloud twenty lines, then translate them, give Jack a few explanatory comments, and then leave him to work out the exact translation. After a few weeks of this, Jack found that he was starting to think in ancient Greek – the mark of someone who has become fluent in a new language.

Lewis flourished under the tutelage of the Kirkpatricks – Mrs Kirkpatrick taught French with the same unusual methodology as her husband. Kirkpatrick called Jack 'the most brilliant translator of Greek plays I have ever met' although his knowledge of the sciences was minimal. '[He] knows nothing of science and loathes it and all its works,' Kirkpatrick wrote to Albert Lewis in May 1916.

Jack's life didn't extend beyond Great Bookham except for occasional visits back to Ireland and time spent with Warnie when his brother was on leave from the Western Front. He had been appointed a second lieutenant in September 1914, and that November was sent to France as part of the British Expeditionary Force fighting the Great War, which had begun in August that year following the German invasion of Belgium. There were trips to London, but for the majority of the time, Lewis turned inward, reading voraciously. In November 1914, he was investigating the work of William Morris; two months later he read *La Morte d'Arthur* for the first time; the summer of 1915, during which he kept a diary, saw him devouring works from Virginia Woolf to *Prometheus Bound* in the original Greek. February 1916 marked his discovery of Spenser's *The Faerie Queene*.

Although it's not perhaps a book that many would find as inspirational as Jack Lewis did, *Phantastes*, by George MacDonald, became a touchstone for him after he picked it up by chance at the local station bookstall in March 1916 (he misremembers the date in *Surprised by Joy*). MacDonald once wrote that his work was for 'the childlike, whether of five, fifty-five or seventy-five' so perhaps it's not so surprising that

Lewis regarded him as his 'master'. First published in 1858, *Phantastes* tells the story of Anodos's travels through Fairy Land, pursued by a shadow self, leading to an act of self-sacrifice and redemption. To Lewis, it had an innocence but also a 'quality of Death, *good* Death'. He would eventually realize that there was a spiritual quality of holiness to the book, which is highly symbolic in style.

During this period, Jack and Arthur Greeves corresponded regularly, discussing – and eventually agreeing not to discuss further – the latter's Christian beliefs (although he was confirmed into the Church in December 1914, Jack Lewis remained an atheist during his time at Malvern and Great Bookham); their shared love of books, with each recommending works to the other; and their sexual fantasies, which in Lewis's case veered towards the sadomasochistic. He signed one letter 'J. Philom.', an abbreviation for philomatrix, the Greek for 'lover of the whip', and admitted to having fantasies about whipping members of Greeves's family.

By late 1916, the Great War wasn't going well for the Allies, and although Lewis could have avoided conscription by dint of his Irish birth or by attending an Irish university, he seemed determined to match his brother and do his bit for the war effort. Knowing that he would become liable for military service a month after entering Oxford, he took the entrance scholarship in Classics in December (claiming that he was a student from Malvern College), and was accepted by his second choice, University College. He still had to take the 'Responsions' exam in March before he could become a member of the university, but would then be allowed to 'come up' to Oxford the following month, joining the Officers' Training Corps (OTC) there. Jack failed the mathematics part of the paper, but was still permitted to go to the university while he prepared to re-sit it. As events transpired, he never did pass the exam; the requirement was waived for those who had been in the service after the Great War, otherwise he would not have been permitted to start his career there.

Lewis's first taste of Oxford in the Trinity term of 1917 matched his idyllic view of it. The university and town were very quiet, since so many of those who should have been cycling around its environs were instead busily fighting to stay alive in the trenches of the Western Front, and Jack was given very impressive rooms that had belonged to a student who was in France. The Dean refused to give him a reading plan, since the OTC would be taking up the majority of his time. He therefore filled his hours with reading in the Library of the Union Society, and spending time on and in the river.

However, on 10 June, with the short university term now over, Lewis was moved from the comparative comfort of University College to Keble College, which was being used as a military barracks. Not only was it much sparser than he was used to, but he was forced to share his accommodation. However, the young Irishman with whom he was thrown by the luck of the alphabet would become one of the most important people in Jack Lewis's life: Edward Francis Courtenay Moore, known to all as Paddy. Less than six months later, the pair were on their way to the horrors of the Western Front.

3

THE GREAT WAR AND OXFORD

Although he managed to spend some of his time living in his University College rooms, Jack Lewis soon had to devote his life to the OTC. During the training, he became increasingly close to Paddy Moore, as well as Paddy's family: Moore's forty-five-year-old mother, Janie, and sister Maureen, had moved from Bristol to Oxford to be near him. The strength of the burgeoning friendship was shown when Jack chose to spend the majority of the month's leave he was granted after gaining his temporary commission on 26 September 1917 with the Moores in Bristol, rather than returning to Little Lea to see his father, causing a further rift between the two generations. It was during this holiday that Maureen heard Jack and Paddy promise each other that should something fatal happen to either one of them while they were on active service, the survivor would look after the other's parent (Janie Moore had separated from Paddy's father in 1907). It was a promise that Jack would keep for over a quarter of a century and would lead most scholars to suppose that their relationship was intimate.

Paddy was posted to the Rifle Brigade and crossed to France ahead of Jack; Lewis spent a few days with his father in Belfast before being sent to the Somerset Light Infantry's headquarters in South Devon in mid-October. On 15 November, he was given forty-eight hours' final leave before reporting to Southampton for embarkation for service at the front; apparently not understanding the importance of the telegram Jack sent him alerting him to his departure, Albert Lewis failed to come to see his son before he left.

Jack Lewis arrived on the front line on his nineteenth birthday, 29 November 1917, and was surprised to find that his former teacher, 'Pogo', was the captain to whom he reported. ('Pogo', alias Captain P. G. K. Harris, had a distinguished war record, receiving the Military Cross and Bar for his bravery in the final weeks of the war.) He was billeted in a town behind the lines, and at some point over the next five months captured sixty German soldiers, all of whom, to Lewis's evident relief, had their hands up in surrender already.

After falling ill with trench fever in February and spending some time in hospital, he returned to the lines in March in time for the First Battle of Arras, which raged between the 21st and 28th, and then the following month for the Battle of Hazebrouck. He gained a great admiration for the sergeants who were able to minimize the danger caused by the inexperienced officers who were being dispatched to the front line, mentioning Sergeant Ayres by name. *Surprised by Joy* contains descriptions of his time in the trenches, but Lewis maintained in later years that 'it is too cut off from the rest of my experience and often seems to have happened to someone else.'

Ayres was killed by the same shell as wounded Lewis during Hazebrouck. Jack received shell fragments in the back, which fractured a rib, as well as causing other superficial tissue damage. Warnie rushed to visit him in the hospital at Etaples, before Jack was sent back to England, arriving at the Endsleigh Palace Hospital on 25 May 1918. Once again, despite pleas from his son, Albert Lewis failed to cross the Irish Sea to visit him.

It seems probable that it was during this convalescence that the relationship with Janie Moore became more than just a friendship. Lewis glosses over the period in *Surprised by Joy*, simply noting that a 'huge and complex episode' was being quite deliberately omitted, since he was neither free to write about it, nor felt it relevant to the thrust of his writing – his journey towards Christianity. Janie Moore by this stage was highly worried about Paddy, who had been reported missing around the same time that Jack returned to England. In September, his death was confirmed (the War Office had written earlier to Paddy's father in Ireland, who had failed to pass the information on to his wife), and Mrs Moore wrote to Albert Lewis praising Jack's 'wonderful power of understanding and sympathy'. When Jack was posted to the Officers' Command Depot in Eastbourne, East Sussex, in October, she and Maureen took digs nearby. She had lost her son; Jack had been motherless since the age of nine: a growing deepness between them was inevitable.

That autumn saw Jack's first professional sale, a lyric cycle he had written before and during his time in the Army initially entitled *Spirits in Prison*, a phrase taken from the First Epistle of St Peter in the New Testament. He was even granted an audience with the publisher William Heinemann himself, who praised the quality of the poetry by an author who was still a few weeks shy of his twentieth birthday (although he did give him notes for improvements, which Jack incorporated). At the suggestion of his father, Jack changed the title to *Spirits in Bondage*, and it was published the following March as by 'Clive Hamilton'. A month earlier, *The Forsyte Saga* author John Galsworthy deemed the poem 'Death in Battle' worthy of inclusion in his literary magazine *Reveille*. This affirmation of his talents, combined with the removal of a threat of return to the front line following the Armistice on 11 November 1918, meant that Jack Lewis was able to consider a future at Oxford and regard himself as a poet.

After a Christmas holiday at Little Lea, Jack returned to Oxford in January 1919 for the Lent term. Now he no longer needed to sit the Responsions, he could begin his studies in earnest. Although he could have also opted not to take the first part of his Classics degree – the Honour Moderations, known as 'Mods', in Latin and Greek literature – he was told that if he wanted an academic career, following the whole course was advisable. His first four terms therefore saw him rereading a lot of material he had previously studied at Great Bookham with Kirkpatrick.

Lewis made friends with various of his contemporaries, including the man he would come to describe as his 'Second Friend', Owen Barfield. Arthur Greeves was the First Friend, a man who shared his tastes in most things; with Barfield, he disagreed on virtually everything, notably religion. However, his key relationship was still with Mrs Moore, who, together with daughter Maureen, moved back to Oxford to be near Jack. Lewis took the obligation to look after her seriously, and, although it was a large drain on his finances, he contributed towards her rent and spent as much time with her as he could, within the confines of his university life (where such a relationship would be grounds for 'rustication' – being sent away from Oxford for a term or more). Lewis's father was not keen on the relationship, and it led to problems during the long vacation from June to October that year, when Jack tried to broker his time between Oxford and Belfast. When he did eventually go home, without Mrs Moore in tow, there were serious arguments with his father, and Jack left early.

At the end of the Lent Term 1920, Jack passed his Mods with First Class honours, and went on a walking holiday with Mrs Moore. He then embarked on the second part of the Classics course (the 'Greats'), continuing to juggle university and domestic life with the Moores. During these studies, he won the Chancellor's English Essay Prize for an essay on optimism, and had the chance to meet W. B. Yeats in person – although Lewis wasn't impressed with the way in which the Irish poet presented himself, in a room lit only by huge church candles, talking about magic and apparitions. He found it hard to comprehend that intelligent people could be sitting having a rational conversation about the supernatural, even if Yeats's poetry, like the fiction of MacDonald, continued to have an effect on him – during this period, Lewis was working on his epic poem *Dymer*, in which the character of the Magician clearly draws on Yeats. In May 1922, Jack Lewis was awarded a First Class degree in Greats.

Turning down the opportunity to become a Classics tutor at Reading University, mainly because he didn't want to move Maureen Moore from the school in Oxford at which she was doing well, and didn't fancy the daily commute to the university, Lewis decided to pursue an Oxford fellowship. He desperately wanted to be free of any financial obligation to his father – who, despite Jack's beliefs to the contrary, was happy to support him until a suitable post appeared – and so took on a job teaching in the English School while he took a degree in English Literature. He wasn't simply providing for himself: by now he was in what his brother later described as 'a joint establishment' with Mrs Moore, which 'bound him to her service' for the rest of her life, while Maureen's school was fee-paying and a drain on their limited resources.

After failing to gain a classical fellowship at Magdalen College in September 1922, Jack began working in the English school, and started studying for the degree, cramming what was normally a two-year course into a single cycle. The following spring, he met fellow Irishman Nevill Coghill, the first of the group that would become known as the Inklings, who presented a paper to the English class that Lewis was attending. The two quickly became friends, going for long walks to discuss the books they were studying and discovering. At the end of the summer, both were awarded First Class Honours in English Language and Literature.

Lewis had achieved this despite some of the domestic pressures on him. As he recounted (although never in a way that indicated that he was complaining), he would regularly sit down to work and be called to deal with some household need of Janie Moore – putting up curtains, going to the shops, or dealing with her brother, 'the Doc', who apparently suffered from brain problems caused by syphilis or post-traumatic stress after his experiences during the war. He was eventually committed in March 1923, and died the following month.

However, the outlook for Lewis's prospects seemed bleak. His scholarship from University College, which had continued during his English degree, had come to an end, and all he had to survive on was the £85 paid by his father annually, and what little he could make from marking exam papers and tutoring a school student. In February 1924, he was told about a possible fellowship in philosophy at Trinity, but realized that this might break up his home life. Despite this, he was eager to take the post, and when a temporary position at University College was offered for the following year, working as a philosophy tutor, Lewis checked to make sure that it wouldn't be an obstacle to his taking the Trinity job, if it were offered. While waiting for further news, he continued work on his poem *Dymer*, and spent time in discussion with Coghill, who was now a fellow in English at Exeter College.

Lewis enjoyed his time acting as philosophy tutor, even though it meant that he was living with Mrs Moore and Maureen only at weekends and in the holidays. Although only four people attended his first lecture, thanks to a mix-up, its reception gave him confidence, and he relished the time spent with the students. However, he was always conscious that it was only a temporary fix to his problems, and the fellowship at Trinity seemed as far away as ever. He therefore applied for any fellowships in either philosophy or English that were being offered.

When a fellowship in English at Magdalen College was mooted, Lewis was dubious about his chances, but the fact he had read both Greats and English told in his favour, since the college believed that few undergraduates would want to read English, which was then still a new subject for university study. After dining at High Table at the college and various interviews, Lewis was elected to the fellowship on 20 May 1925. The first thing he did was to write to thank his father for the faith in him, and the financial support that Albert had provided while Jack was seeking to achieve his goal. For the first time in many years, father and son were no longer at loggerheads, and Jack Lewis had found a post in which he would remain for nearly three decades.

4

FELLOWSHIP AND FATHER

The first years of Jack Lewis's time as Fellow at Magdalen College were marked by the deterioration in health of his father and his own conversion back to religious belief – although not at this point to Christianity. During the latter half of the 1920s was also when he met one of the key influences in his life, J. R. R. Tolkien, who would go on to become as famous in the fantasy field as Lewis himself with his Tales of Middle-earth including *The Hobbit* and *The Lord of the Rings*.

Lewis's responsibilities were to deliver lectures, involve himself as required in the administration of the college, and to act as a tutor to all those who were studying English at Magdalen. In the one-to-one tutorial sessions, Lewis could communicate his love of language and help the maturing students, including, during his first year, John Betjeman, to their own informed opinions on the subject. He also lectured at the women's college, Lady Margaret Hall, and taught philosophy at Magdalen. Coupled with the increasing demands that Mrs

Moore made on him through her perceived increasing ill-health, it meant that Lewis had little time for his own writing.

However, he did manage to complete work on his epic poem *Dymer*. When he showed it to Nevill Coghill in February 1926, his friend was so impressed that he arranged for it to be printed by J. M. Dent & Sons, after Heinemann had turned it down. Unfortunately, this second publication, which was also ascribed to 'Clive Hamilton', didn't bring Lewis any more general acclaim than had *Spirits in Bondage* six years earlier.

May 1926 saw the majority of the country dealing with the effects of the General Strike, which ran from the 4th to the 13th. In Oxford, they had weightier concerns: a newcomer to the Faculty of English was suggesting that the study of Victorian literature should be removed from the syllabus in order to allow proper time for study of the Old English poets. The man responsible was the new Rawlinson and Bosworth Professor of Anglo-Saxon, who had been appointed at the same time as Jack Lewis arrived at Magdalen: J. R. R. Tolkien. Although Lewis had been warned against trusting either Papists or philologists (those who love language, literally), and Tolkien was both, he was charmed by the new arrival, and soon became part of his reading circle, the Kolbitar, who met to read the Icelandic sagas in their original Old Norse language.

The last time that Albert, Jack and Warnie were together came at the end of 1926, before Warnie set sail for China for a new posting there the following April. Just over a year later, Albert retired from his work as a solicitor, but this period of leisure was to be short-lived. In July 1929, Albert was diagnosed with bowel cancer, and across that long summer holiday, Jack dutifully nursed him at Little Lea. With the new term rapidly approaching, Jack agreed to his father entering a nursing home; four days after Jack returned to Oxford, on 25 September 1929, his father died.

By this time, Jack was already on the course that would lead him to become one of the chief proponents of Christianity in the mid-twentieth century. Many of his closest friends – including Arthur Greeves, Owen Barfield, Hugo Dyson and J. R. R. Tolkien – were all Christians, and as he phrased it in *Surprised by Joy*, in the Trinity term of 1929, he 'gave in and admitted that God was God, and knelt and prayed', describing himself as 'the most dejected and reluctant convert in all England'. He had come to this turn of events after rereading Euripides' play *Hippolytus*, and realizing that he couldn't hide from his emotions all his life, nor could he wear what felt to him like an outward suit of armour that was preventing him, rather than protecting him, from a great experience. As far as he was concerned – and he makes this point forcefully in *Surprised by Joy* – his realization of the truths was not linked to his father's last illness and death, which coincided with the way his mind was working rather than causing it. He was worried that readers would feel that he had gained 'redemption by parricide' and use that as an argument against him.

During the autumn of 1929, Jack became closer to Tolkien, and was one of the first people to read his poem The *Lay of Leithian* (which Tolkien never completed). Lewis's criticisms of the work were taken on board by Tolkien, who rewrote the piece to include the suggestions. The following year, Jack bought a house in the Oxford suburb of Headington Quarry, where he would remain for the rest of his life. It was called The Kilns because of the brick-making furnaces that remained in the nine acres of land that surrounded it. He, Mrs Moore and Maureen moved into the property in October 1930; Mrs Moore had previously invited Warnie to live with them, following Albert's death, and he did so for the short period before he departed for his final tour of duty in the Army, which he completed in 1932.

Before Warnie's retirement, Jack Lewis had completed his conversion to Christianity. In September 1931, Jack wrote to Arthur Greeves relating a conversation he had had with Dyson and Tolkien that had gone on until 4 a.m. as the three men discussed metaphor and myth and from there Christianity. Lewis admitted that he had no problem with the idea of a god sacrificing himself in a pagan story, but somehow it was different when it was Christianity involved. The convoluted discussions between the three men culminated in Lewis being much more open to Christian doctrine. According to him, during a trip to Whipsnade Zoo with Warnie, Jack started the journey not believing Jesus Christ was the Son of God, and by the time they reached the zoo, he did – not because he had analysed the situation in particular detail during the trip, but simply because he 'woke up' to the truth.

The 1930s saw Lewis become a fixture on the Oxford landscape, reading, writing, enjoying his teaching duties. Students equally enjoyed his lectures and tutorials when they would find themselves challenged in the same way as Jack had been by Kirkpatrick at Great Bookham. During the vacations, Jack would undertake research and in the summer go on long walking holidays, usually with Warnie, visiting the West Country and Wales.

Although he didn't keep a diary, Jack wrote regularly to Arthur Greeves, mentioning in June 1930 a fantasy novel entitled *The Moving Image* that he was embarking upon, hoping to write four pages a week. Between his various responsibilities, this came to nothing, and no trace of it has been discovered beyond the references in correspondence. He continued work on some of his narrative poems, including *The Queen of Drum* and *The Nameless Isle*, prior to his full turning to Christianity, and after that, he tried to tell the story of his conversion in poetic form, using the trope of a voyage, during the spring of 1932.

After a hectic academic year, Jack Lewis spent some of his summer holiday in 1932 with Greeves in Ireland. Across a fortnight in August, he penned the entire story of *The Pilgrim's Regress*, his updating of John Bunyan's classic story to reflect his own experiences. Greeves was privy to its creation, and Lewis incorporated some of his criticisms – although he retained the intellectual qualities of the book, which matched his own journey, and maintained a more vernacular approach than Greeves approved of. Once Owen Barfield had read it through, Lewis sent the manuscript to J. M. Dent & Sons, who requested him to shorten it before publication. They also wanted to commission illustrations (many editions of Bunyan's *The Pilgrim's Progress* are garnished with woodcuts), but Lewis was able to avoid having these, save the map he created himself.

His next book had been under way for some considerable time before he deemed it ready for publication. Lewis spent eight years researching and writing *The Allegorical Love Poem*, which he offered to the Oxford University Press (OUP) in September 1935. The book was published in May as *The Allegory of Love* (OUP's market research suggested that the word 'allegorical' was off-putting to potential readers). Two further works of literary criticism followed for the OUP before the Second World War: *Rehabilitations* and *The Personal Heresy* (the latter a dialogue with E. M. W. Tillyard).

It was through *The Allegory of Love* that he met one of his greatest friends, and mutual admirers, Charles Williams. According to Lewis's own account, he had heard of the writer on occasion before February 1936 – the author's 'spiritual shockers' had been recommended to Jack, but he hadn't read one – but when he heard Nevill Coghill praising Williams's 1931 novel *The Place of the Lion*, he decided to read it. Within twenty-four hours he had written a fan letter to Williams. The reality was that there was about a two-week gap between Lewis finishing the book and writing to Williams, during which time he recommended it to others. When Williams received the letter, he was amazed, as he was on the verge of writing a letter couched in similarly glowing terms to Lewis, after reading the proofs of *The Allegory of Love*.

By this stage, the group with which Lewis is most associated, the Inklings, had begun to coalesce. It began life as a college literary society, founded at University College by undergraduate Edward Tangye Lean (the brother of *Lawrence of Arabia* director David Lean). He invited Tolkien and Lewis to attend meetings, where unpublished compositions were read aloud and critiqued. This didn't last long, but Lewis, Tolkien and other friends kept the idea going through the 1930s, meeting in Lewis's rooms on Thursday evenings, and in the back parlour of the Eagle and Child pub in St Giles, Oxford, on a Tuesday morning. After his retirement, Warnie joined the group, as did Hugo Dyson, Nevill Coghill, Adam Fox, Owen Barfield, the Lewises' doctor Humphrey Havard, and Lord David Cecil.

The Inklings were the first group to hear portions of Lewis's first science-fiction novel, *Out of the Silent Planet*, which Tolkien recommended to his publisher in March 1938. This was the first of what has become known as the Cosmic Trilogy; what appears to have been planned as the second book in the sequence was abandoned by Lewis a couple of years later (the fragments that are extant were edited and published by Walter Hooper in 1977 as *The Dark Tower*) around the time that he was working on *The Problem of Pain*.

However, everything was to change for Jack Lewis as a result of the declaration of war between Great Britain and Germany on 3 September 1939. By the end of hostilities, he would become one of the most renowned Christian debaters in the world.

5

WARTIME SERVICE

In an article in *The New Republic* in April 1944, broadcaster Alistair Cooke, whose *Letter from America* became a staple for British listeners in the second half of the twentieth century, made an attack on 'the alarming vogue of C. S. Lewis', which he said was a consequence of war's tendency to 'spawn so many quack religions and Messiahs'. It seems that Cooke was offended by Jack being 'pitchforked . . . into the limelight for in doubting times completely unremarkable prophets are pressed into making a career of reassurance.'

One has to wonder if Cooke actually read or listened to any of the material that Jack Lewis wrote during the war, since *The Problem of Pain*, *The Screwtape Letters* and the broadcasts that were written up to form *Mere Christianity* were hardly bland reassurance to Allied forces that God was on their side and that all would be all right with the world. Jack Lewis was uncompromising about what God wanted, and the fact that he was able to communicate that to the listener and reader is what brought him acclaim. As he himself mentioned in *The Problem of Pain*, he could not make the idea of being made perfect through suffering palatable; he could only make the idea not incredible.

Life at The Kilns was fractured by the outbreak of war. Warnie was called back to active duty after seven years of retirement. He was promoted to major in January 1940, but spent several months in a French hospital before being evacuated back to Wales, not long before the remnants of the British Army were picked up from the shores of Dunkirk in late May and early June.

While his brother was away, Jack responded to two separate commissions – to preach before the university at the Church of St Mary the Virgin at the start of October 1939, and to pen a book for a series with the overall title 'Christian Challenge'. Although Jack was used to lecturing in front of a group of undergraduates, ascending into a pulpit was unusual, but he rose to the task, preaching on the topic of culture in wartime, echoing many of the thoughts in his essay *Christianity and Culture* that wartime should not be the excuse to allow a lesser cultural life to take precedence.

Publisher Ashley Sampson, whose Centenary Press had been bought up by Geoffrey Bles in 1930, had read Jack's books and thought he was exactly the sort of writer he wanted for his 'Christian Challenge' series. He asked Jack to tackle 'The Problem of Pain', a perennial sticking point for those questioning the Christian faith: why does God allow suffering? Lewis's book began by querying a number of assumptions people made about God's purpose, which led into a dissection of what pain is and its place in God's plans.

A weekend in the summer of 1940 saw the genesis of one of Jack's most popular works. On Saturday evening, 20 July, while he and Humphrey Havard were listening to Adolf Hitler ranting on the radio, Jack realized how persuasive the German leader was while one was actually listening to him. The next morning he was sitting in Holy Trinity Church at

Headington Quarry (listening to the sermon, according to most stories) and the idea of *The Screwtape Letters* came to him – similarly persuasive letters written by a senior devil to a younger one, instructing him in the ways of tempting humans to sin. He was working on these thirty-one epistles during the autumn, alongside his academic work, and his contribution to the war effort.

Although he was currently too old for active service, Jack was expected to join the Home Guard (as immortalized in the television comedy *Dad's Army*), a group of local defence volunteers. Every Saturday from 10 August 1940 onwards, he donned his uniform and patrolled for three hours at the dead of night around the college grounds. (Even when he became eligible for call-up, Jack's work as a teacher kept him from the draft; he also still had shrapnel in his body from his time in the trenches.)

It was a time of change at The Kilns. On 16 August, Warnie was invalided back to Oxford; eleven days later, Maureen Moore married and moved out. Three schoolgirls were evacuated to Oxford to live at The Kilns, and their presence first set Jack thinking about a tale for children – although it would be nearly another decade before these ideas came to fruition.

In the winter of 1940, Jack was invited to take on a 'travelling lectureship' by Revd Maurice Edwards, the Chaplain-in-Chief to the Royal Air Force. At weekends from the spring of 1941 onwards, Lewis would travel to RAF bases to preach the faith (although he believed that these were singularly unsuccessful); he also accepted an invitation from Sister Penelope, the Mother Superior of the Community of St Mary the Virgin in Wantage, to talk to the junior Sisters. In June, he preached a sermon, now known as 'The Weight of Glory', at the university church, which set out many of the core beliefs that he would expound upon in his most public appearances.

Four months earlier, in February 1941, Jack had received a letter from Dr James W. Welch, the BBC's Director of Religious Broadcasting. Welch had been personally moved by

Jack's insights in *The Problem of Pain* and thought Lewis would be perfect to give a broadcast on 'a positive restatement of Christian doctrine in lay language'. Although Jack disliked the radio (he would occasionally go to the cinema, but generally wasn't impressed with the whole idea of broadcasting), he agreed, but only if he could deliver the lectures in the long summer break, and if he could talk about moral law, rather than Christianity specifically, at least initially. This Welch agreed to, and Lewis thereafter liaised with his assistant, Eric Fenn.

Jack asked Sister Penelope's help with the first batch of four talks, which he wrote and delivered live in August. These received such strong feedback that he was asked to return for a fifth time at the start of September to engage with his critics. The rest of the summer was spent on RAF engagements, writing a second series of talks for the BBC, which had been commissioned immediately, and preparing for college. All the while, *The Screwtape Letters* was appearing in the weekly church paper *The Guardian*, and Jack was dealing with correspondence relating to those.

Lewis had worked on the university authorities to invite Charles Williams to lecture on English Literature, and he attended Williams's talk on Milton in February 1940. This talk was influential on Lewis's own lectures about the poet in December 1941, which were published as *A Preface to 'Paradise Lost'* the following year. *The Screwtape Letters* was also reprinted in book form, first appearing in February 1942.

During the latter part of 1941 and the start of 1942, Jack wrote the second of his Cosmic Trilogy, *Perelandra*, which he described as his favourites among his books – at least until he completed work on *Till We Have Faces* fourteen years later. The second batch of BBC broadcasts, entitled *What Christians Believe*, was delivered in January and February 1942, and a book, combining the text of the first two series, became available in July. The BBC commissioned a third series for broadcast from September to November, although Fenn neglected to warn Jack before he wrote them that they were to be only ten minutes long. Among multiple engagements for the RAF (and their American counterparts following the entry of the USA into the war in December 1941), Jack edited the pieces down, although he retained the originals and used those as the basis of the book version, published in April 1943.

The editors of *The Guardian* were keen to have another contribution from Jack, and he provided a short piece about miracles, which appeared on 2 October 1942. This was the basis of a sermon he preached in Hampstead, London, later that month, and was massively expanded into his book on the topic published in 1947. The Christmas holiday was, in part, spent working on the final story in the Cosmic Trilogy: *That Hideous Strength*. Its descriptions of the Machiavellian machinations within a university college were undoubtedly derived from Jack's own less than pleasant experiences of politics at his own college. Although he was at pains to point out that there was no resemblance between the fictional Bracton College at Edgestow University and Durham University (a similarly small establishment), there were no such protestations about his own home.

Jack was also polishing the lectures he was due to deliver at Durham University. Following his broadcasts about natural law in the first BBC series, he had been invited to give the annual 1943 Riddell Memorial Lectures. He tried these out at the Socratic Society at Oxford – a group of students and others who had been meeting to discuss the 'intellectual difficulties connected with religion in general and Christianity in particular' since the start of 1942. These were then collected and published as *The Abolition of Man* in January 1944. It set out Jack's thesis that there was such a thing as natural law, which he referred to as the 'Tao' and had been applied through the ages, but which was in danger of being ignored, with dangerous consequences for humanity.

During the early part of 1943, Jack completed *That Hideous Strength*, and began work on *The Great Divorce*, which was based on an idea that he had been contemplating for over a decade about souls from Hell taking a 'refrigerium' or holiday in Paradise. Jack read it to gatherings of the Inklings, although Tolkien wasn't very impressed; however, the editors of *The Guardian* were pleased to print it in instalments in the paper from November 1944 to April 1945.

By the time *The Great Divorce* saw print in book form, in January 1946, much had changed. The war in Europe ended in May 1945 and in the Pacific the following August, after the use of atomic bombs at Hiroshima and Nagasaki. On a personal level, Jack lost one of his dearest friends, Charles Williams, who died unexpectedly on 15 May. A collection of essays that Jack and the other Inklings had been intending to give him was published 'as a memorial instead of a greeting'. For Jack, it gave another insight into death: 'It made the next world much more real and palpable.'

6

THROUGH THE WARDROBE

The first post-war term in 1945 saw Jack Lewis pay tribute to Charles Williams with a series of lectures on his old friend's Arthurian poems. He had by this stage completed work on what would prove to be the last of his major Christian apologetics, which was published as *Miracles: A Preliminary Study* in 1947. Various extracts from the book appeared in *The Church of England Newspaper* as well as *The Guardian*, and Lewis was profiled in the former in October 1946 by Ashley Sampson, the man who had first harnessed Lewis's gifts for *The Problem with Pain* just before the war. Sampson didn't pull his punches: Lewis was 'a phenomenon' whose 'theological vision has burst so strangely and with such a wonderful allurement, on our war-torn world'.

It wasn't the only pen portrait of Lewis to appear over the next couple of years. The highly influential *Time* magazine gave him the honour of a cover spot for their feature on him, which appeared in September 1947 just prior to the American publication of *Miracles*. Describing him as 'the man who can put medieval scholasticism into such comfortable modern dress', the *Time* article noted that Lewis was 'not particularly popular with his Oxford colleagues. Some resent his large student following. Others criticize his "cheap" performances on the BBC and sneer at him as a "popularizer".' However, it noted, Lewis was much quieter about his Christian life than might appear at first sight and it mentioned rumours about his living with his elderly mother, although it was known that she had died when he was young. 'One persistent rumour identifies the "mother" as a Mrs Moore, mother of a friend killed in World War I, whom Lewis invited to keep house for him and who is pictured as an aged, bad-tempered old party,' the article speculated.

Mrs Moore was certainly still at The Kilns, and while there is no doubt that she had her difficult side, most Lewis biographers agree that she and Jack had been lovers. However, she found his conversion to Christianity difficult to live with, and as her illnesses increased with old age, so did her bad temper. She spent the majority of 1947 bedridden, with Jack running about after her when necessary. Warnie wasn't a great deal of help – in his diary, he referred to Mrs Moore as 'that horrid old woman'. Warnie himself was to cause Jack some worries: during his annual holiday to Ireland, he went on an alcoholic binge and ended up hospitalized, and Jack had to race to Drogheda to visit him.

The February after *Miracles* was published, a meeting of the Socratic Club heard a 'reply' by Miss G. E. M. Anscombe to 'Mr C. S. Lewis's Argument that "Naturalism" is Self-Refuting'. Although some biographers of Jack have interpreted the ensuing argument as 'misogynist' Lewis against 'feminist' Anscombe, it was really a debate over the manner in which Lewis had made some of his points. Jack was sufficiently persuaded that Anscombe had noted flaws in his clarity (not that she was right, just that he had not expressed himself properly) that he rewrote the relevant portions of *Miracles* prior to its reprint in paperback in 1960 (which explains some of the references to events in 1959 in a book first published twelve years before that).

In August 1948, Jack was visited by American Professor Chad Walsh, from Beloit College in Wisconsin, who was writing a book about Jack (published as *C. S. Lewis: Apostle to the Skeptics* in 1949). At that time, Jack had just started work on his autobiography, *Surprised by Joy*, and was researching and writing his mammoth contribution to the *Oxford History of English Literature* for the Oxford University Press on *English Literature in the Sixteenth Century*. In passing, Walsh mentions that Jack talks of 'completing a children's book which he has begun "in the tradition of E. Nesbit".'

Jack had had vague notions of writing something for children before – among the manuscript for *The Dark Tower* dating from around 1939, there is a single sheet which seems to be the start of a Narnia-esque adventure, introducing four evacuees; and in September 1947 he commented in a letter that the one time he attempted to pen something for children, 'it was, by the unanimous verdict of my friends, so bad that I destroyed it'. This time, though, something clicked.

While dealing with the medical problems of both Mrs Moore and Warnie (who had gone to dry out in a nursing home in February 1949), Jack began dreaming of lions. '[S]uddenly Aslan came bounding into it . . .' he explained some years later to the *Radio Times*. 'Once He was there, He pulled the whole story together, and soon He pulled the other six Narnian stories in after Him.' Portions of the first of these stories, *The Lion, the Witch and the Wardrobe*, were shown to Roger Lancelyn Green in March, who liked them considerably more than Tolkien did – the creator of *The Lord of the Rings* was disparaging about the way in which Lewis treated myth (incorporating Father Christmas, fauns and the White Witch into the story, for example).

It was around this time in the summer of 1949, as Jack was writing Narnia stories considerably faster than they could be published, that Jack himself succumbed to exhaustion, and was ordered to take a rest. However, Warnie, who was becoming increasingly alcoholically dependent, couldn't cope with the idea of looking after Mrs Moore, and he ended up back in hospital instead. Jack didn't get the rest he needed, and became progressively more depressed, particularly when the evening meetings of the Inklings fizzled out that autumn. After Mrs Moore had yet another bad fall, she was sent to a nursing home in April 1950, which alleviated the pressure on Jack, although not on his wallet. He faithfully visited her there every day until her death on 12 January 1951, aged seventy-nine.

By this time, Jack had written four more adventures in Narnia, continuing the adventures of the Pevensie siblings and their cousin Eustace. *A Horn in Narnia* (which was retitled *Prince Caspian* for publication), *The Voyage of the Dawn Treader*, *To Narnia and the North* (better known as *The Horse and His Boy*), were all completed and he was well under way with *The Wild Waste Lands*, which eventually became *The Silver Chair*. Only *The Lion, the Witch and the Wardrobe* had been published, with the others following annually thereafter.

Shortly after Mrs Moore's death, Jack was proposed for the Professorship of Poetry, a Chair at Oxford with a five-year tenure. Although he was a published poet, it wasn't what Jack was best known for, and he was defeated by Cecil Day-Lewis, who was vociferously supported by Enid Starkie, the French scholar of Somerville College. Jack apparently took the news much better than his supporters, and was able to allow himself the luxury of a proper holiday in Ireland that year.

Before then, he had been forced to deal with a woman who had claimed to be 'Mrs C. S. Lewis' and run up huge bills at the Court Stairs Hotel in Broadstairs. Jack took out an injunction of 'Jactitation of Marriage' against the woman, whose real name was Mrs Hooker. This prevented her from 'maliciously boasting' that she was married to Jack, who had told the indignant owner of the hotel when she presented a mass of unpaid bills that he wasn't married. What the apparently confirmed bachelor couldn't have guessed at that point was that when he returned from Ireland, he would meet the woman who would become his wife: Joy Davidman.

Jack was punctilious about responding to 'fan mail', trying wherever possible to send a reply by return of post to those who had been kind enough to correspond with him. This wasn't always practical, and one of Warnie's tasks at The Kilns was to assist Jack with the letters – which meant that when he went off on one of his alcoholic binges, Jack might find himself spending anything up to a couple of hours dealing with mail in the morning before he could contemplate getting on with his own work. This, of course, increased massively once the Chronicles of Narnia (as Roger Lancelyn Green dubbed them) were published, and Jack's readership grew considerably, both in volume and age range.

One letter, which arrived on 10 January 1950, stood out from the rest. It was from an American lady by the name of Mrs W. L. Gresham from the New York area. It no longer exists, so it's impossible to tell what there was about it that 'stood out from the ruck', as Warnie described it, apart from the fact that in general her letters were 'amusing and well-written'.

Much has been written about the relationship between Jack Lewis and Joy Davidman, and perceptions have been altered by the increasing deviance from the genuine story displayed in the stage and film versions of their romance (notably the 1993 movie and its novelization). For those seeking more detail, Brian Sibley's *Shadowlands* is the most accessible account.

Helen Joy Davidman (she never used her first name) was approaching the age of thirty-five when she first wrote to Jack. Born to Jewish parents (who had abandoned their faith before her birth) in New York City, she became an atheist and a Communist during the Depression. With an MA from Columbia University, she was a teacher for a few years before dropping it to be able to concentrate on writing. She worked for the Communist Party as a journalist and critic, and published her first set of poems, *Letter to a Comrade*, in 1938 and her first novel *Anya* two years later, after spending some time as a screenwriter in Hollywood.

While working for the League of American Writers, she met William Lindsay 'Bill' Gresham, a troubled man who already had one short-lived marriage behind him. Gresham had become mentally ill following service in the Spanish Civil War, and turned to psychoanalysis and the Communist Party for support. The two married on 2 August 1942, and they had two children: David, born 27 March 1944, and Douglas, on 10 November 1945.

Gresham was having difficulties with alcohol, and, exacerbated by affairs, was rapidly approaching a mental breakdown, occasionally unleashing physical violence on his wife and children. After a frightening day when Bill thought he was losing his mind, husband and wife sought solace in religion, and became members of the local Presbyterian Church. Both their careers seemed to be improving: Bill's first novel *Nightmare Alley* was published in 1946 and turned into a Hollywood movie; his second book, *Limbo Tower*, appeared in 1949, while Joy's sophomore novel *Weeping Bay* came out the next year.

It was around this time that Joy first encountered C. S. Lewis through Chad Walsh's book about him, which appeared in 1949. She started writing to both Walsh and Lewis, enjoying the intellectual challenge of the give and take with the writers. By this point, Gresham family life had once again deteriorated as Bill took an interest in Zen Buddhism, and embarked on further affairs. Joy had moved out of their bedroom, a tacit acknowledgement that, for her at least, their marriage was over. When her cousin Renee brought her sons to stay, fleeing a violent marriage, Joy began to emulate her style and outlook.

She was working on a book about the Ten Commandments, and brought that with her when she sailed to England in August 1952, after Renee agreed to look after Bill and her sons. Staying with a pen friend, Phyllis Williams, in London, she invited her other regular correspondent, Jack Lewis, to join them for a meal in Oxford. That clearly went well, since Jack reciprocated the hospitality. Further meals followed, and Joy became a regular sight at Jack's side – perhaps to the surprise of his other friends in the male-dominated university community. She was certainly a breath of fresh air in the stuffy environs of Oxford: at her first meeting with Warnie she asked, 'Is there anywhere in this monastic environment where a lady can relieve herself?'

Jack invited her to spend Christmas at The Kilns, during which time Joy received a letter from Bill explaining that he and Renee had fallen in love and asking for a divorce. Given that Joy had intended heading back to New York with a view to saving her marriage, this was something of a shock. She sought Jack's advice, and, perhaps surprisingly given all that he had written about marriage, he told her that she should divorce Bill.

After being on the receiving end of more violence from Bill, Joy realized that divorce was the best option, and agreed, although Bill was unable to follow through for a time because of a shortage of funds. The Greshams were finally divorced on 5 August 1954; the same day Bill and Renee, who had set her own divorce in motion as soon as Joy returned to America, married.

By this point, Joy and her sons had transplanted to England. 'I've become a complete Anglomaniac,' Joy admitted. They arrived in November 1953, and spent some of December in Oxford at The Kilns – where eight-year-old Douglas was delighted to find a huge wardrobe, and even more delighted by Jack's hint that it might even be 'the' wardrobe. Jack had spent the year working on his OUP project, *English Literature in the Sixteenth Century*, as well as the remaining Narnia books. He had had some difficulties working out how to tell the story of Narnia's creation, and had made more than one false start on what eventually became *The Magician's Nephew*. Leaving it aside, he completed writing *The Last Battle* before eventually finishing the chronologically first Narnia book later that year. Shortly before this was submitted for publication in February 1954, Jack's life was shaken up once more.

7

CAMBRIDGE AND MARRIAGE

Whether it was resentment over his perceived popularity with the masses, or concerns that he wouldn't be able to focus on the requirements of the job, Jack Lewis was overlooked for various Chairs at Oxford University over the years. In the end, his elevation to the rank of professor came at 'the other place', as Oxford's greatest rival, Cambridge University, was described. In January 1954, its governing body, the Council of the Senate, decided that the university needed a Professor in Medieval and Renaissance English, and the post was announced as vacant on 31 March. J. R. R. Tolkien was one of the Electors of the Chair, and on 11 May, the decision to elect Jack was unanimous. After some discussion, which centred upon whether or not Jack would need to transplant his whole household from Oxford to Cambridge, something he was not willing to do, Jack accepted the post. Since the Fellowship was not linked to any particular college, Jack was delighted when the Chair was attached to St Mary Magdalene, allowing him, as he explained to Sister Penelope, 'to remain under the same Patroness' as he had been for decades at Oxford.

After a brief holiday in Ireland, Jack returned to Oxford for his final term there, giving his last tutorial on 3 December. September saw publication of his contribution to the *Oxford History of English Literature*, which had taken him the best part of nine years to complete. He spent part of the autumn in London, taking part in a debate alongside Dorothy L. Sayers, and visiting Joy and the boys at their flat; he also found time to give his inaugural lecture in Cambridge, which took place on his fifty-sixth birthday.

Jack took up the Chair officially in January 1955, staying in Cambridge during the week and returning to The Kilns at the weekend. His duties in his new post did not require him to tutor students, and although he no longer had Warnie's help dealing with his correspondence, he had time to start work on a new novel for adults. After discussions with Joy during a visit to The Kilns in March, Jack began to pen what became *Till We Have Faces*, his retelling of the story of Cupid and Psyche. Joy was a great deal of help to him as he wrote, and the book was dedicated to her.

Joy's own book about the Ten Commandments, *Smoke on the Mountain*, was published the same year, and Jack contributed a foreword. To help make ends meet, she was also typing manuscripts for Jack, and assisting Warnie with his own literary works. To further the boys' education, she had arranged for them to go to a private school in Surrey, for which Bill Gresham initially paid the fees. However, after their father defaulted, Jack started to cover the costs. He also paid the rent on a house in Oxford, a mile or so from The Kilns, for her and the boys.

Jack's account of his conversion to Christianity, *Surprised by Joy*, was published in the autumn; around this time, he apparently told Arthur Greeves that he was contemplating marrying Joy in a private civil ceremony. This would allow her to remain in Britain, since the Home Office was refusing to renew her visitor's visa. Jack did not intend to seek a church service; this was purely out of friendship and expediency. They were married at the Registry Office in Oxford on St George's Day, 23 April 1956.

Although Jack had made it clear to Warnie that he didn't expect to live with Joy – she would remain as 'Mrs Gresham' in her own place – events overtook them. Joy was given notice to leave the rented house, but before she and the boys could move in with Jack and Warnie at The Kilns, Joy had an accident on the evening of 18 October 1956, tripping over a telephone wire. The hospital investigations that followed revealed that Joy was suffering from cancer. She was only forty-two but her condition was very serious.

Joy had to undergo three painful operations to remove her ovaries as well as the cancerous parts from her femur and breast, and Jack determined to marry Joy properly, in the eyes of the Church. He went to seek permission from the Bishop of Oxford, on the grounds that Joy's marriage to Bill had been invalid, since Bill had previously been married, and therefore there was no obstacle to a Church of England wedding. The Bishop disagreed – partly, it seems, because he felt that if a public figure like Jack were to marry a divorcee, it would be much harder to prevent others from following suit who didn't have the same technical grounds Jack was presenting. Not happy at the rebuff, Jack realized that to maintain propriety when Joy moved to The Kilns, he would have to make public the earlier marriage. This was done via a very carefully worded message on Christmas Eve in *The Times*, which noted that 'A marriage has taken place between' Jack and Joy, without giving any further details. Writing to Dorothy L. Sayers, Jack commented that, 'What I am mainly acquiring is two (nice) step-sons.' Neither he nor Joy expected her to live for much longer.

Before Joy was allowed to go home to The Kilns, she and Jack were visited by one of his former students, Revd Peter Bide. The young priest had been a participant in spiritual healing through the laying-on of hands, and Jack asked him to lay his hands on Joy. When he was there, Jack asked if he would be willing to marry them, acknowledging that he was putting Bide in a difficult position, since the Bishop had refused permission, and Bide came from a different diocese. However after praying for guidance, Bide agreed, and Jack and Joy were married in the Wingfield Hospital on 21 March 1957. Bind also laid his hands on Joy.

A week later, Joy had been moved to her new home at The Kilns. It seemed as if the end was nigh, a fact that Bill Gresham knew. He wrote to ask Joy to ensure that the boys were sent back to America if she died. She was unable to respond, but Jack wrote back, making it clear that this request was only compounding Joy's pain, and that the boys did not have good memories of their father. He pointed out to Gresham that such a move would alienate them, and he would ensure that 'every legal obstacle' was put in Gresham's way. He concluded by hoping that Gresham would take the chance to recover the love and respect of his children by not pushing this point. Gresham backed down.

However, the event that all of them feared didn't happen, and instead, Joy started to recover. Five months after leaving hospital, she was no longer bedridden but able to sit up in a chair. By November, she was able to walk short distances, and, to her evident delight, no longer governed by her catheter. A year after her marriage, she was fully up and about, according to Roger Lancelyn Green, and that summer, she was able to go to Douglas's school prize-giving.

As Jack now freely admitted, he was in love with Joy – the Eros that he would write about in *The Four Loves* had filled him. He told Dorothy L. Sayers in June 1957 that 'We soon learn to love what we know we must lose'. The one person with whom he was no longer communicating on a personal level was J. R. R. Tolkien, who found out about the marriage second-hand. Jack knew that Tolkien would not approve of his marrying a divorcee, and his silence on the subject widened the gap between them.

Jack himself was beginning to suffer from bone disease, something which he believed had come about as a result of his sharing Joy's burden – as her calcium levels improved, so his worsened.

With Joy's health apparently on the mend, she started to take over responsibility for life at The Kilns. Warnie had worried that the life he shared with Jack there, which had become much easier following the death of Mrs Moore, was coming to an end. However, Joy reassured him that he was still part of the household. He had the occasional alcoholic relapse, but Joy worked with him on his books, and used her experience of living with Gresham to assist him in his fight against the bottle.

Jack and Joy were able to take 'a belated honeymoon' in Ireland in the summer of 1958 before he recorded some talks he had been commissioned to deliver for the Episcopal Radio-TV Foundation of Atlanta, Georgia. These covered a subject that Jack had new insight into following his marriage – the Four Loves (Affection, Friendship, Eros and Charity). The recording sessions were hampered by the well-meaning attempts by the founder of the Foundation, Dr Caroline Rakestraw, to get Jack to 'embrace' the audience. 'Jack said if they wanted an embracer, they had the wrong man,' Joy wrote of the difficult sessions. The talks ended up not being broadcast as originally envisioned, after the bishops involved with the Foundation decided that Jack was altogether too frank on the subject of sex. Jack, who had returned to penning non-fiction with his *Reflections on the Psalms* the previous year, reworked the scripts into his book *The Four Loves*; the original talks were made available on a less well-distributed basis, but were then released on cassette in 1970.

The Archbishop of Canterbury, Dr Geoffrey Fisher, personally invited Jack to be part of a 'Commission to Revise the Psalter' in the autumn of 1958. Between January 1959 and 1962, the commission worked on revising the translation that had been prepared for the Book of Common Prayer, with Jack and T. S. Eliot advising on literary merit. During this time, Jack also consulted on the preparation of the *New English Bible*, which appeared in 1961.

In the summer of 1959, Joy began to think seriously about the possibility of a trip to Greece, somewhere she had always wanted to go. Roger Lancelyn Green offered to help organize this in the spring of 1960. Joy was so much improved – walking up to a mile without too many difficulties – that it seemed as if it wouldn't be a problem.

Unfortunately Jack's period of productivity and happiness was to be short-lived. In October 1959, Joy went for a check-up at the hospital; neither she nor Jack expected it to be anything other than routine. But what they had known was always possible had come to pass: the cancer had returned. Joy had been in remission; it was 'a reprieve, not a pardon', as Jack explained. She began radiation therapy, but by March 1960, the cancerous spots and lumps were no longer responding to treatment.

8

TRAGEDY AND TRIUMPH

'I would rather go out with a bang than a whimper, particularly on the steps of the Pantheon,' Joy Lewis confided to her former husband in a letter informing him that the coach trip that she, Jack, Roger Lancelyn Green and his wife June were planning to take to Greece in the spring of 1960 was still going ahead. It wasn't going to be easy for her – as Green noted in his diary, one of the first things that they learned was the Greek for 'wheelchair', since this was clearly going to be a necessity for Joy.

Jack hadn't told the Greens just how serious Joy's condition was, but it was evident to them that she was suffering. She missed out on some of the expeditions, but was able to take a much larger part in others than they might have believed possible. As an adult, Jack had not travelled abroad other than to Ireland, apart from his military service during the First World War, so this was all new to him too. They climbed to the top of the Acropolis in Athens, visited Mycenae, and had what Jack called 'the last of the great days of perfect happiness' travelling to the temple of Apollo and the Byzantine Church in Daphne.

The tour was demanding: they went to Heraklion and Knossos in Crete, and on to Rhodes. After Joy had an accident getting on the steps of the coach, Jack hired a car, and they followed the rest of the party. As soon as they reached a convenient stopping point, Green would swiftly order four ouzos from a local tavern to be ready once Joy had been assisted from the vehicle. The alcohol helped to dull the pain which Joy was clearly feeling – but she was determined to absorb as much of the experience as she could.

Once they were back in Oxford, Joy went downhill swiftly. Because the cancer had spread, she needed a mastectomy (or being 'made an Amazon' as she called it) on 20 May. A brief period of ease followed, but on 19 June, she was so ill that the next day she told her nurse to call for her son, Douglas, since she was sure that 'I know now I'm dying'. She was taken back to the Acland hospital, refusing an operation and drifting into a coma.

Yet a week later, Joy was back home, and Douglas returned to his school for the end-of-term service, since he was head prefect. She managed to accompany Jack and Warnie on a car ride a few days later, but early on the morning of 13 July, Warnie was woken by the sounds of Joy screaming in agony. She was admitted to the Radcliffe Hospital early that afternoon, and spent the afternoon dozing, or chatting gently with Jack. Mid-evening, the surgeon informed Jack that the end was near, and when he passed this news on to Joy, she said it was the best news they could have. After receiving the final Absolution from her friend Austin Farrer, she told Jack that he had made her happy, and a little later that she was at peace with God.

At 10.15 p.m., Joy Lewis died with a smile – 'but not at me', Jack later recalled.

Her funeral and cremation were held the following Monday, 18 July; they were sparsely attended. Jack believed that his friends' failure to support him showed exactly how they truly felt about Joy; equally, others, like the Greens, were not aware she had died.

Over the next two months, Jack struggled massively with his feelings of grief and wrote down all that he experienced in four children's exercise books that he found in The Kilns. His anger at God, his fears for what had happened to Joy and his eventual acceptance and peace were all recorded, and, at the instigation of Roger Lancelyn Green, were published – although Jack insisted that they appear under a pseudonym. Thus arose the difficult situation where friends of Jack, unaware of his authorship of *A Grief Observed*, suggested that he should read the book to deal with his own situation.

During this period, Jack was also advising on an operatic adaptation of his second Ransom novel, *Perelandra*. Composer Donald Swann recalled a meeting with Jack where, after an hour, Jack asked to be excused as his wife had died the previous night; Swann was overcome at Lewis's graciousness in such difficult circumstances.

Less easy were meetings with Bill Gresham, who had been planning on visiting anyway. He stayed in Oxford for a couple of weeks, spending time with his sons, who barely knew him, and talking with Jack. Warnie disappeared to Ireland, and jumped inside a bottle once more, needing hospitalization. He didn't return until it was time for Jack to head back to Cambridge for the new term, meaning that Jack had to refuse offers of holidays, since he couldn't leave the boys alone at The Kilns.

During the autumn, Jack lectured on 'English Literature 1300–1500' and completed the revisions to an omnibus version of *Screwtape*. The previous year he had been asked to write something for the *Saturday Evening Post*, and he came up with the idea of Screwtape giving an after-dinner toast to a set of young devils. *Screwtape Proposes a Toast* was very different in format from the original *Letters*, but the old devil was recognizably the same.

When he was agreeing the list of complimentary copies that his publishers would be sending out of the combined *Screwtape*, Jack specifically asked that one particular group shouldn't receive a book gratis. This would have gone to a magazine run by followers of F. R. Leavis, who, Jack felt, allowed criticism to become little more than an advertisement of their feelings about a topic. Jack had written a piece in March 1960 criticizing the quality of undergraduate criticism and noting at the end that the undergraduates 'imitate that which, in their elders, has far less excuse'. At the start of October, Lewis's article was taken to task for its comments about the Bible and the classics, and calling its tone 'distasteful' in multiple ways. Jack refused to enter into a debate, even when Professor Leavis himself chimed in defending the undergraduates. Eventually, in February 1961, Jack did respond. Describing himself as 'parchydermatous', he pointed out that '[y]ou waste on calling me liar and hypocrite time you ought to have spent on refuting my position . . . Any man would much rather be called names than proved wrong.'

Jack continued to return home at the weekends to The Kilns, where Warnie had tried to swear off alcohol completely and was working on his fifth book, about the *ancien régime* in France. Jack also threw himself into his work. As well as his lectures at Cambridge, he was still attending meetings of the Commission on the psalter, and giving extra talks, including one on Samuel Pepys to mark the great diarist's birthday.

In the summer of 1961, he was visited by Arthur Greeves, who noticed how ill Jack was looking. Lewis went for a consultation at the Acland Nursing Home, and was diagnosed with an enlarged prostate gland. An immediate operation wasn't possible, as the prostate problem had already affected both his heart and his liver, so he was placed on a low-protein diet and given blood transfusions regularly.

While he was resting at home, unable to return to Cambridge, Jack's book *An Experiment in Criticism* was published to greater acclaim than he had anticipated, since he was attacking some of the trends in literary criticism that seemed prevalent. He remained too ill to resume his lecturing in the spring of 1962, and by Easter the doctors decided that no operation would be needed, as he was coping with his condition. Jack was delighted that he was allowed back to Magdalene for the summer, and resumed his lectures on Spenser's *The Faerie Queene*, as well as his work on the revised psalter.

Returning to The Kilns for the long summer break, Jack turned some of his lectures on Medieval and Renaissance Literature into a book entitled *The Discarded Image*, and the BBC visited him to record an essay about John Bunyan's *Pilgrim's Progress*. The summer's pleasure was rudely interrupted by the suicide of Bill Gresham on 14 September, after he was diagnosed with cancer of the tongue and throat to add to a cataract problem that he had been suffering from for some time. It was Jack's sad duty to once again inform David and Douglas Gresham of another of their parents' deaths.

During the autumn, Jack gave what proved to be his final series of lectures on 'English Literature 1300–1500', and regretfully had to decline an invitation from Tolkien to attend a dinner celebrating publication of a book being presented to him for his seventieth birthday. Christmas was spent at The Kilns, but Jack needed a short stay at the nursing home before he was allowed back to Cambridge.

In the spring of 1963, a long-gestating idea was finally put down on paper. Jack had tried writing about prayer some years earlier, but hadn't been able to find the right way to approach it. The concept of a series of letters between him and an imaginary friend whom he named Malcolm, debating points, rather than simply instructing, opened the floodgates, and Jack wrote the entire book in February and March. He also became embroiled in the debate over the Bishop of Woolwich, John Robinson's book *Honest to God*, which caused a furore for its attempts to redefine the role and purpose of Christianity, although he turned down an offer from *The Episcopalian* magazine in New York to pen a full response. 'I should find it hard to write of such a man with charity, nor do I want to increase the publicity,' Jack wrote of the man he was known to refer to as the 'Bishop of Woolworth'.

In the summer, Jack intended going to Ireland with Warnie and Douglas; as events transpired, Warnie had already made his way there before Jack returned from Cambridge on 7 June. Before Jack could rearrange his plans, he met a young American academic, Walter Hooper, whom he asked to stay and act as his private secretary. At the end of June, Jack heard a chamber recital of Donald Swann's *Perelandra*, for which the libretto had been written by David Marsh, but a few days later he had to go for another blood transfusion, and on 15 July, the day he and Douglas should have travelled to Ireland, Jack had a heart attack while at the nursing home. He was given extreme unction (the anointing of the dying) the next day, but rallied very soon after, and was soon dictating letters to Walter Hooper.

Jack was allowed home on 6 August, with Hooper and a male nurse in attendance. He resigned his Chair at Cambridge, and Hooper and Douglas Gresham brought his belongings back to The Kilns. Hooper had to return to the States for the autumn to complete his teaching before taking up his job with Jack the following January. The nurse, Alec Ross, remained at The Kilns, and Jack's faithful gardener, Paxford, who had been at the house since Jack moved in over thirty years earlier, was still around.

Various friends came to visit Jack that autumn, including the Greens and Tolkien. Jack oversaw corrections to *The Discarded Image*, and made arrangements for the care of both Warnie and his two stepsons. He felt well enough to write an article for the *Saturday Evening Post* about the 'right to happiness', which appeared posthumously on 21 December – after Jack had angrily insisted on the reinstatement of his final paragraph as he had written it when he saw the proofs on 15 November.

Warnie returned to The Kilns at the start of October, and the two brothers were once again company for each other, as they had been six decades earlier. 'The wheel had come full circle,' Warnie wrote in his diary. Jack was 'ready to go', he told his brother, and he tried to see as many of his friends as possible for one final time, even if he tried to keep the true knowledge of his condition as quiet as he could.

Jack made a last visit to The Lamb and Flag for the Monday meeting of the Inklings on 18 November, describing it as 'perhaps the best of all such Mondays'. Two days later, his editor at Puffin Books, Kaye Webb, visited to discuss a re-editing of the Chronicles of Narnia to 'connect the things that didn't tie up'.

He never had the chance to do so. On 22 November, Jack rose as normal, answered some letters, then fell asleep in his chair. Warnie suggested he would be more comfortable in bed, and Jack went. The brothers exchanged a few words over a cup of tea at 4 p.m., but at 5.30, Warnie heard a crash coming from Jack's room. He was lying unconscious at the foot of the bed, and stopped breathing a few minutes later. The Earthly creator of Narnia had passed from the Shadowlands into the new life about which he had spoken for so long.

EPILOGUE

Just over an hour after Jack Lewis died, another famous 'Jack' – US President John F. Kennedy – was assassinated in Dallas, Texas. The same day, Aldous Huxley, the writer of *Brave New World*, died in California. The news from America overshadowed everything else over the next few days and many of Jack Lewis's friends didn't attend his funeral on 26 November because they simply were not aware he had passed away. Many of the Inklings, though, were present, and notice of the service was printed in *The Times* the following day. One notable absentee was Warnie, who simply couldn't cope. Owen Barfield and Alfred Harwood were appointed Jack's executors, with the estate put in trust for his stepsons' education, then for Warnie, and following his death (which occurred on 9 April 1973) to the boys.

Letters to Malcolm was published in January 1964 with *The Discarded Image* appearing in May. *A Grief Observed* was also finally given its correct author ascription, after much soul-searching by Jack's trustees. Various collections of unpublished material were edited by Walter Hooper, who rescued a lot of papers from the flames to which Warnie was consigning them when Hooper happened to visit The Kilns.

Time magazine's obituary for Jack called him 'one of the church's minor prophets', who 'with fashionable urbanity justified an unfashionable orthodoxy against the heresies of his time'. The influence of his Christian writings on such people as Pope John Paul II would suggest that perhaps they were underestimating the power of his timeless appeal. And the continuing popularity of the Chronicles of Narnia has ensured that Jack Lewis will be remembered for many years to come.

2. THE FICTIONAL WORLDS OF C. S. LEWIS

I

BOXEN: CHILDHOOD CHRONICLES BEFORE NARNIA

Perhaps the most important factor to bear in mind when reading and discussing the Animal-Land and Boxen stories, written by Jack Lewis and his older brother Warnie, is that they weren't written for consumption by anyone other than the authors themselves. This was a private world which the two of them created, with its own rules and regulations, its own codes of conduct and logical absurdities that made perfect sense to boys aged between eight and thirteen. They're the creations of young boys who were free to roam where they pleased within their imaginations.

But of course they have taken on an increased significance as a result of Jack Lewis's Chronicles of Narnia. Like them, they feature Talking Beasts; like them, they have frequent interactions between humans and animals. Lewis himself may have written in *Surprised by Joy* that 'Animal-Land [the precursor of Boxen], by its whole quality, excluded the least

hint of wonder' but not for the only time he was too harsh
on his own writing. It may be that, because so much of the
groundwork for the Boxen tales was written in the winter following the death of the boys' mother in August 1908, Lewis
didn't want to look back too keenly, since inevitably it would
bring back those painful memories of a time when his mother
was gone, and his father was so lost in his own grief that he
didn't realize how his sons were feeling.

The earliest surviving piece of Animal-Land is a play, entitled *The King's Ring (A Comedy)* in which 'interesting caric-
tars' (sic) try to find King Bunny's ring, which has been taken
by a mouse called Hit. One of the most intriguing elements
of this is the way in which the Lewis brothers have worked
out a complicated backstory for their characters, which they
expand upon in various other documents, including a history
of Mouse-Land written when Jack was only eight years old.
By the time he and Warnie were writing the Boxen novels
that survive, five years later, politics – or at least a youngster's
view of the grown-up world of politics – was at the forefront
of the stories.

Lewis himself catalogued all the extant stories from Animal-Land and Boxen in 1927, creating an *Encyclopaedia
Boxoniana*. This, along with the thirteen manuscripts that
survived, was published in 1985, twenty-two years after Jack
Lewis died, and twelve years after his brother's death. The
Encyclopaedia tries to bring some semblance of order to the
various stories, noting where they contradict each other, and
regarding some as 'apocryphal'. Lewis's stepson Douglas
Gresham provided an introduction to the published edition,
setting the pieces in context, and Walter Hooper, who was
Lewis's secretary for many years, provides dates for the creation of many of the tales that are included in the book.

Many of the stories feature the frog Lord Big, who was the
de facto ruler of Boxen, even though the country had a sin-
gle-chamber parliament, which was overseen by two kings:
Benjamin VII (a rabbit, sometimes erroneously referred to as

Benjamin VIII by Lewis) and Hawki V (a man). Lord Big had previously been the two kings' tutor, and to an extent they obviously felt he still had some authority over them. (Lewis maintained that this wasn't a direct commentary on the way their father behaved towards him and Warnie, but the parallels can be drawn.)

The main Boxen novels, *Boxen* and *The Locked Door*, chart two of the various problems that the Boxen rulers faced: attempts to change the make-up of the Clique who governed the country; and difficulties that arose after trade contracts were altered to favour other parties (in a story which will have echoes for *Star Wars* fans in the set-up for *The Phantom Menace*, the first Episode in George Lucas's epic saga).

Than-Kyu (an island state between Turkey and Pongee) is the location for a short story (described as a 'sketch' by the authors) relating an incident from Lord Big's youth when he managed to upset the Imperial Deputy Governor of the island by kicking him. The man gains his revenge by failing to advise Big of a rule stating that foreigners can only stay for six days – after which time, the frog is thrown off the jetty.

The Sailor charts attempts at reforms in the Boxonian Navy, and features the young bear naval officer, James Bar, who has problems with Alexander Cottle, a young cat who has been selected by Lord Big to implement them.

Littera Scripta Manet ('The Written Word Abides') is a four-act comedy featuring Bar, this time described as 'a puppy', alongside Lord Big ('a grumbler'), King Benjamen ('an idler') and Rajah Hawki ('Another'). It's based around an indiscretion in Big's past that Bar discovers and the latter's attempts to blackmail the Boxen leader: is Big the father of Gladys Green ('a hussy' according to the list of characters), with whom Bar is living? Big refuses to pay up unless Bar marries Gladys – and Bar immediately denounces the idea of marriage as 'a relic of the dark ages' which 'should have been abolished when its fellow evils were swept away. It belongs to the realm of magic, the burning of witches, religious intolerance, torture, despotic power, the office of the Little Master.' As a result, Big thrashes Bar but the play ends with Bar consenting to marry Gladys.

The small fragment of *Tararo* that remains suggests that a war with the Prussians is coming to Boxen and this coincides with the final story, *The Life of Lord John Big*, which incorporates incidents from the previous stories to provide an overview of the frog's career and makes copious reference back to these.

Readers coming to the Boxen novels expecting them to be a prototype of Narnia are likely to be disappointed, in particular for those people hoping to find Christian parallels similar to those found within Lewis's later fiction. The animal inhabitants of Boxen interact with the humans without any particular import being given to their physical form as animals, whereas the Narnian Mr and Mrs Beaver, for example, in *The Lion, the Witch and the Wardrobe*, act like beavers in our world, except that they have been given the power of speech by Aslan. In that respect, there's more of a resemblance to Kenneth Grahame's animals in *The Wind in the Willows* than those of Narnia.

Because of this, the stories are often dismissed out of hand as not being worthy of reading. However, viewed as a child's perspective on an adult world – particularly the 'talky' world of politics (to which the young Lewis boys were exposed thanks to their father's strident views being expressed in their hearing on countless occasions) – they are fascinating.

2

THE PILGRIM'S REGRESS

The first fiction that Jack Lewis published after his conversion to Christianity was a thinly veiled account of his own travels from religion to atheism and back to Christianity. It is therefore often discussed with his other two autobiographical works – *Surprised by Joy* and *A Grief Observed* – rather than as a piece of fiction, as John Bunyan's story, *The Pilgrim's Progress*, upon which it was clearly modelled, is more normally looked at as a religious tract. However, it should be noted that Lewis himself, in the preface to the third edition, reminded the reader that the story wasn't purely autobiographical, and just as the Narnia tales wrapped up their Christian message within the story of the Pevensies and their friends, so *The Pilgrim's Regress* is a tale in its own right.

Lewis subtitled the story 'An Allegorical Apology for Christianity, Reason and Romanticism' and in it he is describing how he looked for that elusive quality, Joy, and how he discovered that Christianity provided the object of the 'unsatisfied desire'. He was also writing *The Allegory of Love* at the same time, and in that defined allegory as 'start[ing] with an immaterial fact, such as the passions which you actually experience . . . then invent[ing] *visibilila* [visible manifestations] to express them.' The parables in the Bible were allegories used by Christ in his teaching, and Lewis followed in the footsteps of those who tried to use allegory to appeal to the imagination, rather than the intellect.

In the first part of John Bunyan's original, published in 1678, Christian, an Everyman, travels from his hometown 'The City of Destruction' to 'The Celestial City' – i.e. from this world to Heaven. He is weighed down by a great burden, representing his sin, and encounters many obstacles along the way including Mr Worldly-Wiseman, Mr Legality and his son Mr Civility; Giant Despair in his Doubting Castle; and Vanity Fair, where Christian's companion is killed as a martyr. The second part, which appeared six years later, follows Christian's wife and family on the same journey.

Lewis's story is set in contemporary times, between the two World Wars, and reflects the different problems which he felt Christians, especially himself, faced when trying to achieve Joy. Like Bunyan, he creates his own geography with many versions of the *Regress* including a map.

Our Everyman is named John, who was born in the land of Puritania. Everyone there fears the Landlord, who rules through his Stewards; if they disobey they face harsh punishments, such as eternal life stuck in a black hole full of snakes and scorpions. As a child, John is fascinated by a vision he receives of a beautiful Island in the West, which never leaves him.

When he's older, John leaves the town and meets a 'brown girl' who persuades him that she is the true object of his desires, but he realizes eventually that she isn't. He returns to Puritania, but feels guilty about the girl, and resolves to leave. On the road, he meets Mr Enlightenment, who fills his mind with worldy knowledge, and explains that the Landlord doesn't exist; he invites John to the city of Claptrap, but John refuses. However, he is buoyed by the news about the Landlord, then meets Mr Vertue and Miss Media Halfways. Vertue says they must follow the path (even though he's made the rule up himself); Media takes him off-path to visit her father in the city of Thrill. John is almost convinced by the Halfways that he has found the Island in his and Media's love for each other, but Media's brother Gus tells him she is just another 'brown girl', and that he can show John something much better.

Gus takes John to the city of Eschropolis, where he meets the Clevers and learns about their art. However, when he challenges their suppositions, they chase him out, calling him 'puritanical' and 'bourgeois'. The owner of the city, Mr Mammon, refuses to give him any help. John is then arrested by two guards and brought before Mr Sigismund Enlightenment. According to him, the Island represents John's primeval desires, and imprisons him within a Giant known as the Spirit of the Age. He is rescued from there by Lady Reason, who tells him that she can't answer his questions, as he must discover the answers for himself. Frustrated by this, John leaves her company, and continues on his way.

When he encounters a Grand Canyon, which appears impassable, he runs into Vertue once more. The two are offered help by Mother Kirk, who calls herself the daughter-in-law of the Landlord. She explains the canyon appeared when the first two tenants ate forbidden wild apples. Rather than follow her rules, John and Vertue look for another crossing, and arrive at the home of Mr Sensible, where they stay the night. The next day Sensible's servant Drudge disappears, and Sensible shuts up his house. John and Vertue are surprised to find Drudge helping them.

John tires and is carried by Drudge and Vertue until they reach the house of Three Pale Men: Messrs Neo-Angular, Humanist and Neo-Classical, who offer them lodging out of duty. Drudge and Vertue continue the quest while John rests, but Drudge has decided to stay with a giant, Savage. Vertue too was tempted to stay with Savage but resisted. John and Vertue's next stop is at the home of Mr Broad, who doesn't interest John, although his neighbour, Mr Wisdom, does. They stay there to allow Vertue to rest.

Wisdom's daughter Contemplation reawakens John's imagination, showing him how to fly by moonlight, but John soon realizes that Wisdom's lessons may cause him to lose hope. Once Vertue is recovered, they set off again, but the two argue. A Man helps John to follow Vertue's path and then appears to John in a dream when John starts to wonder if the Landlord is merely a metaphor. After another dream, John starts to realize that it is the Landlord himself he has really been searching for, and that's why he has been unable to cross to get to the Island.

John meets an old hermit named History who explains much about the true nature of the Landlord. He tells John that the vision of the Island came from the Landlord, since the Landlord uses many different ways to get people to come to him. He must reconcile with Vertue, and return to Mother Kirk.

He dreams that he sees Contemplation, who takes him to the Landlord, whom he still fears. Reason forces him out of the cave where he is resting, and Death tells him that the cure to Death is dying: because John surrenders to him, he is Death's master. John goes to Mother Kirk, who tells him to swim across the river in the Canyon. Accompanied by Vertue, he does so, ignoring the ghosts of Humanist, Media, Enlightenment and Halfways, who try to persuade him otherwise. Once on the other side, John is visited by Wisdom once more, who tries to tell him that what he is experiencing cannot be true. The Landlord's voice tells him that he is within a myth, but it is the Landlord's myth.

John and Vertue meet other pilgrims and they are given a guide, Slikisteinsauga, who takes them back east. On the way they see that all the lands they have travelled through are just shadows: the black hole is for those who will not accept the Landlord's help, since he won't force people to accept his will. John and Vertue have to fight dragons they encounter without the guide's help. Once they have triumphed, they end up back in Puritania; John has found what he desired (the Island) in the Landlord.

For the benefit of those not so well versed in the various schools of thought of the early twentieth century, Lewis provided headers at the top of each page of *The Pilgrim's Regress*, which explained the reality of what John was encountering allegorically within its pages. For later editions these were placed in short sections at the start of each chapter. These give a great deal of help for readers coming to it eighty years later, as some of the ideas have sunk from view during the intervening period – no doubt something of which Jack Lewis would approve.

The Pilgrim's Regress was first published in May 1933 by J. M. Dent and was well received in many quarters, particularly for the poetic fragments that appear in the latter part of the book, once John has found his way towards salvation. Those who felt attacked by it, particularly Broad Churchmen and High Anglicans, were less favourably disposed, and Lewis admitted in a letter the following year that in places it was over-bitter and uncharitable.

One of the direct results of its publication was Lewis finding Arthur Sampson, who was so impressed with *The Pilgrim's Regress* that he asked Jack to write *The Problem of Pain* for a series he was publishing. His colleague, Geoffrey Bles, would become the publisher of most of Lewis's future work. It was dedicated to his boyhood friend Arthur Greeves, in whose home in Ireland it was written in 1932.

Like its seventeenth-century forebear, *The Pilgrim's Regress* is not an easy book to read, but provides valuable insight into the way Jack Lewis viewed his life up to that point. Reading it in conjunction with *Surprised by Joy*, the reader finds someone who hasn't just accepted Christianity: he has challenged it, fought against it, and only come to terms with it when it is clear that he must.

3

THE SCIENCE-FICTION NOVELS

In addition to the fame which he has rightly garnered for the creation of the land of Narnia, C. S. Lewis also penned three highly enjoyable science-fiction novels, collectively published as the Cosmic Trilogy. *Out of the Silent Planet*, *Perelandra* (also known as *Voyage to Venus*) and *That Hideous Strength* (*The Tortured Planet*) appeared before and during the Second World War, and are set a few years in the future (roughly from 1940 to 1946). Like a lot of science fiction from that period, their depictions of the planets have been superseded by scientific discovery, but these stand up better than many, partly because Lewis was already consciously working to a rather different set of principles.

Jack Lewis had enjoyed reading science-fiction stories as a boy, including the 'scientific romances' of Jules Verne and H. G. Wells, and there are references to the latter's *The War of the Worlds* and *The First Men in the Moon* within the trilogy. When he was six he even wrote a story entitled 'To Mars and Back'.

However, when he read David Lindsay's 1920 novel *A Voyage to Arcturus* some fifteen years after it was published, Lewis realized that other planets would make a great backdrop for spiritual adventures. He wasn't particularly impressed with either the philosophy Lindsay espouses in the book (calling it borderline diabolical on occasions), or the writing style, but the concept appealed. Around the same time, Lewis also read Olaf Stapledon's *Last and First Men*, which was first published in 1930. This masterpiece of science fiction follows mankind's progress as it outgrows Earth and moves through the solar system; at times it is ruled by giant brains (an idea that Lewis pillories in *That Hideous Strength*), and it usually emerges victorious over the indigenous life on the other planets. In *Out of the Silent Planet*, the Stapledon-esque philosophy is adopted by Weston, and contrasted with the Malacandrians (Martians), who have the technology to travel to Earth but choose to die with their planet.

Lewis was also an opponent of the view espoused by Professor J. B. S. Haldane in his essay 'Last Judgement' in his book *Possible Worlds*: man should live for ever, and would not continue to follow ethical paths since 'God's ways are not our ways'. Haldane later believed the Cosmic Trilogy was an attack on science, but Lewis disagreed with this: he was against what he described as 'scientism', a view that mankind had to survive and it didn't matter if we lost our humanity in the process. His novels were designed to provide a Christian point of view that countered the Haldane/Stapledon model.

The background to the adventures of Professor Elwin Ransom derived from an idea of the universe in which the planets each have a reflection of the classical deities and the attributes associated with them – Venus is charity, Mars is courage. Each is ruled by an Oyarsa, a term derived from a medieval scholar of Plato's works, who embodies these attributes, but in a Christian context. Earth is 'bent' because of the actions of one of the Oyarsu, who tried to take power from Maleldil, the lord and creator of them all, who assumed physical form on Earth to battle the bent Oyarsa (the parallels with Christianity become clearer in discussions in the second and third books). They speak Old Solar, an ancient language, and refer to the planets by their Solar names: Malacandra is Mars; Perelandra is Venus; Thulcandra (the Silent Planet) is Earth.

4

THE COSMIC TRILOGY: *OUT OF THE SILENT PLANET*

One night during a walking tour of the Midlands, philologist Dr Elwin Ransom seeks shelter at the estate of physicist Professor Weston. He arrives as Weston and another man, Dick Devine, whom Ransom knew and disliked at school, are trying to force a slow-witted young man into a building. When Ransom intervenes, Devine recognizes him and suggests to Weston that Ransom might be more use to them, so they offer him a bed for the night.

Devine drugs Ransom and the two men take him on board their spherical spaceship, bound for the nearby planet Malacandra. Although Ransom is excited by the idea, and enjoys the wonder of space travel, he is perturbed by a conversation he overhears. They can't decide whether to let him remain conscious or drug him before handing him over to something called the 'sorns' as a sacrifice. Ransom takes the sharpest knife from the galley, and hides it, ready to escape when he can.

After they land on Malacandra, Ransom begins to observe the differences between the two worlds, and when the sorns – tall, spindly creatures that he thinks of as 'spooks on stilts' – arrive, he makes a run for it. He travels far from the landing point, deducing from the gravity and the warmer temperature of the water that he may be on Mars.

Although he's initially frightened when he sees a different species, his fear turns to wonder when it tries to communicate with him, and his philology training kicks in. He starts to communicate with the creature, a hross named Hyoi, and accompanies Hyoi to his home in a valley.

Ransom spends some time there, getting to know the language and customs of the people. He discovers that Earth is called Thulcandra, 'the Silent Planet', but the reason for the name is known only to the seroni (the proper name of the sorns), who live on a higher level than the hrossa. When the hrossa learn that he escaped from bad (or 'bent') men, they decide he should go to see Oyarsa, the ruler of the planet, who lives in Meldilorn and knows everything and everyone. Ransom asks if Oyarsa made the planet, and learns that Maleldil the Young One made and rules the world, living with the Old One who is 'not the sort that has to live anywhere'. The other species on the planet are the pfifltriggi, frog-like creatures who work as artisans and miners, and the eldila, spiritual beings who are almost invisible to Ransom. The philologist also learns that gold is widespread on Malacandra, explaining Devine's reason for going there.

The human is invited to join in a hunt for a hnakra, a predatory animal which is rarely seen. On the way, Ransom hears an eldil speaking in his head, telling him he must go to Oyarsa, as the two 'bent' humans are following him, and if they find him anywhere else there will be evil. This is proved all too true shortly afterwards: Hyoi is shot by Weston and Devine, and the other hrossa send him to Oyarsa, believing that Hyoi has been killed because Ransom didn't obey the eldil straightaway.

On the way he meets a seroni named Augray and realizes his fears about them were groundless. Augray explains that Oyarsa is the greatest eldil, put there when the planet was made, and carries Ransom to his meeting with Oyarsa. On the journey, they meet other seroni, who ask Ransom about Thulcandra, which Ransom learns has no Oyarsa of its own. Instead, the seroni reason, when they learn about such things as slavery and prostitution, that everyone on Thulcandra wants to be a little Oyarsa themselves.

Meldilorn is an island in the middle of a lake, with huge trees, and as Ransom crosses it on foot to meet Oyarsa, he meets a pfifltrigg who makes a sculpture of him. He sees a representation of the planets, confirming he is on Mars, and notes that the picture of a winged, wavy figure, representing Oyarsa, is missing from the ball for Earth – in fact it's been cut out from the design.

After spending the night with the pfifltriggi, Ransom is summoned to Oyarsa. Although he is invisible to Ransom, the Earthman can sense his presence as Oyarsa explains that Thulcandra used to have its own Oyarsa, brighter than many of his colleagues, who became 'bent'. A great war followed, which ended with him bound in the air of his own world. The Oyarsa believes that Maleldil hasn't completely given up on Thulcandra and its Oyarsa and has 'wrestled' with him there.

The reason Weston and Devine brought Ransom is also clarified. The Oyarsa had seen them arrive on their first visit four Earth years earlier, and had sent the sorns to teach them the Malacandrian language. The men refused to learn and wouldn't come to visit the Oyarsa but instead stuffed their ship with gold and fled. They thought that the Oyarsa wanted a sacrifice, hence bringing Ransom.

Ransom explains that he believes Weston has come to Malacandra because he wants humanity always to survive and will wipe out the indigenous population so that mankind can move there, and onwards as necessary. Before he can tell the Oyarsa about Maleldil's battles on Earth, hrossa bring

Weston and Devine in under guard. Weston tries to intimidate the hrossa (he can't see the Oyarsa either, although he can hear it) and then bribe them; they laugh at him. The Oyarsa sends Weston to have a cold bath in case he is overheated and thus talking nonsense, while the bodies of three hrossa that the humans killed are scattered.

Devine realizes that the Malacandrians are far more powerful than they'd thought and advises caution, but Weston is filled with his own importance. Ransom has to translate and in doing so shows the true scale of Weston's ambitions. The Oyarsa realizes that Weston is only concerned about 'the seed' of man, rather than how men may look or think in the years to come – he wants the concept of man itself (its DNA, so to speak) to continue regardless of anything else. The Oyarsa cannot let them remain on Malacandra, so, even though the orbits of Mars and Earth aren't well placed, they must go. It will provide ninety days' worth of oxygen and food, and on the ninetieth day, the ship will disintegrate. They can take the chance, or stay and be killed.

Ransom decides to go back to Earth with the others; the Oyarsa removes the weapons from the ship and the eldila ensure that Weston and Devine don't kill him. Although they cut it fine, the humans land on Earth just before the ship disintegrates, and Ransom finds the nearest pub for a pint of beer.

Some months later, Ransom invites C. S. Lewis to visit him, when the latter raises a query about the word Oyarses, and they decide to tell his story as fiction. Ransom approves Lewis's manuscript (with some additions) and notes that Weston has shut the door to space travel – if mankind is to go to other planets, time travel will need to be involved.

Out of the Silent Planet wasn't an immediate hit. Both J. M. Dent & Sons and Allen & Unwin turned it down before The Bodley Head picked up the rights. It was published in 1938, dedicated to his brother Warnie as a 'life-long critic of the space-and-time story'. Many of its readers didn't pick up on the Christian analogies within its pages – Lewis noted in a letter to Sister Penelope at Wantage that only two of the reviewers 'showed any knowledge that my idea of the fall of the Bent One was anything but an invention of my own!' Although it gained around sixty reviews, mostly complimentary, *The Times Literary Supplement* compared it unfavourably with H.G. Wells's writing.

Although there was some controversy over this – with one Lewis scholar maintaining that some, if not all, of it was a forgery perpetrated by Lewis's secretary Walter Hooper – it seems clear now that Lewis's first planned sequel to *Out of the Silent Planet* would pick up on the comments about time travel that conclude the first book. All that remains of this are lengthy fragments published as *The Dark Tower* in 1977, which would suggest that Lewis began work on it in 1938, shortly after publication of *Out of the Silent Planet*.

A group of scientists, including Ransom and the narrator (Lewis) meet at Cambridge, discussing the impossibility of time travel, with one of them, Orfieu, demonstrating a 'chronoscope' – an instrument that can look through time in the same way a telescope looks through space. He doesn't know where exactly they are looking at, only that there is a large tower there in what he calls 'Othertime'. Ransom is sure he's seen it before somewhere. Inside is a man, Asiatic in complexion, with a very black beard – and a huge sting in the centre of his forehead that drips poison, which he uses to turn people into automata. At one stage, the three men watching are convinced the other man can see them through the chronoscope.

Ransom is convinced the Dark Tower is in Hell although the others don't agree. Orfieu's colleague Scudamour has a double in Othertime, with whom he has a degree of sympathetic resonance, feeling the man's pain. But the double then grows a sting. They also realize that the Dark Tower is a double for a new university library in Cambridge, which makes some think Othertime is in the future, and the Tower is a copy of the library, although Scudamour wonders if it's not an amalgamation of their world and a future one.

When he sees a double of his fiancée about to be stung by his own double, Scudamour jumps through the chronoscope into Othertime and somehow swaps places with his counterpart. The girl calls him The Lord of the Dark Tower and the Unicorn of the Eastern Plain and isn't like his fiancée save in appearance, although she was linked to the original of the Unicorn as Scudamour was with his girl. Mysterious White Riders attack, keen to destroy the Unicorns, and Scudamour investigates his surroundings, learning that the Othertimers believe in multiple realities which can cross. Experiments have been tried . . .

. . . which is where the manuscript breaks off, as Scudamour learns how the Othertime version of the chronoscope (and presumably Orfieu's own) worked. There are no indications as to how Lewis would have continued the story, or how a Christian theme would have been threaded throughout it.

Lewis referred to the unfinished work in conversations with Alastair Fowler when the latter was his student in the 1950s, and showed him the manuscript, telling Fowler that 'he had been unable to carry it further'. As an intriguing sidestep to the Cosmic Trilogy, *The Dark Tower* is worth reading; it's a theme that has been explored in much science fiction (at its heart, Scudamour's crossover is only an elaborate version of *The Prince and the Pauper*, or the shepherdess and the princess in MacDonald's tale), and it would have been intriguing to see where Lewis took it. Certainly one idea continued into his later work – that one could travel through an object into another world. Another object like, say, a wardrobe . . .

5

THE COSMIC TRILOGY: *PERELANDRA* (AKA VOYAGE TO VENUS)

C. S. Lewis has been summoned to Dr Elwin Ransom's home, but on the way is assailed by doubts. When he finally gets to the apparently empty cottage, he finds a coffin-like box, and an eldil awaiting him. Ransom arrives, and explains that the doubts were a deliberate attempt to put Lewis off by the Black Archon of Earth; Ransom is being sent by Maleldil to Perelandra (Venus) to stop the Black Archon's attack on that planet, partly because he speaks Old Solar, the ancient language, which he learned from the hrossa on Malacandra. Lewis seals a naked Ransom in the coffin, which disappears. Over a year later, Lewis and his friend Humphrey are summoned back: Ransom's coffin glides back to Earth, and a younger-looking professor comes out, with an injured heel. He tells them his story:

When Ransom arrives on Venus, he discovers that it is an ocean-filled paradise. He swims to one of the islands of vegetation that float, without roots, around the ocean, and rests. When he awakes, he finds a small dragon curled around a tree, but realizes that it isn't capable of communication. His island floats around the ocean until he encounters a green-skinned lady on a neighbouring island. He tries to swim to it, but the current sends him back to his own island; however, by the time he wakes again, a number of the islands, including the lady's, have butted up against each other.

The Green Lady apologizes for laughing at him the day before 'because she was young' and explains that she is human in appearance since Maleldil took that form on Earth, and all new creatures will take that form. There is only one other like her on Venus, whom she describes as the King; she calls herself the Queen or Mother. She realizes that Ransom (whom she calls Piebald) isn't the King (i.e. the Adam) of his world, and is bemused by his questions, wondering if he has been sent to teach her about death.

During a day spent wandering, Ransom spots a fixed island, and the Green Lady is horrified to learn that Ransom's people sleep in such places: it's forbidden to them. They travel there on the back of fish after seeing something land from the heavens. From a viewpoint on the fixed island, they spot a spherical spaceship, and Ransom realizes that Weston has arrived. Weston uses a raft to reach the shore, and starts to speak to the Green Lady in Old Solar (which he never bothered learning on Malacandra). She leaves the two men on the Fixed Island. Weston accuses Ransom of seducing her, but these thoughts haven't crossed his mind.

Weston claims he has had a change of heart since returning from Malacandra and is now aware of a Force that guides men, which overrides all petty moral and ethical concerns. He calls this Force into him, but is then possessed by some demonic agency that he fights briefly but in vain, leaving him writhing in agony.

The next day Ransom is surprised to find that Weston has been strong enough to leave the island; he travels by fish to another island, where he sleeps until he's woken by the sounds of Weston and the Green Lady arguing. Weston is trying to persuade her to stay on the fixed island, or even consider doing so, and doesn't really sound like the hectoring Weston Ransom knew on Malacandra. But he's unsuccessful and she leaves him.

Ransom wakes to find mutilated corpses of frog-like creatures: Weston has been tearing them apart. Seeing him, Ransom realizes that something infinitely evil has travelled within Weston to Perelandra. The Green Lady is innocent, and the temptation of Eve in the Garden of Eden is about to be re-enacted unless Ransom can prevent it.

A great debate ensues, in which Weston – or, rather, the thing within him – tries many arguments to persuade the Green Lady that disobeying the rule about staying on the fixed island may not be wrong. Weston's strongest argument is that there would have been no Jesus if there had been no Fall, to which Ransom says that good was made from something bad and asks Weston if he was pleased that Maledil became man. Weston can only howl in response; the lady sleeps. Ransom realizes that it is no longer Weston and thinks of it as the Un-man. To unbalance Ransom, it keeps calling out his name, and the Earthman guesses that it may not need sleep, even if he does. (Luckily for Ransom, the lady requires sleep, so the Un-man has to stop from time to time.)

The Un-man persists in his temptation, painting a picture of women whose rebelliousness has roused an otherwise sluggish race to greatness. The Green Lady listens but is not convinced. Ransom equally persists in trying to present counter-arguments, as well as preventing the Un-man from killing defenceless creatures. Occasionally the real Weston, broken by the experience, can be heard, but Ransom is never sure if this is a trick or not. The Un-man teaches the Lady vanity and pride in clothing that he creates from feathers, and from there he tries to persuade her to put herself first.

Ransom wonders where Maleldil's representative is in all this, and it finally dawns on him that it's he. The only person in a position to stop the temptation on Perelandra is he. After a lot of internal debate with a Voice putting Maldeldil's point, Ransom realizes that he must kill Weston – even if it costs his own life, as his God sacrificed his own life in a similar battle.

Everything else bar the Un-man is asleep when Ransom awakes. A huge fight begins between the two, with the Un-man eventually turning tail and fleeing. A long chase ensues, during which Weston temporarily gains control of his body and reveals the true nature of Hell to Ransom. The latter is distracted by pity for Weston, over whom the Un-man takes control once more and tries to drown Ransom. A final fight follows, and Ransom throttles the Un-man. Ransom climbs to the surface from the subterranean cavern in which they have ended up, but Weston's corpse is reanimated by the Un-man and follows him, accompanied by a giant insect. Ransom hurls a stone at Weston, killing him finally, and throws the body into a sea of lava.

Ransom finally reaches the surface and realizes he has been bitten on the heel by the Un-man during the fight. He climbs to the top of the highest mountain, where he finds another transport coffin – and two eldila. They are the Oysaras of Malacandra (whom Ransom met on Mars), and Perelandra. They choose guises to present themselves before the King and Queen of Perelandra, to whom the Oysara is passing over dominion, now a second Fall has been prevented. Ransom is awestruck by the resemblance of the King to an unwounded Christ. The pair are given the names Tor and Tinidril, and they reveal the plan for Perelandra – as well as a desire to set matters right on Earth. When Ransom wakes next, a year has passed and his journey home begins.

As noted in the last chapter, *Perelandra* wasn't Jack Lewis's first attempt at a sequel to *Out of the Silent Planet*, but when he realized that he wasn't getting as advanced with *The Dark Tower* as he would have liked, he switched tacks and instead told a story set on another of the inner planets, despite stating at the end of *Out of the Silent Planet* that Weston had shut the door to the planets except through the past.

This isn't the only inconsistency between the two books: the epilogue to *Out of the Silent Planet* makes it clear that the names that Lewis uses in the manuscript – Ransom, Weston and, presumably, Devine, although this isn't made explicit – are pseudonyms that have been adopted in order to prevent Lewis and 'Ransom' from being sued. However, during what might be termed Ransom's 'Gethsemane moment' in *Perelandra*, when he doubts that it's down to him to deal with the Un-man, one of the crowning arguments that the Voice presents is that Ransom's name is important, because he can be the ransom for the world on which he stays. The argument rather falls apart if Ransom's real name is anything other than a synonym for 'ransom'.

Some of the other differences between the set-up of *Out of the Silent Planet* and *Perelandra* are explained within the text – or, at the very least, mentioned. The languages on Malacandra are no longer equal, as they were in *Out of the Silent Planet*; Old Solar is the key language, and the others followed during the equivalent of the Cambrian period.

Whereas many of the readers and reviewers of *Out of the Silent Planet* regarded it as a piece of science fiction, and didn't pick up on the religious subtext, it is much harder to miss in *Perelandra*, particularly given how many times Ransom makes explicit reference to the Fall in the Garden of Eden, and the events and reasons behind the incarnation and passion of Jesus Christ. Entire chapters are given over to religious arguments over the meaning of temptation and the Fall; in many ways they seem the key battle of the book, rather than the epic chase sequence between Ransom and Weston that culminates in the double death of Weston.

As ever, Lewis owes a debt to stories that have come before.

Olaf Stapledon's *Last and First Men* provides the floating islands of vegetation on Perelandra, although Lewis's internal vision of these was his starting point for the novel to which he added the story of the Fall, retelling the tale recounted in Milton's *Paradise Lost*, on which he had been lecturing since 1937, but with a revised ending. This time the story of Adam and Eve is told with the serpent defeated. The green pigmentation of the Lady and King derived from the seventeenth-century writer Richard Burton's *Anatomy of Melancholy* in which he talks of green men 'that fell from heaven'. Lewis himself reckoned that the climax to the story was operatic in form – and perhaps unsurprisingly gave his blessing to Donald Swann's version (see part 4, chapter 5) – and saw parallels with Dante's *Purgatorio* as well as Wagner's Ring cycle. The Fisher King also received an incurable wound in various versions of the Arthurian legend.

Perelandra was under way in November 1941, and complete by the summer of the following year. It's also set then – Ransom leaves a memorial for Weston, which gives his dates as 1896 to 1942. After completing it, Lewis rewrote the first two chapters – the material featuring himself – before sending it to his publishers. Dedicated to 'some ladies at Wantage' (referring to the nuns of the Community of St Mary the Virgin at that town in Oxford rather than 'wanton ladies', which is how it was translated in the Portuguese edition!), it was published in April 1943, and was described by *The Commonweal* as 'far superior to other interplanetary adventures'.

Respected science-fiction author Arthur C. Clarke (who would go on to write *2001: A Space Odyssey*, whose descriptions of astronaut Dave Bowman's visions are in places similar to the first attempt by the Oysaras to show themselves to Ransom) wasn't impressed with Lewis's views on science fiction and interplanetary flight – particularly the views that Lewis ascribed to those involved in it, as personified in Weston. Clarke felt that the scientists had higher ideals than Lewis supposed, but Jack believed that 'a point of view (not unlike Weston's) is on the way' describing a race that tried to increase its own power by technology was 'a cancer in the universe'.

Jack's friend and biographer George Sayer regarded *Perelandra* as the most rewarding of Lewis's novels for Christians; until he wrote *Till We Have Faces*, Lewis himself regarded *Perelandra* as his best work. It is filled with lyrical passages, which transport the reader to this mythical Venus – even by contemporary standards, Lewis's imagination was working overtime compared with the realities of the planet's environment, as he had with Mars – which becomes the background for an archetypal battle between good and evil.

6

THE COSMIC TRILOGY: *THAT HIDEOUS STRENGTH*

Sociologist Mark Studdock and his wife Jane live in the Midlands university town of Edgestow. Mark is an ambitious research fellow at Bracton College; Jane is bored and lonely, stuck in their flat. A newspaper story about a guillotining reminds her of nightmares she's had about a severed head, and an old man being dug up out of a churchyard who then speaks something vaguely Spanish.

A group within the college force a sale of part of its land, the unspoiled Bragdon Wood, to a new scientific group, NICE (National Institute for Coordinated Experiments). Mark meets Lord Feverstone (a.k.a. Dick Devine, Weston's partner on Malacandra), who offers him a job at NICE: it's at the cutting edge, aiming to create a new type of mankind.

Jane runs into Mrs Dimble, the wife of one of her former tutors, whose husband is an expert on Arthur and Merlin – Bragdon Wood contains 'Merlin's Well', beneath which the mage is meant to be sleeping. When Dr Dimble mentions that Celtic would have sounded like Spanish, Jane tells them about her dreams, and they offer a psychoanalyst's details. The next day, Mark goes with Feverstone to NICE's current headquarters at Belbury, while Jane visits Dr Grace Ironwood.

Mark meets the key NICE personnel. The Deputy Director, John Wither, seems to be the real power since the official Director, novelist Horace Jules, is just a useful figurehead. Professor Filostrato, a famous physiologist, confirms that NICE's work is dealing with the destiny of the human race; the head of NICE's private police force, 'Fairy' Hardcastle, a butch lesbian, warns Mark that Wither and Professor Frost are the ones to worry about. At dinner, another member of Bracton College, William Hingest, confirms he is leaving NICE, telling Mark that it's too much of a conspiracy for his liking.

Dr Ironwood lives at St Anne's Manor, which is still a working farm. According to her, Jane is a visionary and very important to the future of the human race. She wants Jane to help her 'company'; annoyed, Jane leaves, but that night she dreams of Hingest's murder. The following day, both Mark and Jane learn of the scientist's death but that evening, Mark glosses over aspects of the NICE job offer, while Jane remains silent about her visions.

Mark is manipulated into working for NICE, writing articles to rehabilitate a guillotined radiologist, François Alcasan. Jane meets members of Dr Ironwood's 'company', who are led by a man now known as Dr Fisher-King (in fact Elwin Ransom), but she isn't yet sure about joining, particularly as they require her to gain Mark's approval.

NICE has moved into Edgestow, and as a fog envelops the town, the place descends into chaos with even Hingest's funeral affected by machine noise and workmen swearing. Mark becomes part of NICE's inner group – Feverstone, Hardcastle, Filostrato, a former preacher named Straik, who believes NICE is doing God's will, as well as Professor Frost and John Wither – and is told that Hardcastle's force are planning a riot in Edgestow, and his job is to spin the coverage in their favour.

Jane's dreams feature Professor Frost whom she previously saw with the guillotined man, and when she sees Frost in the flesh in Edgestow, she heads to St Anne's. There Dr Fisher-King explains that he can't let her join the group properly because of Mark's allegiance to NICE. Jane returns to Edgestow but becomes caught up in the riots. She is tortured by Hardcastle, but luckily the riot worsens and she manages to get away from the NICE police.

At NICE, Mark falls out of favour for refusing to invite Jane to stay, and is told it was a suggestion by 'the Head'. NICE has found a way to bring the dead back to life, and the Head is the actual disembodied head of Alcasan. Mark is introduced to the Head – which Jane witnesses in a dream – and agrees to try to bring Jane there. However, when Hardcastle talks about having met Jane, Mark's hackles rise again.

At St Anne's, the resident sceptic, Archie MacPhee, tells Jane about Ransom's past journeys. She learns Ransom is the Pendragon of Logres, the heart of England, and a group of like-minded people have accreted around him at St Anne's. They guess that NICE are aiming towards creating disembodied brains as a form of immortality, but Ransom says that NICE's activities in Bragdon Wood are more important. Jane's dreams have confirmed that NICE intend to dig up Merlin, who is only sleeping, not dead; together they will be unbeatable by anything except Armageddon.

Mark runs away from NICE, but is arrested for Hingest's murder and taken back to NICE headquarters. In an effort to turn Mark to their side, Frost reveals the truth: Macrobes (the dark eldila confined to Earth) are in charge, and have their own diabolical plan. Left on his own, Mark starts to pray.

Both NICE and the St Anne's group search for Merlin, who has woken early and left his resting place. Merlin swaps his clothes with those of a tramp, and the NICE team take the tramp back with them. Merlin makes his own way to St Anne's and after some persuasion, agrees to help them against NICE. The false Merlin at NICE reveals he's the tramp to Mark (who's left to guard him), but the others believe they need a linguist to be able to talk to him.

Mr Bultitude, a tame bear who resides at St Anne's, is kidnapped by NICE personnel for use in their vivisection experiments. Another of the group's husbands is sent there for 'remedial treatment' rather than being released from prison. Jane has two mystical experiences, firstly encountering the spirit of the Perelandran Oyarsa, and then a second with God. Merlin is given all of the powers of the other planet's Oysaras (Oysereu), and goes to NICE claiming to be an interpreter.

Unknown to Wither and Frost, Merlin hypnotizes the tramp to relay his instructions, and, although they're dubious, the two NICE leaders go along with the tramp's orders. Wither takes Merlin and the tramp on a tour, while Frost tries to complete Mark's initiation into NICE by getting him to destroy a Cross. Mark refuses, but before anything else can happen, everyone has to get ready for a formal banquet with the NICE Director who is visiting. At that, everyone starts spouting gibberish – the curse of Babel is upon them.

Chaos reigns: Merlin releases the animal and human prisoners. The Director and Hardcastle are killed. Merlin sends Mark to St Anne's. When Wither, Straik and Filostrato go to the Head's lab, the Head keeps demanding more decapitated heads. Filostrato is first to die, then Wither kills Straik before being killed by Mr Bultitude the bear, who then eats the Head. Frost commits suicide in a fire. Feverstone follows Merlin into Edgestow, but is buried in rubble by an explosion as the town is destroyed.

At St Anne's, the victory celebration is accompanied by explanations: Ransom became the Pendragon, the leader of the secret world within England, but is now heading back to Venus. There will be a new Pendragon. And Mark and Jane are reunited.

*   *   *

The final volume in Lewis's Cosmic Trilogy is set on Earth, in stark contrast to the interplanetary wanderings of the first two stories. Readers expecting it to focus firmly on Elwin Ransom and his battle against the evil Oysara on Tellus – which is how things are left at the end of *Perelandra* – may be disappointed to find that the Cambridge philologist doesn't appear for some time, but it's fair to say that his presence is critical to the story. The revelation that Lord Feverstone is Dick Devine, the secondary villain from *Out of the Silent Planet*, comes (perhaps too) early in the story, making it clear from the outset to those who have read the earlier stories that there's something definitely not right about NICE.

Lewis subtitles *That Hideous Strength* 'A Modern Fairy-Tale for Grown-Ups' and points out in his introduction that he's really following the conventions of the genre by starting the story in a humdrum environment familiar to a lot of his readership. It's set 'after the [Second World] War' which was still raging, not necessarily in the Allies' favour, at the time Lewis wrote the story. Internal dating suggests that it's 1946, six years after the events of *Out of the Silent Planet* in 1940, although various scholars have suggested that it fits better with 1948. The NICE police are compared to the Gestapo in Nazi Germany and the Ogpu (the Soviet secret police, which was actually dissolved in 1934); the railway on which Curry travels at the end of the tale hasn't yet been nationalized (i.e. it's pre-1947).

That Hideous Strength, as Jack acknowledges in his preface, tackles similar themes to his book *The Abolition of Man* (see part 3, chapter 4), and Jack's objections to 'progressive' education, particularly as shown in a book called *The Control of Language*. He believed that if the appropriate emotional responses to situations were not followed, mankind would lose its humanity. The group at Bracton are referred to as 'the Progressive Element', and it's clear that their beliefs, or indeed lack of them, are what allow the dark eldila to control NICE

– and Mark recognizes that the attempt to get him to destroy a cross before he is allowed fully into the inner circle of NICE reflects this cauterizing of the emotions.

The title comes from a reference to the Tower of Babel – the Old Testament biblical story about an attempt to build a tower to the heavens, which prompts God to curse everyone to speak in a different language so they can't work together – and the relevance is demonstrated at the climax of the story when the NICE inner circle start to talk utter nonsense. It also deals with the use and misuse of language: Mark is hired to manipulate the readers of newspapers to believe NICE's policies through his stories, and the discussions he has about this with Hardcastle and Dr Dimble show Lewis's beliefs in the inherent dangers of such writing. According to George Sayer, the NICE members themselves were based on people with whom Lewis had contact at Oxford: the account of the board meeting near the start reeks of verisimilitude. Equally, the character of MacPhee, the sceptic who always asks questions, was a tribute to Jack's teacher at Great Bookham, William Kirkpatrick.

The idea of keeping a corpse alive had struck Lewis as the possible subject of a play to write in 1923 after he had read about German experiments before the Great War. The theories within the story about the Logres, and how England is caught between the sway of the Logres (the Celtic word for 'England') and that of Britain ('behind every Milton, there is a Cromwell', Ransom explains), is based on the writings of Lewis's friend Charles Williams, who died in May 1945, shortly before the novel was published. The Logres represent the spirit of that Arthurian golden age whose influence keeps England from degenerating into simply being part of Great Britain. Williams's outlook on good and evil permeates the book, and the collection of his poems, *Taliessin through Logres*, published in 1938, features many of the same themes (although in considerably denser text). If Ransom resembled Tolkien in the first two books, as some claim, he is nearer in thought and outlook to Williams in this final appearance, but Tolkien isn't forgotten – there are references to Numenor and the West, as featured in Tolkien's then-unpublished novels.

That Hideous Strength wasn't well received, although Lewis's own comment in a letter that it was universally damned is unfounded. George Orwell was annoyed by the presence of the supernatural; others felt that the addition of the Arthurian element of the Logres and Merlin was superfluous. Comparison with Aldous Huxley's *Brave New World* in *The New York Times* was in Lewis's favour: Orville Prescott noted that Huxley's books are 'bitter' and his mood 'one of cynical despair'. Lewis, on the other hand, was sounding 'a militant call to battle'.

Lewis abbreviated the book himself for publication in America as *The Tortured Planet;* some of the most evocative parts of his descriptive prose are excised (the idea of Merlin hiding behind the hedgerows of time, for example) and the odd piece of Latin corrected, but if you haven't read the original, you don't feel cheated by the shortening. 'I believe I have altered nothing but the tempo and the manner,' Lewis wrote in the preface. It was dedicated to J. McNeill – Janie McNeill, a friend of his from Belfast, who wasn't best pleased: 'I hate it!' she told her friend Mary Rogers. 'I wish he'd dedicated any book other than this to me!'

While it lacks the sense of wonder of the first two books in the trilogy, *That Hideous Strength* is a science-fiction thriller, which throws Arthurian legend and the occult into the mix. Of all Lewis's unfilmed works, this is the one that would lend itself to television treatment – with shockingly little updating required.

Postscript to the Cosmic Trilogy
In *The Dark Tower and other stories*, Walter Hooper reprints Lewis's other brief pieces of science fiction alongside the large fragment from the second Ransom adventure. 'The Shoddy Lands', 'Ministering Angels' and 'Forms of Things

Unknown' are all short stories of varying quality. In 'The Shoddy Lands', the narrator believes that he is given an insight into the superficial life of a woman to whom he's just been introduced, and was an experiment by Lewis to write about looking at yourself when you're not looking at yourself (i.e. catching your own reflection when you're doing something else). The story appeared in *Magazine of Fantasy and Science Fiction* X in February 1956.

'Ministering Angels' is a response to an article suggesting that the first settlers on Mars would need to have suitable female company sent up to minister to their needs. There's a Roald Dahl feel to this story, with a nice Christian twist at the end, and you can't help a wry smile at the situation. This appeared in *Magazine of Fantasy and Science Fiction* XIII in January 1958.

'Forms of Things Unknown' wasn't published in Lewis's lifetime, but, like the previous two stories, was included in the collection *Of Other Worlds*. It plays off a line in *Perelandra* about myths in one world being facts in another (Ransom encounters a Cyclops on Malcandra, for example). The fourth man to land on the moon, Lieutenant John Jenkin, dismisses the idea of animated stone but can't explain what happened to his three predecessors until he encounters statues there, whose hair is moving in the breeze . . . except, of course, there is no air on the moon. Hooper believes Lewis may have held this back from publication because readers wouldn't get the punchline, but anyone familiar with *Clash of the Titans* will understand immediately.

7

THE SCREWTAPE LETTERS/
SCREWTAPE PROPOSES A TOAST

Adding a second story to the Cosmic Trilogy wasn't the only fiction occupying Jack Lewis's mind during the early years of the Second World War. Between May and November 1941, a series of letters appeared in the Church of England weekly newspaper *The Guardian*, apparently sent from a Senior Devil by the name of Wormwood, to his nephew Screwtape, a Junior Devil who was clearly in need of some assistance in his infernal task. Inspired by hearing Adolf Hitler talking on the radio in tones that were so persuasive and unflinching it seemed possible to believe almost anything while he was speaking, the thirty-one *Screwtape Letters* cover the whole gamut of human experience.

After a reminder by the editor of the work that the Devil is a liar, we meet Wormwood and Screwtape. The younger devil is responsible for keeping a human away from the temptation of the Enemy (i.e. God), but his problem is almost immediately increased when his Patient becomes a Christian. Wormwood points out that this isn't necessarily a fatal situation, and recommends focusing him on the flaws of his fellow Christians, encouraging a poor relationship with his mother, and pushing him towards prayer to his own imaginary version of God, rather than the true Enemy.

Between the fourth and fifth letters, war is declared in Europe, which delights Wormwood, although Screwtape points out that wars sometimes encourage men towards rather than away from the Enemy. Uncertainty over whether he will be called up keeps the Patient from thinking about the Enemy, and Screwtape suggests that Wormwood should push him towards bearing malice towards his neighbours while thinking benevolent thoughts about those too far away for him to focus on properly.

After advising that the Patient should think of devils as almost comedy figures while moving towards their aims, Screwtape is concerned when the Patient's religious interests start to wane: the Enemy wants to make 'loathsome little replicas of himself' and does his best work when his children are struggling. He points out to Wormwood that the concept of pleasure belongs to the Enemy but sexual temptation is more tempting when the subject is less religiously inclined. With care, he can be made to believe that the peak of his spiritual interest when he was converted was simply a phase he went through.

Screwtape exhorts Wormwood to develop his Patient's scepticism, and to gain more worldly friends. This way he can look down on the Christians as being not worldly wise enough, and the new friends as insufficiently spiritual. If he develops a conscience, he can believe it's a puritanical impulse – something that Screwtape notes has brought many to their Father Below. The different forms of humour provide more opportunities, particularly anything that pushes the Patient towards dismissing sacred things. He should carry on going to church, but learn not to take it overly seriously – his conscience may prick at this, but it won't lead him to repent properly, and thus give the Enemy control.

However, when the Patient does repent, and begins to become genuinely humble, Screwtape is worried, and suggests making him proud of his humility. He should focus on the uncertain future (there's been a lull in the war), rather than the present or eternity. He should try different churches, particularly ones which don't follow biblical teaching, or are inconsistent – Low Church or High Church, it doesn't matter which. And Screwtape advises that the Patient become a glutton 'of delicacy' rather than 'excess', quoting the example of a little old lady who 'only' wants quite specific things, no matter what she's offered.

On the subject of love, Screwtape notes that people are selfish, so true love is not possible for them. When they 'fall in love', they are focusing on their own pleasure. Ideally, therefore, the Patient should fall in love and then marry someone who will make his continued life as a Christian difficult – Wormwood should give him false expectations about women, so he'll marry the right person for their needs. Everything that the Patient has – his body, his time – is his to dictate use of: the concept of his belonging to the Enemy shouldn't cross his mind.

The Patient gets a new girlfriend just before Letter XXII and, to Screwtape's anger, she is a Christian girl. His anger is intensified when he realizes Wormwood has betrayed one of his earlier indiscretions about the Enemy to the Secret Police, and he becomes so furious that he turns into a centipede! Once calmed down, he advises Wormwood to try to undermine the faith of the new Christians he is meeting through his girlfriend by focusing on the historical Jesus, and the political benefits of Christianity. Both will keep him away from proper worship.

When Screwtape talks to his colleague Slumtrimpet, who is in charge of Wormwood's Patient's girlfriend, he learns that she thinks unbelievers are inferior. The Patient is to be made to think the same way and take pride in his superiority. They should look for something new in their faith so they are not 'merely' Christians. The courtship period is also a good time to sow seeds of resentment, with the Patient and his girlfriend apparently being unselfish but each being offended when the other doesn't notice it.

The concept of Time concentrates Screwtape's mind when he talks about prayer. The idea that God is outside time and thus not constricted by it is missed by humans, who don't understand the correlation between that and the efficacy of prayer. Time may not be on the tempters' side, they realize, when bombing raids begin in the Patient's city – he is still in the wrong spiritual condition for them. More time equals more opportunities to tempt him but for now they decide to aim him towards cowardice. That will mean he will put his faith in precautions he takes, rather than in the Enemy.

Unfortunately for Screwtape and Wormwood (particularly the latter), the Patient copes well with the first air raid, but is killed in the second – and is taken straight to the Enemy. All Wormwood can now look forward to is being devoured in Hell for failing in his task.

The format of the *Letters* came to Lewis while sitting in his local church on a Sunday morning in 1940 listening to a sermon, shortly after hearing an address on the radio by Adolf Hitler. Jack Lewis's Hell is a bureaucracy populated by devils, one that he likened to that found in a police state 'or the offices of a thoroughly nasty business concern'. Prefaces to the book point out that Jack didn't believe in 'the Devil' as a power equal and opposite to God, but in Satan, the leader of devils, who is the opposite of St Michael, the chief angel. Although inspiration came quickly, and he was able to choose the topics without too many problems, he found writing the actual letters themselves difficult, since he had to put himself in the position of Screwtape, someone who could find no trace of beauty without wanting to eradicate it. According to his stepson Douglas Gresham, that made it Jack's least favourite book to write.

This sort of satire wasn't new – Lewis himself recognized a debt to a 1922 book by Stephen McKenna, *Confessions of a Well-Meaning Woman*, which featured the same moral inversion: 'the blacks all white and the whites all black'. It confused some of its readers: in the postscript to *Screwtape Proposes a Toast*, Lewis recalled that one country clergyman cancelled his subscription to *The Guardian* because much of the advice seemed to be 'positively diabolical'. It fared better with other reviewers who understood Lewis's points well. The *Saturday Review of Literature* referred to it as 'a spectacular and satisfactory nova in the bleak sky of satire' and the *Manchester Guardian* noted that the book 'is sparkling yet truly reverent . . . a perfect joy.'

Lewis refused the £2 weekly fee for the *Letters*' publication in *The Guardian*, instead providing a list of widows and orphans to whom it should be sent. The book version was published in February 1942 in the UK, and a year later in the United States, dedicated to his great friend J. R. R. Tolkien. Minor changes were made during the book's printings: a reference to seeing the number 73 bus going past the British Museum was altered, after numerous correspondents pointed out that it didn't. (Lewis jokingly claimed that this error would 'prove' that the book was written 200 years later than it really was – in the same way that religious texts are pulled apart to see if they really can date from their supposed era.)

When *The Pilgrim's Regress* was reprinted, Lewis provided 'headers' to explain the allegories. He fought off suggestions of anything similar, such as an index of sins covered, for *Screwtape*, pointing out that the whole idea of the book was to provide the reader with self-knowledge '*under pretence* [sic] of being a joke'. An index would 'give the bluff away' and worldly readers whom Lewis was aiming to catch would avoid the book.

Over the next fifteen years, Lewis resisted all temptation to continue Screwtape's moral lectures, noting in 1953 that '[t]he very fact that people ask for more proves it was the right length'. However, when he received an invitation from the *Saturday Evening Post* to pen something for them, 'that pressed the trigger'. The result was *Screwtape Proposes a Toast*, which first appeared in the newspaper on 19 December 1959. Screwtape has been invited to give a speech at 'the annual dinner of the Tempter's Training College for young Devils', and in the way of alumni returning to their seat of learning to pass on their realms of knowledge, he talks about past glories and the promise of better things to come – even if, at the end of the 1950s, there aren't rich pickings to be had among human souls, such as Henry VIII or Hitler. The *Toast* explains the problems that can be caused by the idea of democracy, and the difficulties that can be exploited in the education system – a theme that Lewis had been writing about for twenty years in both his non-fiction and fiction (*That Hideous Strength* and the first two Narnia stories featuring Eustace Scrubb).

Even before it appeared in the paper, Lewis had discussed a book version, possibly to be called 'The Whole Screwtape'; which combined the *Letters* with the *Toast*. He agreed to write a new preface over the 1959/60 Christmas vacation, and there were various discussions over the title, with his publishers keen that the buying public not be deceived into thinking that most of the book was new. Lewis was more concerned that the order be presented correctly, and everything was eventually sorted out to all parties' satisfaction. Lewis provided a copy of the pen-and-ink portrait of Screwtape that he had drawn for the first American edition of the *Letters* to be used on the cover of the combined *Screwtape*, and requested that *The Cambridge Review* not receive a review copy since they would 'blackguard any book of mine'.

The final book ended up with the unwieldy title *The Screwtape Letters and Screwtape Proposes a Toast* for its appearance in the UK in February 1961 and the following year in America; the 'and' was altered to 'with' for later US editions. The *Toast* was also reprinted as the centrepiece of a collection of short writings that appeared in January 1965.

Although the epistolary nature of the book sometimes works against Lewis being able to expand on his themes – which leads to his returning to some of them later on – the short, sharp format means that Lewis doesn't waste a word. Both the *Letters* and the later *Toast* are easily accessible, and unsurprisingly, some of Jack Lewis's most popular works.

8

THE GREAT DIVORCE

The Screwtape Letters indicated how the Devil could inveigle himself into the minds of ordinary folk; Lewis's next piece of fiction saw him return to the allegorical sphere of writing, which had been so successful in *The Pilgrim's Regress*. His novel *The Great Divorce*, published in 1945, once again looks at human life from an unusual perspective, this time from the point of view of a group of passengers who we realize are visiting Heaven and are being given a second chance. It gave Lewis the opportunity to answer many of the questions which he felt Christians were being faced with, and to present situations which would be familiar to many of those who read it – particularly those whose first encounter was within the pages of *The Guardian*, in which, like *Screwtape*, it originally appeared.

The narrator, who we can deduce from the final section is Lewis himself, is wandering around a dreary grey town, lit by a perpetual grey twilight, without ever finding a 'nice' area. He joins a queue of people waiting at a bus stop, many of whom are arguing with each other, then boards the bus, which proceeds to fly off. After chatting with some of his fellow passengers – including a poet who committed suicide partly because of the alliance with the communists during the Second World War, an intelligent-looking man who tells him (and the reader) about their departure point, Hell; and a fat clean-shaven man who has his own theories on the subject – he realizes that the bus is being filled with an unearthly light. This is a precursor to their arrival in Heaven, where it becomes clear that all on board are ghosts – as they realize when they discover everything in Heaven is too heavy for them to pick up, despite their best endeavours.

Angels come to greet them, but there's no one specifically for the narrator, who proceeds to listen in to a conversation between a Big Man and an angel who used to be a murderer but repented. The former can't believe it's fair that a murderer is saved and he isn't, and returns to the bus in disgust. The narrator briefly meets two lions, and then eavesdrops on an angel talking with the fat clean-shaven man. The town from which they left is Hell if you don't leave, but only Purgatory if you choose to repent. The man doesn't believe this, and argues semantics with his angelic friend, before also deciding to return to what he still won't accept is Hell.

The intelligent-looking man wants to take an apple from one of the trees in Heaven back with him, but when he finally manages to pick the smallest one up, he's warned to put it back, since he can't take it to Hell. Better to stay in Heaven and learn to eat them, he's advised.

The narrator isn't impressed with this attitude, and finds a hard-bitten man, who explains that what is failing to impress *him* is the whole business of Heaven and Hell. He thinks they're just 'advertising stunts', set up by a 'World Combine'; it's part of the 'same old lie' he's been fed since he was a child. Listening to this, the narrator wonders if he might be right and the angels are just making fun of those who have travelled there from Hell. The narrator continues onwards and finds a well-dressed woman hiding from her angel, because she is ashamed about what she's wearing. She won't believe the angel when he says it's of no consequence, and eventually the angel loses patience and summons a herd of unicorns that stampede through.

The next person the narrator encounters is someone he knows: Scottish writer George MacDonald, whom the narrator has admired. MacDonald explains that they are in 'Not Deep Heaven', a place where the denizens of Hell can visit. They meet various people whose motivations are dubious: one woman is constantly complaining, another thinks she can attract the angels by looking sexually attractive, and a famous artist, who likes the idea of Heaven, but can't accept that everyone is equal and he won't be famous there.

After this, they meet a domineering wife, who wants the angel with whom she is talking to return her husband to her so she can continue badgering him in death as she did in life. The angel, unsurprisingly, refuses, much to the woman's annoyance.

They then witness a meeting between an angel and his sister, a ghost. The woman hoped to meet her son, who died young and with whom she has been obsessed for the rest of her life, staying angry with God for taking him. Her brother explains that she chose to live in the past, and let her loss define her.

A more positive encounter follows: a man has a wicked red lizard perched on his shoulder, and eventually allows the angel to kill the lizard, despite the lizard's most persuasive arguments. This permits him to become an angel himself, the only one of the ghosts to remain in Heaven.

An angel named Sarah Smith is fêted as one of the 'Great Ones' for her good works on Earth, where she was kind and humble. She is there for two ghosts – a Tragedian (an actor), led on a chain by a dwarf, who are both aspects of the same man, her former husband. The dwarf tries to blackmail her with his self-pity, and won't listen to her arguments. Finally he becomes so resentful that he disappears, leaving just the Tragedian.

The narrator then sees a giant chessboard, and understands that the pieces are people in the world, watched over by larger figures, which are their immortal souls. When he asks whether people are simply playing out choices that had already been made, he's told not to ask more from a vision than a vision can give . . . The narrator is still alive, and only dreaming all this. He wakes with a start, as a clock strikes three and an air-raid siren is howling.

Jack Lewis mentioned the idea to his brother Warnie in April 1933, but it was another decade before *The Great Divorce* saw print, dedicated to his typist, Barbara Wall, 'Best and most long-suffering of scribes.' The idea of the 'Refrigerium' – a holiday for the inhabitants of Hell – derived from the writings of the seventeenth-century Anglican, Jeremy Taylor, whose work Lewis read in the summer of 1931, and can be traced even earlier, to the fourth century AD. The idea of a guided tour of one of the eternal realms pays homage to Dante's *Divine Comedy*; in the classic poem, the writer is guided by his spiritual ancestor, the Roman poet Virgil. Here the narrator meets someone that he too wishes to emulate, his teacher, MacDonald. Lewis presented *The Great Divorce* to a meeting of the Inklings in April 1944; at the time, he called it *Who Goes Home?*, the cry of the policemen in the House of Commons after the chamber has finished sitting. (This title was used for the serialization of the book in *The Guardian*.) The new title reflects a reversal of William Blake's *The Marriage of Heaven and Hell*, and ends with one of Lewis's central tenets: 'All that are in Hell, choose it.' It concludes with a conscious nod to *The Pilgrim's Progress* when the narrator wakes to realize it was all a dream.

When it was published, it attracted some complaints: A. C.

Deane in *The Spectator* described the work's 'glittering yet
distasteful pages', and said it lacked 'consciousness of infinite
love and supernatural redemption'. *The Times Literary Supplement* nailed one of the book's strengths: 'Those who find
themselves in agreement with the arguments put up by the
Ghosts for not being saved will be unable to finish the book.'

Some of the same themes that Jack Lewis would later use
in the Narnia stories appear in *The Great Divorce*: the idea
of a preview of Heaven, which can be found in *The Voyage of
the Dawn Treader* and the end of *The Silver Chair*; and the
concept of the Shadowlands – our world being simply a pale
copy of the original – are both rehearsed here.

The Great Divorce is the shortest of Lewis's books for
adults, and often betrays its roots as a series of articles, which
does make it easier to dip in and out of than some of his
other works. Lewis's last novel for adults for over a decade
is certainly more provocative than *The Pilgrim's Regress* or
Screwtape – in the latter, the turning upside down of the usual
rules can sometimes mask the core truths – and seventy years
later, many of the archetypes whom Lewis portrays are easily
recognizable.

9

THE CHRONICLES OF NARNIA

While his science-fiction trilogy is known to fans of the genre, and his religious writings are essential reading for most Christian scholars, the main reason Jack Lewis is known by the general public is his seven-book series the Chronicles of Narnia, published annually between 1950 and 1956, and never out of print subsequently. Audiences have been enthralled by the land of the White Witch and Aslan the lion ever since *The Lion, the Witch and the Wardrobe* first appeared. Generations of children's first encounter with them came as bedtime reading, and television adaptations in 1967, 1979/80 and 1988 increased their popularity. With the rapid advances in computer-generated techniques, it was no surprise when the estate of C. S. Lewis eventually consented to a series of films from Walden Media, which began in 2005.

Although they are names that have entered the English language through their use in Lewis's books, both the words Narnia and Aslan existed before Lewis appropriated them for the Chronicles. Aslan is the Turkish word for lion; Narnia (or Narni as it is now known) is a small town in Italy, between Rome and Assisi, which boasts a thirteenth-century fortress and has the largest Roman bridge ever constructed, the Ponte di Augusto.

Many thousands of words have been published analysing the stories, and those interested in delving deeper into their meaning are recommended to read the books by Lewis's secretary, Walter Hooper, notably *Past Watchful Dragons*, which includes long excerpts from earlier versions of the stories, referenced in this volume. Hooper's interpretation of these aborted tales may not always align with Lewis's intentions but by presenting the complete texts, the reader can make up their own mind.

The following sections do not discuss the various alterations made to the stories for their adaptations into different media: these can be found in the relevant portions of part 4. However, since the Walden Media films do deviate – sometimes, particularly in the case of *Prince Caspian* – quite markedly from the original text, a summary of each adventure is provided as it appeared in the Chronicles.

These are discussed in chronological order within the fiction, rather than the order in which they were originally published, following the list that Lewis himself suggested when a young reader wrote to him querying the order in 1957. Anyone coming to the Chronicles for the first time, though, may well do best to read *The Lion, the Witch and the Wardrobe* before anything else – and then perhaps go back to *The Magician's Nephew* for the prequel, and continue on from there in chronological order.

10

THE CHRONICLES OF NARNIA: *THE MAGICIAN'S NEPHEW*

It's early in the twentieth century, a time when Sherlock Holmes is still residing in Baker Street. Young Polly Plummer is surprised to find Digory Kirke living next door to her; he is staying with his mad magician uncle, Andrew Ketterley, and his aunt Letty since his father is in India and his mother is very sick. The two decide to investigate a passage in the eaves of the terraced houses, believing that they can drop through into an empty house.

However, they end up in Uncle Andrew's laboratory; he tries to keep them there, but eventually relents if Polly will take one of the glowing yellow rings on the table. When Polly picks it up, she vanishes. Uncle Andrew tells Digory that she has been sent to another world, following in the paw-steps of a guinea pig he dispatched earlier. The rings were made with dust from another world, via Atlantis, and passed to him by his fairy godmother. He believes that the green rings will return the user to Earth.

Digory agrees to use the yellow ring to find Polly, and is transported to a pool inside a wooded area, where there are lots of pools. Although both Polly and Digory initially have amnesia, they see the guinea pig and their memories return. After checking that the green rings really do work (but using the yellow rings to reverse course before they arrive back in Uncle Andrew's study), they decide to investigate the other pools, and see if they lead to yet further worlds.

They arrive in a world covered in red light, which is apparently uninhabited. They go through a series of halls until they find one filled with what seem to be statues. Those at the start look happy; the ones at the end are miserable, with a gradual change visible on those between. The final woman is a large woman who Digory thinks is very beautiful, although Polly doesn't share his opinion. There's also a pillar with a golden bell and a hammer, with an inscription warning that striking the bell will cause danger, but that anyone who doesn't will go mad wondering what might have happened.

Over Polly's objections, Digory strikes the bell. The building starts to collapse but once the dust has settled, they realize that the woman has woken. She tells them that she is Jadis, former queen of the empire of Charn; she destroyed her world to prevent her sister from taking over, by using 'the deplorable word'. She interrogates them about Earth, and deduces that Uncle Andrew must be the ruler, since he created the rings. She orders them to take her with them, and manages to grab hold of Polly's hair as she travels to the Wood Between the Worlds.

The youngsters try to get away from her to return to London, but Jadis begs for mercy, and when Digory hesitates for a moment, she grabs his ear and accompanies them back to Uncle Andrew's attic room. Uncle Andrew is delighted at her arrival; Jadis is less impressed with Edwardian London, and decides that she will be Empress of the World. After Digory apologizes for not listening to her advice earlier, Polly agrees to help him if she can.

While Uncle Andrew takes Jadis out to get appropriate finery and jewels, Digory overhears his aunt Letty saying that the only way to cure his mother is a visit to the land of youth. Digory wonders if one of the pools will lead there, but before he can do anything further, Jadis arrives back in a hansom cab, pursued by another cab with police officers and a jeweller (whom she has robbed) inside. Digory tries to grab Jadis to take her back but when he and Polly do so, they are accompanied by Andrew and the cabby (and his horse). Jadis is still holding a steel bar that she broke off a lamp post to attack a policeman with but she is weakened by the Wood. Digory immediately takes the party through to a new world, which is in total darkness. The cabby suggests singing a hymn; Digory and Polly join in – as does another voice, singing an incredibly beautiful song (which Andrew and Jadis loathe). The stars begin to appear and sing along, and then day breaks, and the humans realize that a huge lion is singing.

Jadis tries to attack the lion – Aslan – as it creates all the plants and animals on this new world, but is ignored. Two of each animal are then given the power of speech (although Uncle Andrew cannot understand any of this). Aslan then makes the cabby's nag Strawberry a talking horse and appoints the cabby, Frank, as the first King of Narnia, alongside his wife Helen, whom he calls across the worlds.

Digory asks Aslan to help his mother, and the lion sends him on an errand to fetch an apple which will keep Jadis out of Narnia. Polly and Strawberry (now with wings) help him, and despite Jadis trying to tempt him to either eat an apple himself or take one back for his mother, Digory brings back just the one apple as instructed. The apple is planted and a tree from it bears fruit the next day; Aslan gives Digory one for his mother, which will cure her. The steel bar grows into a lamp post.

Andrew, Digory and Polly are returned to London, where no time has passed. Andrew runs to hide, while Digory and Polly retrieve all the rings and bury them along with the core of the apple that has cured Digory's mother. When the tree that grew from there eventually was blown over, Digory had the wood made into a wardrobe, which he kept in the manor house in which he lived as an old professor . . .

Originally entitled *Polly and Digory*, *The Magician's Nephew* was the penultimate book in the Chronicles of Narnia to see print, but reading the stories in chronological order – as Jack Lewis suggested – it comes first, relating the genesis of Narnia. The biblical parallels are clear, particularly in the latter part of the book, as Aslan 'sings' the world into being (in much the same way as in Tolkien's *The Silmarillion*) in the same order as 'our' universe is created in the first chapter and a half of the Book of Genesis, and then there is temptation over an apple. There are also links with Lewis's own discussions about the battle between the concepts of natural law and sovereignty, which he debated in his 1944 book about sixteenth-century English Literature.

In modern terminology, *The Magician's Nephew* is a pre-quel to *The Lion, the Witch and the Wardrobe* (Lewis wouldn't have described it as such: the term was first used in 1958) and Lewis was working on it for some time before he considered it ready for publication. Various elements are set up for *The Lion* . . . including the wardrobe itself, built, as we learn here, with wood from another dimension; the talking animals; and the White Witch herself, Jadis, who has already destroyed one world and is quite happy to extend her reign of terror to wherever she finds herself. The old professor's understanding regarding Narnia makes much more sense when we realize that he was present at its creation (and you realize how much he's concealing when Peter and Susan first go to ask his advice after Lucy's first trip through the wardrobe), and we discover why Sons of Adam and Daughters of Eve are so important to the Narnian monarchy – it derived from them originally. The lamp post that guides Lucy when she first arrives in Narnia was the catalyst for the story in the first place: Jack Lewis's friend (and later biographer) Roger Lancelyn Green asked him how the lamp post had come to be there.

In *Past Watchful Dragons*, Walter Hooper includes a large piece of an early part of Lewis's work on *The Magician's Nephew*, known as the 'Lefay Fragment'. Although this too features Digory, the set-up is quite different from the final version of the story. Digory lives with his aunt Gertrude after his parents' death, and, thanks to a big oak in his garden, he is able to talk to the animals and the trees. However, when the girl next door, Polly, encourages him to cut a limb off the tree to make a raft, he loses the ability. He is visited by his godmother, Mrs Lefay, who tells Digory that he looks like Adam must have done shortly after being turfed out of the Garden of Eden, and suggests that he should visit a furniture shop, whose address she provides on a card. On that intriguing note (would he perhaps have found the Wardrobe there?) the fragment finishes mid-sentence.

Lewis hit various snags while writing *The Magician's Nephew*. After restarting the book, this time in the manner with which we are familiar, he had reached the three-quarters mark when he showed the manuscript to Roger Lancelyn Green. Green was critical of a section that showed Digory visiting the dying world of Charn and spending time with 'Piers the Ploughman' and his wife. When Lewis revised the book for eventual publication, he removed this section.

There are some links to other fiction as well as the Narnia stories. The way in which the children travel between the worlds, described most clearly as Digory follows Polly to the Wood the first time around, is very reminiscent of the way in which Ransom travels in Lewis's first science-fiction novel, *Out of the Silent Planet*. The narrator of *The Magician's Nephew* references the Bastable family in the opening sentence, the heroes of a number of E. Nesbit's tales, which Jack had enjoyed reading as a child when they first appeared in the opening decade of the twentieth century. Mrs Lefay bears a name that will ring bells with anyone familiar with the

Arthurian legend – Morgan Le Fay is another name for Morgana, the antagonist in many versions of the story, including the twenty-first century BBC incarnation.

According to Lewis's own 'Outline of Narnian History', the terrestrial portions of *The Magician's Nephew* are set in 1900, earlier perhaps than the internal evidence suggests. Digory was born in 1888, Polly a year later. For Narnia, it's year one, and a thousand years will go by before there is a proper visitation from Earth – although Lewis does note that in Narnian Year 460, pirates from our world manage to pass through, as mentioned in *Prince Caspian*. Digory reappears in *The Lion, the Witch and the Wardrobe*, and again in *The Last Battle*, where Polly also is seen.

The Magician's Nephew was published in the UK in May 1955 and in America five months later. Dedicated to the Kilmer Family, an American family with whom Lewis corresponded regularly, it was well received by critics. Described by the *New York Times Book Review* when it was published as 'one of [Narnia's] best crops', it still draws readers in, although there is a good argument to be made for reading it after the other books in the series (although before *The Last Battle*), as it does tie together so many of the elements from those books.

11
THE CHRONICLES OF NARNIA:
THE LION, THE WITCH AND THE WARDROBE

Four children – Peter, Susan, Edmund and Lucy Pevensie – are evacuated to a house in the countryside to get away from the bombing of the cities by the Germans at the start of the Second World War. They are warned by the housekeeper, Mrs Macready, not to disturb the Professor, but they are able to make up their own games – including hide-and-seek, during which Lucy, the youngest, hides in a wardrobe in the spare room. To her amazement, she finds herself in a snowy landscape, illuminated by a lamp post. She meets Mr Tumnus, a faun, who takes her to his cave and makes her tea.

Tumnus explains that she is in Narnia, which is ruled by an evil queen who has brought a hundred years of winter, but never Christmas. There are those who are waiting for Aslan to return. Tumnus knows he ought to prevent Lucy from leaving and pass her over to the queen, but in the end, he decides to help her back to the wardrobe.

None of Lucy's siblings believes her but when Lucy goes back into the wardrobe, Edmund follows, and also finds himself in Narnia. He, however, encounters the Queen of Narnia, travelling across the snow in her reindeer-pulled sledge. Enchanted by her magical Turkish Delight, Edmund promises to bring the others to the queen. Once she has gone, Lucy returns from visiting Tumnus, and they go back home – but Edmund refuses to back up her story, maintaining he was just going along with her story.

After they seek the Professor's advice (he asks them which of the younger two is the more credible and suggests they follow their instincts – or mind their own business), Peter and Susan have to hide in the wardrobe with the other two to avoid a tour party. They all arrive in Narnia, and Edmund quickly gives himself away. They find that Tumnus has been arrested and follow a robin that leads them to a talking beaver. The beaver and his wife feed the quartet, and tell them about the prophecy that the queen's reign will end when two sons of Adam and two daughters of Eve sit on the thrones at Cair Paravel. During the meal, Edmund sneaks out to go to the queen.

Realizing their brother will betray them, the other Pevensies join the Beavers heading to the Stone Table to meet Aslan. On the way they meet Father Christmas, who gives them magical gifts: a sword for Peter, a horn as well as a bow and arrows for Susan, and a magical healing potion for Lucy. The queen's power is waning, if Father Christmas can appear and the snow that has covered Narnia for a century is starting to thaw.

The queen has realized this too: alerted by Edmund, she sends her secret-service agents – wolves led by Maugrim – to the beavers' house, and then to the Stone Table. She heads for the Table, taking Edmund with her, and meets a group of creatures that have been given a feast by Father Christmas, and turns them to stone. When Edmund tries to intercede on their behalf, she turns on him, and he realizes that he is in trouble.

The beavers and the other three Pevensies reach the Stone Table ahead of the queen and Edmund, and meet Aslan. Lucy asks whether Edmund can be saved, and Aslan says it may be harder than she thinks. Maugrim, the wolf, eavesdrops on the meeting and chases Susan up a tree. She blows her horn for help, and Aslan sends Peter to fight Maugrim. He slays the wolf and is knighted by Aslan.

Although the queen considers killing Edmund to prevent the prophecy from coming true, she decides to sacrifice him at the Stone Table. When they reach there, Edmund is rescued by Aslan's forces, and the lion tells his siblings there is no need to deal with what has happened. The queen demands safe passage and reminds Aslan that under the 'Deep Magic' every traitor belongs to her as lawful prey, and she has the right to a kill. The two negotiate in private, and Aslan announces that the queen has renounced her claim on Edmund, but doesn't explain how. Whatever the reason, it has made the queen very happy.

That night, Lucy and Susan can't sleep, and follow Aslan when he secretly leaves the camp; he allows them to ride on him as he travels up the hill to the queen's camp. The girls hide and watch in horror as Aslan is muzzled, shorn and killed on the Stone Table. The queen believes that he has died in vain: she will still kill Edmund, and Narnia will be hers for ever.

Once the queen and her minions have abandoned Aslan's body, the girls try to untie him, and as the sun rises, their efforts are helped by field mice that chew through the bonds. They are heading back to the camp, still dejected, when they hear a cracking sound and turn to see the Table split in two and the body gone. Aslan is alive: an even Deeper Magic states that if a willing victim dies in a traitor's place, the Table will crack and Time will run backwards.

The queen's forces have attacked Aslan's people, who are

led by Peter. Aslan, Lucy and Susan head to the queen's castle, where she has kept her enemies, frozen as statues. Aslan's breath revives them and they race to join the battle. The day is won when Aslan himself pounces on the queen.

The Pevensies are crowned at Cair Paravel, and their reign of peace and harmony begins. Some years later they are hunting for the White Stag when they find the lamp post – and find themselves back in the Professor's house. When they recount their adventures, the Professor tells them that one day they may go back . . .

The first, and for many, the best of the Chronicles of Narnia, *The Lion, the Witch and the Wardrobe* is Narnia's equivalent of the Passion and Resurrection of Christ. Although the parallels aren't exact, it is hard to escape the similarities between the victim who was slain for mankind's sins, according to the Bible, and Aslan's willingness to be sacrificed in Edmund's place. The victim's body is tended to by women after death, and they are the first to witness his resurrection. The state of Narnia before this sacrifice is more allegorical, if you're trying to make more of the analogy between the two – the queen (i.e. Satan)'s grip is on the land, and although there are promises of good times, they never arrive. The eternal winter also spoke to Lewis's other great obsession with northernness: in Norse tradition, the Fimbulwinter is the prelude to the end of the world.

Lewis had begun writing the first draft of a children's story as early as September 1939, when three schoolgirls were evacuated from London and sent to live with Lewis and Mrs Moore at The Kilns. Only a small portion of this exists, and relates how four children – Ann, Martin, Rose and the youngest, Peter – were sent to live with a relation of their mother's, a professor who lived in the country. Their father was in the Army, their mother was doing important war work. Little more is known about their adventures, although there are suggestions that Lewis did complete the story, but then destroyed it because his friends unanimously said that it was bad. (The scrap was found on the back of part of the manuscript for a short-lived sequel to *Out of the Silent Planet* entitled *The Dark Tower*; see part II, chapter 4 for the questions over its validity – and accordingly of this fragment found with it.)

At the start of 1949, though, Jack tried again. In an essay entitled 'It All Began With A Picture', he recounts how an image he had had in his mind since he was sixteen began to recur: it was a faun carrying an umbrella and parcels in a snowy wood. Now, aged forty, he decided to make a story to accompany the picture. Until he dreamed up the concept of Aslan, he wasn't entirely sure how the story would unfold, but once he did (after many dreams about lions, he later noted), Aslan 'pulled the whole story together'. In March, he read the first two chapters to Roger Lancelyn Green, who approved, and Lewis completed it that month. Green himself had penned a story entitled *The Wood That Time Forgot*, from which Lewis borrowed certain elements, including an apparently kindly character who is in fact a fallen angel and tries to persuade one of a group of children to turn against her fellows.

J. R. R. Tolkien wasn't as kind as Lancelyn Green had been. He too had read the manuscript for *The Lion, the Witch and the Wardrobe* and was not impressed by such items such as the titles of the books that Mr Tumnus had in his cave. It's fair to say that Lewis's respect for Tolkien's fantasy fiction wasn't reciprocated.

The Lion, the Witch and the Wardrobe: A Story for Children was published in October 1950 in the UK, with an American edition following a month later. There were minor differences between these: in the US versions, Edmund and Susan are interested in snakes rather than rabbits in the first chapter; the queen's Chief of Secret Police is named Fenris Ulf; and the description of the 'fire-stones of the Secret Hill' is replaced with 'the trunk of the World Ash Tree'. The last two changes increase the debt the story owes to Norse mythology: Fenris

Ulf is one of Loki's children, while the World Ash Tree, Ygg-drasil, is where Odin hangs for nine nights, after wounding himself with his spear. All of these changes were removed in 1994 when HarperCollins took responsibility for all editions worldwide.

The book was illustrated by Pauline Baynes, whose draw-ings for Tolkien's *Father Giles of Ham* had impressed Lewis. Tolkien himself had commented that friends thought they 'reduced my text to a commentary on the drawings'. Baynes herself thought that Lewis had gone to a bookshop and asked for a recommendation of an artist; whichever way it hap-pened, Baynes's forty-three pictures fit the story perfectly (and indeed reading any edition without them somehow feels wrong!).

The story begins in AD 1940 for the Pevensies and the Professor, lasting a few days in terrestrial time. In Narnia, though, it's the year 1000, and Jadis has been back in charge for the last 102 years. The High Kings and Queens reign for fifteen years, vanishing from Narnia in 1015, a year after Susan and Edmund visited the court of Calormen, and King Lune of Archenland found his long-lost son Cor – a story that is told in the fifth published Chronicle, *The Horse and His Boy*. It will be nearly 1,300 years before the Pevensies return to Narnia, during which time the Telmarines conquer Narnia, and Caspian I and his descendants take the throne.

Lewis was no doubt pleased by the review in the *Guard-ian* on 23 February 1951, which compared it favourably with Hans Christian Andersen, and Lewis's own inspiration George MacDonald. Equally, he was probably delighted by the seven-year-old boy who reviewed the book for the Chil-dren's Christmas Number of *Time and Tide* in December 1950, who said that 'this book is very nice. It could not be better.'

12

THE CHRONICLES OF NARNIA:
THE HORSE AND HIS BOY

As far as young Shasta knows, he is the son of Arsheesh, a tough fisherman on the coast of Calormen, a land far to the south of Narnia, separated from it by Archenland. But when one night he overhears a Calormene nobleman, known as a Tarkaan, offer to buy him from his father, he discovers that Arsheesh isn't related to him at all: he simply found Shasta as an infant in a small boat that landed on the shore nearby. Discussing his options out loud with himself in the stable, he is amazed when his horse joins the discussion, since he has never heard of a talking beast. The horse, Bree, explains that he is a talking horse from Narnia, who was captured by the Calormene and has remained silent ever since. He suggests that he and Shasta escape to Narnia together, and once the two adults are asleep, they sneak away.

They travel together for some weeks, and Bree realizes they will need to travel through the capital city, Tashbaan, to cross the great river. He thinks they're being followed by another horse, possibly ridden by a Tarkaan, which stops when he stops. When they pause in a fog, they hear a lion's roar, and race away, as does the other horse. After crossing a river, they pause, but the lion roars again, and this time the two horses almost collide. Bree discovers that the other horse can also speak; Hwin and her rider, Aravis, a Tarkheena of around Shasta's age, are also trying to escape to the north. Over Aravis's objections, they team up.

Aravis explains that she has been promised in marriage to a much older Tarkaan, Ahoshta, and would have rather died than gone ahead. Hwin persuaded her not to do so, and helped her to escape. They came up with an elaborate plan to put everyone off their scent, and made a clean getaway.

Once they reach Tashbaan, they agree a rendezvous at the tombs on the far side in case they are separated, and disguise themselves as peasant children with pack horses. They've arrived at the same time as a party of Narnian lords, led by the 'White Barbarian King', Edmund. Shasta is mistaken for a runaway Narnian and taken with them to the Tisroc's palace where he learns that the Narnians think he is Prince Corin of Archenland, who disappeared the day before. Queen Susan is there because the Tisroc's son Rabadash wants to ask her to marry him; she has travelled there with an entourage including Mr Tumnus. Susan doesn't want to marry Rabadash, but is worried in case he kidnaps her to force her hand. Tumnus suggests that the Narnians invite the Tisroc to a banquet on the Narnian yacht in a couple of days' time; they can then be on board ostensibly preparing for the feast, but in fact they will sail away the night before the feast.

Shasta is woken by the arrival of Corin, who appears to be his mirror image. Corin had disappeared to deal with a boy who had insulted Queen Susan. The real prince allows Shasta to use his escape route to get away. However, when Shasta reaches the agreed meeting place at the tombs, no one else is there. Although he's scared by the thought of staying in a supposedly haunted place, he's reassured by the presence of a large cat, which curls up next to him.

Aravis, meanwhile, has been recognized by an old friend, the Tarkheena Lasaraleen, who brings her to the Tisroc's palace and promises to help her, even if she can't quite understand why Aravis can't see the benefits in being betrothed to a much older man. As the girls move through the palace, they have to hide to avoid detection by the Tisroc, and overhear the Tisroc, Rabadash and Ahoshta agree to send an army to conquer Archenland and then continue on to take Narnia.

When the two youngsters and their horses are reunited, they head off through the desert between Tashbaan and Archenland to try to warn of the impending attack. They are chased by a lion, which seems about to kill Aravis after scratching her before Shasta shouts at it to leave them alone – which it does. They meet a hermit, who can see visions and tells Shasta to run ahead to warn King Lune of Archenland.

Shasta finds the king, and is initially mistaken for his son Corin, but explains the situation. He's given a horse, but since he has only ever ridden Bree, he's confused by the reins and spurs, and falls behind the others. In a dense fog, he realizes that he is close to the enemy, so lets his horse take another route. He then senses someone else in the fog with him, and eventually learns that it's Aslan, who has been with him in various guises throughout his travels. When he wonders if he imagined the encounter, he sees a pawprint in the ground which is filled with fresh water.

Shasta crosses the border, and is found by some dwarves. They pass his message on to Cair Paravel using various talking animals, and King Edmund and Queen Lucy soon appear, along with Corin. The two boys are told to keep out of the forthcoming battle. During this, Rabadash is defeated, and turned into a donkey by Aslan after he refuses to speak politely to him; his curse will eventually be lifted, but if he strays from the Temple of Tash, it will be permanent.

The hermit tells Aravis, Bree and Hwin that Shasta is

alive, and the battle is over. They agree to head into Narnia, although Bree is worried about the way his tail now looks, since it had to be docked to maintain their disguise in Tashbaan. They encounter Aslan, who tells Aravis he wounded her so she knew how her servant felt when she was lashed for letting Aravis escape. Shasta arrives, and explains that he is really Prince Cor, Corin's older brother, and invites them to come to King Lune's castle. Shasta and Aravis marry each other; Bree and Hwin also get married, but to other horses.

The Horse and His Boy was one of the four stories that Jack Lewis completed even before *The Lion, the Witch and the Wardrobe* was published, but it was delayed until fifth for publication, so that the 'Caspian trilogy' (*Prince Caspian, The Voyage of the Dawn Treader* and *The Silver Chair*) could be released in order. It's an oddity among the Narnia books: it's set during the reign of the four Pevensie siblings (all the other books run in a discrete order rather than overlap), and it doesn't centre on visitors from our world to Narnia. Edmund, Lucy and Susan all play important roles – High King Peter is away dealing with giants in the Northern Lands, which is partly why the Calormenes believe that Narnia is vulnerable to attack – but the focus of attention is firmly on Shasta, Aravis, Bree and Hwin.

For those keeping track, it's approximately Narnian Year 1014, a year or so before the Pevensies' fifteen-year reign of the land comes to an end with their mysterious disappearance – so in 'real' terms, this takes place during the final chapter of *The Lion, the Witch and the Wardrobe*, which concludes with the Pevensies returning to our world in 1940.

Various different biblical parallels have been ascribed to this story. There are specific instances, such as Shasta washing himself using the water from Aslan's pawprint, which equate to Christian practices (in this case baptism). The story of Shasta's arrival in Calormen in the first place has echoes of the story of Moses in the Old Testament, in which the baby

Moses was placed in a basket of rushes, discovered by the Pharaoh's daughter when she was bathing, and grew up to become his nation's leader. The earlier tale of Joseph's life in Egypt is also relevant: like Shasta, he was sent to live away from home in a 'pagan' land, and then helped his homeland to deal with a disaster. The story of Esther is also apposite to this: like her, Shasta isn't aware of everything that is being done for her by the deity. And of course Aslan is acting as a guide and shepherd to Shasta, as set out in Psalm 23.

It's at this point (which is a comparative rarity in the Narnia books) that Aslan is reminiscent of all three parts of the Holy Trinity (God the Father, Son and Holy Spirit): he speaks to Shasta in three different voices, one so low that the earth shakes; a second 'loud and clear and gay'; and the final one like the susurration of the wind through the leaves.

Biblical teaching is also present, and Lewis himself noted that the book is about 'the calling and conversion of a heathen'. Although the title of the book deliberately makes it appear as if Bree is the more important character than Shasta (one of Lewis's other proposed titles was The Horse Stole the Boy, 'which might allure the "pony-loving" public', the author suggested), it's actually the latter who plays the more important role. As the story progresses, we realize that Bree is quite proud and self-obsessed – his worry about going to Narnia after his tail has been docked as part of their disguise is an indication of this. He wants to make a good impression when he meets other talking animals, and isn't sure whether rolling around on the ground is something that proper talking horses do. Even after his encounter with Aslan, he's still not quite got the message (and one has to wonder if that's why he and Hwin eventually go their separate ways).

There are, of course, other influences visible in The Horse and His Boy. The idea of twin princes separated was most famously used by Mark Twain in The Prince and the Pauper, but there are hints of the Roman gods Castor and Pollux in Cor and Corin – like Cor/Shasta, Pollux was a horseman, while his brother was a boxer, as we are told Corin grows up to be.

Originally entitled *Narnia and the North*, *The Horse and His Boy* was written between March and July 1950, and the eventual typescript was dedicated to David and Douglas Gresham, the sons of Joy Gresham, who would become Lewis's stepsons a few years later, following their visit to The Kilns in December 1953. The illustrations were completed by Pauline Baynes, and were complimented by Lewis in a letter in January 1954, in which he particularly praised the detail in the pictures of Tashbaan ('we only got its full wealth by using a magnifying glass') and the comedy of the pictures showing Rabadash turning into an ass. The endpapers of the original edition contained a map showing the relative positions of Tashbaan, the Desert and Archenland, drawn by Baynes.

The Horse and His Boy was published in September 1954 in the UK, and a month later in America. It was hailed as 'a beautifully written tale' by *Kirkus* and 'far above other modern fairy tales' by the *New York Herald Tribune Book Review*. It's perhaps more suitable for a slightly older audience than the earlier Chronicles – as with many children's series, including the Harry Potter books, the reading age required for the stories does progress. Children who read the first Narnia story in 1950 were ready for something a bit meatier four years later, and Lewis provides this in a story that hues closer to the Arabian Nights than his other work.

13

THE CHRONICLES OF NARNIA: *PRINCE CASPIAN: THE RETURN TO NARNIA*

A year or so after their adventures through the wardrobe, the Pevensie siblings find themselves pulled back into Narnia from the railway station where they were waiting for their trains back to boarding school. It takes them a bit of time to realize where they are, since they have arrived on an island, with an ancient apple orchard and some ruins overgrown with weeds. However, when Susan finds a gold chess piece, they work out that they are in the ruins of Cair Paravel, anything up to a millennium after their last visit. As memories start to come back, they recall the treasure room, and make their way there. Inside are their gifts from Father Christmas, apart from Susan's horn, as well as jewels and armour.

The next day, they decide to head for the mainland but before they can find a way, they see some soldiers about to throw something overboard from a boat in the river, something clearly still alive. Susan shoots at the soldiers, and two of them run off into the woods. Inside the bundle is a dwarf, who thinks that the Pevensies must be ghosts: 'new Narnians' avoid the area. Over breakfast, the dwarf, Trumpkin, explains what has been happening in Narnia:

Trumpkin has been sent to Cair Paravel by Prince Caspian, who ought, by rights, to be Caspian X of Narnia, following the death of his father when Caspian was still an infant. His uncle Miraz has acted as Protector as Caspian grew up, but the young prince was brought up with tales of Old Narnia – the victory of High King Peter over the White Witch, and the talking beasts (which have vanished from New Narnia). When Caspian mentioned these to his uncle, Miraz denied their truth, and replaced the nurse who told Caspian the stories with a new tutor, Dr Cornelius, who Miraz doesn't know is a half-dwarf, astronomer and magician. When Cornelius realizes how much danger Caspian is in after Miraz's wife has a baby boy of her own, he wakes the prince and sends him to the border with Archenland. He gives him some supplies as well as Queen Susan's horn, and tells him to use it to call for help from High King Peter, or even Aslan himself.

Caspian flees on his horse, but is knocked unconscious during a lightning storm. He wakes to find that his future is being debated by three creatures: the badger, Trufflehunter, who advocates letting him live; a dwarf, Nikabrik, who wants all humans dead; and Trumpkin, who is more moderate. Caspian persuades Trumpkin and Trufflehunter that he is the legitimate heir, and is given a tour of the Old Narnians – whom Nikabrik is convinced Caspian will betray to the Telmarines – including the squirrel Pattertwig, and the mouse Reepicheep. Although Caspian initially thinks of living in hiding with the Old Narnians, he is persuaded to come out fighting for his cause, with the support of the various creatures.

Dr Cornelius arrives to inform them that Miraz is trying to

find Caspian, and suggests regrouping at Aslan's How, which was built over the site of the Stone Table. Caspian and his troops try a surprise attack on Miraz's forces, but it's unsuccessful, so they decide to use the horn. Pattertwig is sent to Lantern Waste – where Lucy first appeared – and Trumpkin to Cair Paravel.

Trumpkin takes a bit of persuading that the youngsters in front of him are the help that the horn summoned, but eventually agrees to accompany them to Aslan's How. They travel downriver and finally reach an impassable point. Lucy believes she sees Aslan in the trees, directing them in a different direction from the one Peter and Trumpkin favour, but the others – except Edmund – don't believe her, and they waste time travelling the wrong way, and encountering enemy forces.

That night Aslan wakes Lucy and asks why she didn't follow him earlier. Lucy realizes she should have done, despite the others' objections, and obeys his instructions to wake the others and tell them to follow her. She takes what appears to be an impossible route down a gorge, but the others conclude that she must be following someone because otherwise she wouldn't have found the path. At the bottom, when Aslan drinks from the water, Edmund starts to see him, followed by Peter and Susan when they reach the top on the other side. Trumpkin needs a little more persuading, since he doesn't believe in lions – at least at first.

At Caspian's camp, Nikabrik is stirring up trouble, claiming that no help is coming and that the dwarves have borne the brunt of the attack. Suggesting that Aslan is dead, he brings two guests – a werewolf and a hag – into the camp, who start to invoke the spirit of the White Witch. Before too long, though, Peter, Edmund and Trumpkin arrive, killing the hag, the werewolf and Nikabrik.

Peter challenges Miraz to single combat and two of Miraz's own 'supporters' decide to take the opportunity to rid themselves of Miraz and seize power themselves. During the fight

Miraz trips, and Peter helps him to his feet; the two Lords stab the Protector in the back and claim it's Narnian treachery. However, before a full-scale battle can break out, tree people, roused from their slumber earlier by Aslan's singing, plunge through the ranks of Peter's army towards the Telmarines. The latter decide that this is the end of the world and flee – only to face Aslan, who most believed was a myth.

Lucy uses her cordial to restore Reepicheep, although without his tail until Aslan agrees to its regrowth. Caspian is knighted and crowned as king, and the Telmarines are offered a chance to return to our world, from where they originally came. They pass through a doorway, followed by the Pevensies – although Peter and Susan have been told that they are too old to return to Narnia . . .

Although the manuscript of *Prince Caspian* had been completed long before *The Lion, the Witch and the Wardrobe* was published in 1950, this may not have been the way that Jack Lewis had originally planned the return of his characters to Narnia. Some of his notes regarding future Narnia stories are reprinted in *Past Watchful Dragons*, although a close reading of them would indicate that he was looking at various different possibilities, rather than, as has been assumed by most readers, plotting *The Voyage of the Dawn Treader* as the second story.

The notes are divided into four sections: the first, headed 'SHIP', talks about two children finding themselves on an ancient ship which is travelling backwards through time, whose help is needed for a sick king. 'A very green and pearly story', it definitely fits *The Voyage of the Dawn Treader*. The second paragraph, 'PICTURE', suggests that one of the children goes into a picture, and something comes out. This idea is partly used in *The Voyage of the Dawn Treader* but also foreshadows the ending of *The Silver Chair*. 'INVERTED' is not used: a child from our world goes into a fairy-tale king and queen's court (although you could argue that this is a precursor to the idea in *Prince Caspian* that the everyday Pevensies are interlopers in the Old Narnian court). The final paragraph, 'SEQUEL TO L.W.W.', is the nearest to *Prince Caspian* as it unfolds: Men are now tyrants in Narnia, and a dwarf reveals the history. This very much covers the early part of the eventual second book. Elements from the Lefay Fragment (see part II, chapter 10) also are brought into *Prince Caspian*, notably the character of the squirrel Pattertwig.

Prince Caspian shows what happens when people turn away from the true faith and have to be brought back to the right path: Lewis himself called it 'restoration of the true religion after a corruption'. Miraz's claim to the throne is considered on a par with the Antichrist. This is a theme that Lewis comes back to, much more strongly, in the final book in the Chronicles, *The Last Battle*, with the character of Shift. It's also about the testing of faith: the sequence where Lucy sees Aslan, but chooses to follow what her brother and Trumpkin propose, but is given a second chance, is similar to the moments in the Sermon on the Mount where Jesus warns his listeners that they will lose friends and family members if they follow him. Nikabrik chooses to follow the wrong path to defeat Miraz – trying sorcery rather than believing in Aslan – and pays the price. The Old Testament story of Nehemiah – who was sent by God to restore the Israelites' faith after generations under Babylonian rule – also has some parallels to the efforts to bring the old religion back to Narnia.

Lewis drew on his own past for some elements of *Prince Caspian*. Growing up in early-twentieth-century Ireland, he would be used to seeing ruined castles, and he had learned the folk stories about the Irish at the knee of his nurse, Lizzie Endicott, in the same way as Caspian is taught about Narnia.

It's AD 1941, according to Lewis's own notes, when the Pevensies return to Narnia, even though nearly 1,300 years have elapsed there since their departure in 1015, and it's now 2303 in the Narnian calendar. Just over three hundred years earlier, the Telmarines (who first appeared in Narnia around

460 Narnian Time) had conquered Narnia, with Caspian I becoming ruler in 1998. Although a similar one-year period elapses for the human children in our world between this and the sequel, *The Voyage of the Dawn Treader*, only three years pass – Lewis's way of indicating that time is elastic.

Prince Caspian: The Return to Narnia was completed by December 1949 and first published in October 1951, one day apart either side of the Atlantic. It is dedicated to Mary Clare Havard, who at the time was a young teenager, the daughter of one of Lewis's friends. Jack showed her the manuscript of *The Lion, the Witch and the Wardrobe*, and took her criticisms (notably her querying of the lamp post in Narnia) seriously.

Lewis had proposed calling the story simply *Drawn into Narnia* or *A Horn in Narnia* but his publisher, Geoffrey Bles, wanted a snappier title; Lewis was able to ensure that a version of his preferred title was still part of the end result to convey the theme of the book. Pauline Baynes produced the illustrations once more, creating a map of 'Narnia and Adjoining Lands' for the endpapers, based on a map that Jack Lewis had drawn himself. Lewis had to ask for one drawing to be altered: Baynes had inadvertently shown a character rowing a boat in the wrong direction, and he requested her to make the children look a little less plain and 'pretty them up a little'.

Prince Caspian was hailed as 'a first-rate story' by the *Church Times* while the *New York Times Book Review* praised it for lacking 'the cuteness and archness that mar so many books written for children'. The structure is a bit odd, with a large portion of the early part of the book told as a flashback – and you can see why the makers of the Walden Media movie version decided to intercut the two plot strands – but this presents the reader with a new Narnia adventure that is familiar but very different from *The Lion, the Witch and the Wardrobe*. As Aslan points out, he doesn't repeat himself – something that Lewis was careful to maintain throughout the Chronicles. The next adventure would find two of the Pevensies, as well as an unwilling fellow traveller, all at sea.

14

THE CHRONICLES OF NARNIA: *THE VOYAGE OF THE DAWN TREADER*

Edmund and Lucy have been sent to stay with their cousin, Eustace Clarence Scrubb, while their parents and Susan are away, and Peter is studying with Professor Kirke. Eustace is a typical 'modern' boy, not interested in fantasy and adventure, and disbelieves the Pevensies' tales of Narnia. He dislikes a painting of a ship that's been hidden in Lucy's temporary bedroom – and dislikes the real ship, the *Dawn Treader*, even more when the painting comes alive and the three children find themselves on board.

Lucy and Edmund are delighted to find the ship belongs to King Caspian, now in the fourth year of his reign, and that their friend Reepicheep the mouse is with him. Their mission is twofold: to map the islands and seas beyond the immediate vicinity (and maybe find out more about the ocean across which Aslan travels to Narnia), and to find seven lords who had been banished by Caspian's uncle Miraz. Eustace threatens to sue all and sundry for every problem that he faces, much to Reepicheep's displeasure.

The first island looks idyllic but the three humans, Caspian and Reepicheep are captured by pirates who plan to sell them. Caspian stays incognito, but is recognized by Lord Bern, who buys him, and over the next three weeks, helps Caspian to restore order, ending the slave trade.

Leaving Lord Bern in charge, the ship heads east, and after some clear weather, they encounter a dreadful storm. Surviving that, they find an island covered with canyons and waterfalls. Eustace heads off and gets lost in the fog. He eventually finds the beach but sees a large creature (a dragon, although he doesn't realize it) coming out from a cave. It dies in front of him, and Eustace shelters from a storm in its cave, which is filled with treasure, including a bracelet, which he puts on his arm.

The next morning when Eustace wakes he discovers he is now a dragon. He locates the others and is finally able to explain his plight. A few days later, he becomes a boy once more: as he tells his friends, the preceding night he kept tearing layers of scales off only for them to regrow. But then Aslan appeared and offered to take them off completely; Eustace agreed, even though he was warned it would be painful.

The journey continues, and the next obstacle is a giant sea serpent which wraps itself around the ship. Eustace tries to fight it off, but ends up breaking his sword; Reepicheep exhorts everyone to work together to push it off. The next island looks promising: they find Narnian relics, and a statue of a man made of pure gold standing in a lake. However, they realize that the water in the lake turns anything it touches to gold, and the man is no statue, but Lord Restimar. Edmund and Caspian grasp the potential of this and begin arguing, which only stops when first Lucy and then all of them see Aslan. They decide to name it Deathwater rather than Goldwater Island and leave it untouched.

Their next stop is an island inhabited by invisible creatures, the Duffers. They ask Lucy to read a spell to make them visible and beautiful once more: they were made ugly by a magician whom they've not seen for some time. Lucy enters an ornate palace and finds the spell book, which she finds captivating, since the pictures within come alive to show the effects of the spells. She resists until she finds one that will make her beautiful, and outshine her sister. But as she starts to say it, she sees Aslan's face staring at her from the book, and hurriedly turns the page. Another spell allows her to overhear two girls gossiping about her, one of whom she considered a best friend.

Lucy finally finds the spell to restore visibility to things that were invisible – and immediately sees Aslan in the flesh. The lion chides her for eavesdropping, then introduces her to Coriakin, the wizard who turned the Duffers from ordinary dwarves into monopods. The Duffers decide to remain as they are, renaming themselves Dufflepods.

After leaving them behind, the crew encounter an island where dreams come true – or rather, all nightmares become reality. It's covered by an incredibly thick and dark mist, and they only learn of its existence when they answer a call for help from Lord Rhoop, who has managed to escape. The ship has great difficulty getting away until Lucy prays to Aslan to help them. He appears and encourages everyone to row hard. This they manage, but Lord Rhoop is incapable of telling them what he saw and it seems as if the island has now vanished for ever.

On their final island, they discover an open space similar to Stonehenge, where three men sit in a very deep sleep at a banqueting table. No one wants to touch the food in case that's what affected the men, but Reepicheep persuades his friends to spend the night there. They meet a woman who wonders why they've not eaten from Aslan's Table, and explains that the men were enchanted because one of them had picked up the knife that the White Witch used to kill Aslan (in *The*

Lion, the Witch and the Wardrobe). Only someone returning from Aslan's country can wake them. The woman introduces them to her father, another 'retired star' Ramandu, who says that they must sail to the end of the world and leave one of their members behind.

As they sail on, the water becomes sweet and provides all the food they need, and they then enter a sea filled with lilies. Finally they reach a waterfall that goes up, marking the boundary with Aslan's country. Caspian decides he will stay, but is persuaded of his responsibilities. Reepicheep paddles on in his coracle into Aslan's country, and the children meet a lamb, who invites them to breakfast; it turns into Aslan, who tells the Pevensie siblings that this is their last trip to Narnia. However, they can find his country from their own world, and must learn to recognize him by his name there.

The three humans are returned to Eustace's home and Caspian marries Ramandu's daughter. The only person really unhappy is Eustace's mother, who doesn't like his new attitude at all.

Another of the stories that Jack Lewis completed before the first publication of *The Lion, the Witch and the Wardrobe*, *The Voyage of the Dawn Treader* went through a few alterations along the way to its eventual release in 1952, although Roger Lancelyn Green noted that the manuscript he read had very few corrections and had been written in a 'white heat of inspiration'. Its genesis can be found in the notes referred to in the previous chapter – a combination of a ship that is travelling backwards through time to find a cure (the healing aspect of which becomes a small plot point at the end) and the idea of people from our world using a painting as the way to enter Narnia (although the idea of someone coming out in return isn't present here). The latter point owes a debt to George MacDonald's 1875 story *The Wise Woman* (sometimes called *The Lost Princess*), in which a young princess goes into a picture of a country hillside filled with sheep and a young shepherdess does the same with a picture of the princess's home.

As with *The Lion, the Witch and the Wardrobe*, there were also some changes between the British and American editions (or rather, those published before 1994), notably early on, where Lewis changed a description of Eustace being too stupid to make something up, to simply being incapable of doing so. Then in chapter 12, dealing with the emergence of the *Dawn Treader* from the black mist over the Dark Island, in the American version Lewis adds a comment from the narrator, equating the feeling that the crew experienced with the realization when you wake up and hear ordinary sounds that what has just felt so vivid was really just a dream. The fate of the Dark Island is also changed: in the British original, it disappears for good; however, American audiences were informed that it simply fell behind them as they travelled further forward. (This alteration has led to discrepancies in the plot descriptions of this story in various accounts.) Unfortunately, he didn't catch one error that slipped through into all editions: the Duffles' weapons are invisible when Lucy first encounters them, but in the next chapter, the plates and dishes they are carrying can be seen.

Only a few months have gone by for Edmund and Lucy, making this 1942 according to Lewis's own chronology (although the references to the Second World War are gone, making this dating a little suspect), but Caspian is in the fourth year of his reign over Narnia, making it around 2306–7. The next book is set at the end of Caspian's reign, half a century later, during which time he has a son, Prince Rilian, and Ramandu's daughter, his queen, is killed.

For Lewis, *The Voyage of the Dawn Treader* was about 'the spiritual life (especially in Reepicheep)' but to tell that story, he uses a form he would have learned about from his nurse Lizzie Endicott: the Immram, a tale of a hero's sea voyage to the Otherworld in Irish storytelling tradition. The *Dawn Treader* is heading east rather than the traditional west of these stories – heading into the dawn rather than away from it. His characters are on a pilgrimage to Aslan's country, dealing with various obstacles along the way. Rather than draw parallels with stories from the Old and New Testaments, Lewis is using allegory more, creating another *Pilgrim's Progress*, with his characters encountering doubt and temptation, needing to work together and persevere in order to overcome problems that they could not deal with on their own. It's a theme that he tackles in his adult novel *The Pilgrim's Regress* (see part II, chapter 2), while the glimpses of Aslan's country mirror the view of Heaven given to the inhabitants of Hell in *The Great Divorce* (part II, chapter 8). There are a few moments which are perhaps direct nods to biblical stories: Ramandu is dumb until a live coal is laid on his lips by a bird, in exactly the way indicated in a prophetic passage from Isaiah (6:6).

Lewis is perhaps more blatant in the final chapters than anywhere else previously in the Chronicles about Aslan's identity. Whereas a child, particularly those who had been to Sunday School, as many of his original readers would have done, could pick up the parallels in *The Lion, the Witch and the Wardrobe* between Aslan and Christ, here he tells Lucy and Edmund quite clearly that he is present in our world, but by another name. His appearance as a lamb is also a direct reference to Christ's title of 'the Lamb of God' (*agnus Dei*).

The Voyage of the Dawn Treader was completed in the first couple of months of 1950 but not published until September 1952 on either side of the Atlantic, dedicated to Geoffrey Corbett, the foster son of his great friend Owen Barfield (later editions amend this to Geoffrey Barfield, a name he adopted when adult). The *New Yorker* felt that it 'surpasses even the preceding volumes', although Chad Walsh in the *New York Times Book Review*, who had indicated that *Prince Caspian* had been 'a let-down', felt that it wasn't quite 'up to the very high level of *The Lion, the Witch and the Wardrobe*.' Pauline Baynes's illustrations for the original British version included a map of the Bight of Calormen and the Lone Islands of the Great Eastern Ocean; this, however, didn't appear in any paperback editions in Britain, or any American versions at all until 1994.

The introduction of Eustace allows Lewis a chance to give a fresh perspective on his Narnian tales and it's a bittersweet moment when we realize that we're not going to encounter Lucy and Edmund again (although modern-day readers will be aware they reappear in *The Last Battle*). Reepicheep is one of Lewis's best characters, making this one of the most readable of the Chronicles.

15

THE CHRONICLES OF NARNIA:
THE SILVER CHAIR

Eustace Scrubb is still a pupil at Experiment House, a modern school where children can do what they like, and nobody stops bullying. When he finds fellow pupil Jill Pole crying, they end up talking about Narnia, and Jill wishes she could go there. To escape the bullies, they open a door that's normally locked – and find themselves in Aslan's country, high on a cliff. In panic, Jill grabs Eustace's arm, but he falls over the edge.

Aslan immediately appears, using his breath to guide the boy down into Narnia. The lion tells Jill she has to rectify the situation, and help Eustace, since Aslan has called them there (even if Jill thinks it's the other way around) to help find the missing Prince Rilian. There are four signs to look for: Eustace will meet an old and dear friend when he arrives, and if he does they will get help; they must journey out of Narnia to the north until they reach the city of the ancient giants; they must do what the writing on the stone tells them to; and the lost prince will be the first person to ask them to do something in the name of Aslan. Once Jill has them clear, Aslan blows her into Narnia.

Jill arrives as Eustace is watching an elderly king embark on a journey; only after he's departed do they learn that it's Caspian X, Eustace's friend from the *Dawn Treader*, and seventy years have passed since he was last in Narnia. They are invited to a parliament by the wise old owl Glimfeather, where they are briefed on Prince Rilian's disappearance ten years earlier. He had been trying to find the serpent that had killed his mother but instead was entranced by a lovely woman in green. After many men died searching for him, Caspian forbade any further quests, but declared that he would go himself. The owls suggest a marsh-wiggle by the name of Puddleglum will be the children's best guide.

The pessimistic Puddleglum lives in a wigwam in the marsh, and believes the ruined city is best accessed via Ettinsmoor, due north from them. They evade some rather stupid giants in the wild wastelands, and cross the moor before arriving at a canyon, which is spanned by a huge bridge. Jill thinks it's a giants' bridge; Puddleglum is inclined towards a magical explanation. They cross it, and meet two people: a beautiful lady in a dazzling green dress, and a silent knight in black armour. They tell her they're looking for the ruined city, although Puddleglum stops them from saying why; the woman sends them on to the city of Harfang, inhabited by 'gentle giants' who will offer them bed and board, particularly if they tell them that the lady of the 'Green Kirtle' has sent them for the Autumn Feast. Jill and Eustace are keen to take advantage, as winter is setting in, and they eventually reach the castle, although Jill falls into a trench along the way that seems to lead nowhere.

The giants are delighted to receive them – almost too delighted. That night Jill dreams about Aslan and the signs, and sees the words UNDER ME beneath her window. The next day, they look out of her window, and see the territory they've crossed in a new light – they'd been clambering over the ruined city, and they can see that the trench Jill fell in was the 'E' of 'ME'. Puddleglum is sure that means they need to search *beneath* the city. They also discover that being sent for the Autumn Feast means that they will be the food being served – Jill finds a cookbook with a recipe for serving Man. They manage to get away from the giants, and down a hole into the Marches of Underland.

The Marches' Warden, accompanied by gnomish Earthmen, takes them across the Sunless Sea to the Queen of the Underland's quarters at the Dark Castle, where they meet the Black Knight once more. He has never heard of Rilian or Narnia, and explains that 'UNDER ME' comes from an ancient poem. Puddleglum is the only one now convinced that they are still on the right track, since they've done what Aslan told them to do.

The knight explains that he has to be bound into a silver chair each night because he has been enchanted and becomes violent. He invites them to watch his condition, as long as they promise not to free him, even if he begs them to. However, as soon as the enchantment starts to take hold, he changes his story and claims that he is now in his right mind. Jill, Eustace and Puddleglum aren't sure what to do – until the knight begs them to free him in the name of Aslan. This they do, and he destroys the chair.

As soon as Rilian ceases to be enchanted, the queen appears and tries to re-enchant him, and capture the others. Again, Puddleglum is the one who resists and Eustace and Rilian begin to fight back too. Puddleglum stomps out the fire which is burning the queen's magic incense, and tells the queen exactly what he thinks of her. She turns into a serpent, which Rilian, Eustace and Puddleglum decapitate. With the help of the Earthmen, who had also been enchanted by the queen, they escape from the Underland, while the Earthmen head back to their own land, Bism, deeper underground.

The travellers head back to Cair Paravel arriving in time for Caspian to return from his voyage, bless his son, and then die. During the mourning for the dead king, Aslan reappears and takes Jill, Eustace and a revived and now-young Caspian to the cliff where the humans arrived. Caspian asks if he can visit their world, and Aslan allows him five minutes there to help sort things out. The lion blows down a wall, prompting hysterics from the head teacher, but by the time that the authorities arrive, he has replaced it, and the head is moved from her job (becoming a school inspector and eventually an MP!). Experiment House is changed for the better.

The Silver Chair – alternately known as *Night Under Narnia* and *The Wild Wastelands*, suggestions Lewis made before wiser heads at Geoffrey Bles prevailed – is the first of the Narnia stories that Jack Lewis completed after the publication of *The Lion, the Witch and the Wardrobe*. It was penned between the Christmas vacation of 1950 and March 1951, when Roger Lancelyn Green presented some suggested alterations to it – Lewis, in particular, was concerned about the properties of a wood fire, and whether Puddleglum simply stomping on it would be sufficient to extinguish it.

The story charts 'the continued war against the powers of darkness', Lewis explained. Aslan needs Jill and Eustace to do what he tells them to do, otherwise he won't prevail – it's clear from the first meeting between Jill and the lion that their victory is by no means assured. He suggests that they could end up dead, or back in their own world by other means (presumably, although it's not stated, through some enchantment).

The book is also a vehicle for Lewis to attack then 'modern' forms of education. Early on the narrator informs the reader that this isn't a 'school story' (like the writings of Frank Richards or Enid Blyton), but it certainly is about schools. In Lewis's non-fiction work *The Abolition of Man* (see part III, chapter 4), written in 1943 and based on lectures he delivered in February that year, he tackled what he saw as the wrong way in which the English teaching system was debunking values and denying absolutes. His final science-fiction novel, *That Hideous Strength*, also criticizes this, and the sections in *The Silver Chair* set in Experiment House, or talking about the lack of education that Jill and Eustace have received, are very cutting about the uselessness of their upbringing. He also gets in a few scathing comments about bullies in general, which recall his own bad experiences in his short time at Malvern College.

The Silver Chair draws inspiration from many sources, as well as Lewis's perception of the spiritual journey. Early parts of Edmund Spenser's incomplete epic *The Faerie Queen* are recognizable in the battle between Rilian, Puddleglum, Eustace and the queen when she tries to enchant them and then turns into a serpent. George MacDonald's fairytale *The Princess and the Goblin* is also structurally quite similar to the overall tale. Lewis had read widely in his youth, and it's entirely possible that everything from H. Rider Haggard to Jules Verne's tales of underground cities subconsciously influenced him.

Although some of the characters in the books may be modelled on key influences in Jack Lewis's life (such as William Kirkpatrick 'becoming' Professor Kirke), one was positively identified by the author to Walter Hooper. Puddleglum was based on Fred Paxford, who was the gardener at Lewis's home The Kilns for the entire thirty-three years that Jack lived there. The 'lovable pessimist' was a devoted friend and from all accounts worthy of the tribute in *The Silver Chair*. The name of the character apparent derived from a translation by John Studley of the Latin phrase *Tacitae Stygis* as 'Stygian puddle glum'.

The story is set seventy years after *The Voyage of the Dawn Treader* (or so Eustace suggests), although in his chronology, Lewis diminishes the gap to fifty years, setting it in 2356, making Caspian in his seventies, rather than his nineties. It's still apparently 1942 on Earth, although, as with the previous novel, there are no indications that the Second World War is still continuing. Narnia has just under two hundred years left before *The Last Battle* and the end of its existence; Jill and Eustace will survive a further seven years.

The Silver Chair was published in September 1953 in the UK, and a month later in America, illustrated as ever by Pauline Baynes, who additionally contributed 'A Map of the Wild Lands of the North' for the first edition, which appeared in subsequent paperback editions, and in hardbacks from 1992 onwards. It was first available in the US in the 1994 paperback versions. Lewis thought these were the best that Baynes had done to date, although he did criticize one which had an out-of-proportion Aslan in the foreground, and another showing a gnome who looked like 'a brat out of Dickens's London'. It was dedicated to Nicholas Hardie, the son of Lewis's colleague Colin Hardie, a Fellow and Classical Tutor at Magdalen College, one of the Inklings who demonstrated an excellent ability to carve some of the treasured hams that were sent to Lewis by admirers in the US.

The book contains some wonderfully comic and heroic touches, especially Puddleglum's speech to the queen when he defies her attempts to persuade them all that Narnia and the Overworld is simply a figment of their imaginations. Summing up the creation of such fictional worlds, he defends the right of 'four babies playing a game' to create their own play-world, which puts the real world to shame. It's one of the best moments in the whole Chronicles of Narnia. (And for those of us of a certain generation, there's only one Puddleglum actor who we can hear saying it – the frankly marvellous Tom Baker.) In some ways, it's the last hurrah of Narnia, because when we return there in the final book, everything has changed. And not for the better.

16

THE CHRONICLES OF NARNIA: *THE LAST BATTLE*

It is the last days of Narnia. The manipulative ape Shift and his less intelligent donkey friend Puzzle find a lion's skin which Shift makes into a 'lion costume' for Puzzle to wear. When Shift suggests that Puzzle could do a lot of good if people thought that he was Aslan, the donkey reluctantly agrees.

Three weeks later, King Tirian and his unicorn friend Jewel are delighted by the news that Aslan has returned to Narnia. However, the centaur Roonwit tells him that the stars are foretelling disaster, not a new time of peace. A dryad then arrives to inform them that the talking trees in Lantern Waste are being cut down. Tirian sends Roonwit to summon an army, while he and Jewel investigate. They learn that the logs from the trees are being sold to the Calormenes, apparently at Aslan's instigation, and when they see two Calormenes mistreating a talking horse, they furiously kill them.

Tirian and Jewel initially flee, but the king soon realizes

that they have done wrong, particularly if the instructions did come from Aslan – although this doesn't fit with the Aslan they know from the old tales. They decide to hand themselves over to the Calormenes to be given to Aslan for judgement. They are taken to a stable with the door closed; outside it sits Shift, hailed as 'mouthpiece of Aslan', who is passing on messages apparently from the lion. These are really serving his own agenda, and that of the Calormenes, whose representative sits beside Shift. According to Shift, Aslan has ordered that creatures are to be sent to Calormen to work there; the money they earn will make Narnia 'a country worth living in', with roads, cities, schools – as well as whips, kennels and prisons. When an old bear says they just want freedom, Shift says freedom isn't doing what you like: it's doing what Shift tells you to do. And to cap it all, Shift explains that the Calormen god Tash is the same as Aslan: they are different names for the same person (Tashlan).

Tirian shouts out that Shift is lying; before he can explain, Shift orders him gagged and tied to a tree for Aslan to deal with. That night, some talking animals provide him with food and drink, although they won't untie him in case it angers Aslan, whom they believe they have seen coming out of the stable. By the light of a fire, Tirian sees the fake Aslan, and, remembering the help the real lion has given previous Narnian royalty, calls for aid from him or any of the Friends of Narnia over the centuries. To his surprise, he sees a vision of seven humans, one of whom calls himself Peter the High King.

Ten minutes later for Tirian, but a week later for them, Eustace and Jill appear to untie him. They were going to meet Peter and Edmund, who had recovered the magic rings Digory and Polly had used so they could come to the aid of the Narnians, but just as their train got into the station they were pulled into Narnia. Disguising themselves as Calormenes, they return to Stable Hill and rescue Jewel; Jill persuades Puzzle to come along with them. They free some dwarfs, but they won't help Tirian expose Shift and the Calormenes.

Only one dwarf, Poggin, will assist, and he tells them that Ginger the Cat concocted a story to help explain Tirian's disappearance: supposedly Aslan appeared and swallowed him up. Shift is now drinking heavily, and Ginger and the Calormene captain Rishda are taking control: they are both enlightened and thus believe that neither Aslan nor Tash exists. However, as Tirian and his party quickly learn, Tash is as real as Aslan – and is heading into Narnia.

They decide to rendezvous with Roonwit and his army, but on their way, they are told by an eagle that Roonwit is dead, and Cair Paravel has fallen to the Calormenes. Sadly Tirian concludes that Narnia is no more. They decide to make a stand at Stable Hill, proving that Puzzle was a false Aslan. Jill and Eustace have no option but to stay, and wonder what will happen if they die in Narnia.

However, Rishda and Ginger are one step ahead: they get Shift to tell the assembled crowd that Tashlan is angry because there is a false version of Aslan around. Shift then explains that anyone who goes into the stable can meet the real Tashlan, and Ginger goes first. What he sees in there scares the ability of speech out of him. Emeth, a Calormene, wants to go next and won't be dissuaded from entering. A moment after he does, a body is thrown out, which Rishda claims is his, but isn't. A boar is pushed towards the entrance, but doesn't want to go, and at that point Tirian and his small force start a fight.

All seems lost until Tirian pulls Rishda inside the stable, where they meet Tash, who takes Rishda for his own until he himself is banished by new arrivals: the seven friends of Narnia – all those who had visited before, bar Susan ('no longer a friend of Narnia'), looking in the prime of their lives. They, and their parents, were all either on the train or waiting at the station platform when there was a dreadful roar and they appeared in the stable.

Tirian realizes that the stable's 'inside is bigger than its outside' and Lucy explains that Calormene soldiers had been waiting to deal with anyone who came through but Tash dealt with them. Only Emeth and the dwarfs were spared – although the dwarfs can't see the 'new' interior, and think they're still in the stable.

Aslan then appears and calls Father Time to bring Narnia to an end. Every creature comes to the stable door; some are allowed through, others are sent into Aslan's shadow and disappear. Dragons and giant lizards then destroy Narnia, a sea covers the world, and the sun envelops the moon, which itself is then snuffed out. Aslan tells Peter to shut the door.

On their way farther up and farther into the land beyond the door, they meet Emeth, who was saved by Aslan, as well as Puzzle. The land resembles Narnia, but is somehow a better, clearer version, and Digory realizes that the old Narnia was a shadow copy of this real world. They go up the waterfall at the end of the world past a lake to a great wall. A door opens to reveal Reepicheep – and all the other great figures of Narnian history, as well as a 'real' version of England. Aslan explains that they have all died, and the great adventure is now beginning . . .

The Magician's Nephew – the book published immediately before *The Last Battle* – told the story of Narnia's creation. *The Lion, the Witch and the Wardrobe* deals with the Passion and Resurrection. *The Last Battle* is the end of the world, derived from the gospel prophecies relating to the end times as well as the biblical book of Revelation (also known as the Apocalypse). Although scholars may argue over what portions of the Old and New Testaments are relevant to the other books in the series, there is no getting around this one, making it the most overtly Christian of all the Chronicles.

The biblical version relates how a false god will appear (the Antichrist) in the years before the end of the world, just as Puzzle does here. Shift's actions are an extrapolation of St Matthew 24, St Mark 13, and St Luke 21, which talk of 'false Christs and false prophets' whose great signs and wonders will deceive even the wisest before the return of the Son of

Man. Emeth's late entry into Aslan's kingdom derives from St John 10, which explains that there are sheep from another fold who need to be gathered in. The division of creatures between those that will be saved and those that enter the shadow comes from St Matthew 25.

Lewis is uncompromising in his account of who is going to receive eternal life, and those who are doomed. His use of the Calormenes has laid him open to some considerable criticism, as it would appear that he is equating Islam (the Calormenes are distinctly Middle Eastern in origin) with devil worship – the discussion whether Tash and Aslan are the same is one of the underlying themes of the book, and is resolved in Aslan's discussion with Emeth at the end, where the lion is clear that Tash is his opposite. There is some casual racism – the use of the word 'darkies' to describe the Calormenes stands out for a modern audience more than it would for Lewis's initial readership.

There has also been a lot of discussion about the fate of Susan (see the next chapter for some of the fictional responses that have appeared). Although it's clear that Susan couldn't return to the Narnia that she visited before, since it no longer exists, there is no reason to indicate that later in life she can't turn back to belief in Aslan, and be allowed entry to the 'real' Narnia. 'There is plenty of time for her to mend,' Lewis pointed out in a letter a year after *The Last Battle* was published. Lewis is very dismissive of the way she has changed in her teens, which is a tad hypocritical, some might think, given that at the very age Susan is meant to be, Lewis himself was virulently against Christianity.

Lewis doesn't just draw on Christianity for *The Last Battle*. Plato is named by Professor Kirke towards the end of the book, and the Greek philosopher Socrates's Dialogues are the basis for the idea that everything good and true in the material world is a version of something in the eternal world of Ideas or Forms – the more that visible things imitate the eternal ones, the better they are. Plato's *Republic* is the source of the shadowlands metaphor – all we can see currently are the shadows of the reality that we are not in a position to look at as yet. This idea of a true creation being imitated in our world also informed *That Hideous Strength*.

Two hundred years have passed since Jill and Eustace were last in Narnia at the end of *The Silver Chair*, although 'more than' a year has passed on Earth. This is where Lewis's own chronology comes unstuck, as he claims that the train accident is in 1949, which simply makes no sense, given that *The Silver Chair* is supposedly in 1942. If seven years had gone by, the children wouldn't be children any more, but equally, British Railways didn't exist prior to 1947. There is ironically more elasticity in Lewis's time frames given for the Earth portions of the Pevensies' adventures than in their Narnian equivalents – on internal evidence, only three years or so have gone by, but we've gone from the height of the Blitz in 1940 to 1949. He wasn't the first fantasy writer to come unstuck on such things, and won't be the last!

The Last Battle, originally known as *The Last Chronicle of Narnia*, was published in March 1956 in Britain and six months later in America, although it had been completed in March 1953 while Lewis was suffering from a bad attack of sinusitis, prior to the author finishing writing *The Magician's Nephew*. It won the prestigious Carnegie Medal for the best children's book of 1956, an award that Lewis felt was one he shared with Pauline Baynes since he was sure 'the illustrations were taken into consideration as well as the text'. The book bears no dedication. It was described as 'one of the best' of the series by the *New York Times Book Review* while Charles A. Brady noted that Lewis 'evangelizes through the imagination'.

The Last Battle isn't a comfortable read: it starts off rather like *The Horse and His Boy*, set purely within Narnia, with no involvement from people from our world. But unlike that adventure, *The Last Battle* begins on a downbeat note and proceeds to get steadily worse. Even the arrival of Eustace and Jill is overladen with gloom – Lewis foreshadows the eventual news of their deaths in the train crash virtually from the start, with Eustace making some comments about the bump being worse than he might have expected. By the time we reach the last battle itself, readers will be excused for wondering whether all is lost (and modern-day readers will be used to TV shows, such as the recent versions of *Robin Hood* and *Merlin*, where the final episodes end on a very downbeat note). Although it is the end, something much greater is shown, even if we are never going to get the details – at least in this world.

One of the last things that Jack Lewis promised, when Puffin Books editor Kaye Webb came to visit him two days before he died in November 1963, was to re-edit the books, to 'connect the things that didn't tie up'. He never had the chance to do so, and for all their occasional inconsistencies, the Chronicles of Narnia remain as he wrote them six decades ago, and still live up to the description Charles Brady gave: 'the greatest addition to the imperishable deposit of children's literature since the *Jungle Books*.'

17

ADDITIONS TO THE CHRONICLES OF NARNIA

When a book captures the imagination, you don't really want it to finish, and that can apply even more so with a series of novels featuring a character or situation which clearly has more potential beyond what the original author showed. The adventures of Sir Arthur Conan Doyle's Sherlock Holmes have continued for many years with varying degrees of success. Authorized new tales of Ian Fleming's secret agent James Bond have been appearing since 1968.

However, very few new tales of Narnia have followed the publication of *The Last Battle*. True, there has been 'fan fiction', stories written and distributed among those who love the Chronicles, which pick up on references in Lewis's originals and weave new adventures, but these have been actively discouraged by the estate of C. S. Lewis.

There have been two stories published which are still available, one authorized, one very definitely not, as well as five tales which have slipped under the radar of all but the most devoted Narnia enthusiast.

This quintet was published in 1988, licensed by Iron Crown Enterprises from the Episcopal Radio-TV Foundation Inc., and were part of the 'Choose Your Own Adventure' genre: the reader becomes an active participant in the story, faced with a choice at the end of short sections of narrative. Choose the wrong way, and you faced doom and destruction; navigate your way successfully, and appropriate good fortune was yours. Very popular for a time, versions were written for many genre series, including *Doctor Who*, James Bond, Indiana Jones and *Star Wars*.

Return to Deathwater by Curtis Norris picks up on elements of *The Voyage of the Dawn Treader*, and features a brief mention of Eustace at the start. Young Chris Porter is on a school trip (presumably with Experiment House) from where he is summoned into Narnia, some generations after Caspian's time. A strange mystery on the Island of Deathwater holds two lovers apart and endangers all who venture there. The mystery troubles young King Favian's dreams; Aslan has come to him, and therefore he seeks Chris's help. With the aid of a Talking Mouse named Cheekimeek, Chris must conquer his own pride and fears to find the cure for Deathwater that Aslan has promised, and reunite the lovers.

Anne Schraff's *The Sorceress and the Book of Spells* is set during the reign of the Pevensies. It begins with the heroine, Robin Traverstock (who has some anger-management issues), swimming in the sea and being transported to the Eastern Sea of Narnia. Arriving at Cair Paravel, Aslan tells her that the Sorceress of the Western Wilds has acquired a magic book, *Runes From The Sceptre Of Grace*, which she is using to stir up a war between Narnia and Archenland. When the Pevensies are discredited, she can take over. Aslan sends Robin to recover the book and defeat her before she is able to cause any more mischief.

Leap of the Lion seems to cover some of the same ideas as

The Last Battle (with one of the endings mirroring it). Curtis Norris's story features Jesamy Haverfield, who is at the same school as Susan and Lucy Pevensie. When Jesamy is pulled into Lantern Waste, he learns that Narnia is in disarray, because its people have turned away from Aslan. A Calormene named Haadreh the Wise has taken advantage of the situation and built his Temple on top of Narnia's most sacred spot, cast the lawful King Daliar into prison, taught nonsense, and taxed and oppressed everyone. Jesamy has to find Aslan and let him know that many Narnians are still faithful. Unlike some of the stories, this presents a sequence in which the hero goes off on completely the wrong quest from the start. This also contains some Americanisms such as jello, which were more carefully pruned from the other books.

The Lost Crowns of Cair Paravel by Gerald Lientz begins with a cameo from Polly Plummer, the heroine of *The Magician's Nephew*. She is now a teacher in London, with whom Kim Spencer, the narrator, is staying after a school trip. Polly takes against some of Kim's schoolmates – Theodore and Rupert Barfield and Eliza Chesterton – after they eat an apple from the Narnian tree, which tastes horrible to them (the book is set prior to the storm that destroys the tree). Kim believes Polly's story of Narnia and that night is transported to a cloud where she meets Aslan. There, the Hundred Years Winter, when the people of Narnia are in despair, is coming to a close. Kim Spencer must recover the lost crowns of the last King and Queen of Narnia, and restore them to their proper places in the long-abandoned castle of Cair Paravel, ready for the arrival of the Pevensies. The story explains how Jadis was able to take control of Narnia: according to legend, a fierce dragon, Featherflame, killed the monarchs, and destroyed a tree known as the Shield of Narnia, which kept her out. The crowns are now protected by Flamesteam, another dragon, a follower of Aslan.

The final book published was *The Return of the White Witch* by Rob Bell, which acts as a direct sequel to *The Lion, the Witch and the Wardrobe*, explaining what happens in Narnia immediately after the Pevensies return to England. The narrator this time is Verne Wycliffe, who feels abandoned by her parents because they're concentrating on the imminent arrival of a new baby. Verne and her friend Jeremy Trevisian are exploring the area near Brindlethatch Manor but get separated in a cave, and Verne arrives in Narnia. Mr Tumnus is now Regent but he has become set in his ways, and hasn't noticed that Narnia is in danger. A warlock intends to resurrect the White Witch, and only Verne can stop Narnia falling back under her spell.

The first four books were released in a box set, with *The Return of the White Witch* intended as the start of a further trio of adventures. The other two, *The Magician's Rings* by Anne E. Schraff (which one can assume was linked to the rings that Uncle Andrew created in *The Magician's Nephew*, which the Pevensies were intending to use in *The Last Battle*) and *Keeper of the Dreamstone* by John Ruffner, should have appeared in December 1988 and February 1989 respectively, but were not published. On the penultimate page of *The Return of the White Witch*, there is an advertisement seeking 'a few good writers' for the series, but if anyone responded to Iron Crown Enterprises, their stories never appeared.

In 2005, a new story appeared for Puddleglum, the marshwiggle featured in *The Silver Chair*, written by children's author Hiawyn Oram. It was part of a proposed series called 'Step Into Narnia', which, as the cover of *The Giant Surprise* proclaimed, was 'inspired by the stories of C. S. Lewis'. The project was planned for some time before *The Giant Surprise* was published, and it appears that four books were initially proposed. Very few details are known about the other three: there are references on internet bookseller Amazon to *The Rainbow Dragon*, dating it to 1989, long before the series was planned (perhaps on the assumption that it was supposed to be part of the 'Choose Your Own Adventure' series), but the story was never published. The penultimate page of *The Giant Surprise* refers to ogres and dragons, so it would seem likely these would have been the focus of a couple of them.

The 'Step Into Narnia' series (or just 'Narnia', as it is confusingly called on the final cover) was presented as 'new adventures specially created for much younger children . . . and prepare them to enjoy the original books'. In Oram's book, illustrated by Tudor Humphries, we return to the marshlands where Jill Pole and Eustace Scrubb first meet Puddleglum in *The Silver Chair*. We are quickly introduced to his niece Lally, 'the brave little Wigglet' who helps Puddleglum when Giant Dribble and Giant Crackerwhack stomp through the marshes fishing for mice and capture two of their murine friends, Greep and Graypaw. While Lally distracts the Giants with games, Puddleglum searches for the mice, and find them in the giants' castle.

It's an admirably simple story, beautifully illustrated by Humphries, with lots of onomatopoeic words that children will enjoy joining in with whoever is reading it to them. While one might wonder at the implications of suggesting to children that making rock and dirt sandwiches is a good idea (although chances are most of them have at some point anyway!), it captures the slow-wittedness of the giants and their ability to be distracted.

The Giant Surprise is a nice little tale, set in Narnia, rather than a continuation of the Chronicles – which may be why it was not as well received as it might have been. *Christianity Today*'s reviewer, in particular, was cutting about the text, in an effort to back up a mistaken point about the book being part of a 'brand'. On the other side of the coin, Peter Chattaway at *Patheos* noted that 'I'm all in favour of short stories that bring the characters to life for their own sake, without necessarily serving some larger "theme"', although he admitted he had yet to read this book.

When the plans for the series were first announced in 2001, they became embroiled in a controversy when it was misreported that HarperCollins were intending to re-edit the original Lewis books to remove the Christian content. A leaked memo from an executive involved said, 'Obviously, this is a biggie as far as the estate and our publishing interests are concerned ... We'll need to be able to give emphatic assurances that no attempt will be made to correlate the stories to Christian imagery/theology.' This referred to the new stories, it seems, not the originals.

At the time, *Christianity Today* said it would be 'lamentable for any new Narnia books to be commissioned at all, in Weblog's opinion', particularly if they were lacking in Christian content. Christopher Mitchell, then director of the Marion E. Wade Center in Illinois, the home of the Lewis archives, nailed the biggest challenge any continuation of the Chronicles faced: 'The minimum they'll have to achieve, to stay true to Lewis's intention, is to make good attractive, while not making the bad any less bad,' he told the *National Catholic Register*. 'It's always easy to create believable evil characters. Making goodness believable and attractive is hard. And the new books will be judged from the perspective of the classics.'

Whether the new stories didn't fit in with the plans for promoting the Walden Media movies, or *The Giant Surprise* was a test to try out the market which failed to perform as well as the publishers hoped, is unknown, but it does have the kudos of being the only official continuation of the Chronicles. It also gained a brief moment of glory later when the Narniaweb.com website claimed that it would form the basis of the fourth official movie – although astute readers quickly spotted that the date of the story was 1 April 2011.

A year before readers were taken back to meet Puddleglum, though, Susan Pevensie had made a fresh appearance in a short story. 'The Problem of Susan' was written by prolific author Neil Gaiman, who had apparently delayed publication for some time because he was worried about copyright implications. (As events transpired, he wasn't sued.)

'The Problem of Susan', which first appeared in the anthology *Flights: Extreme Visions of Fantasy*, is definitely not a tale for children. It features an interpretation of the bargain between the White Witch and Aslan in *The Lion, the Witch and the Wardrobe* that culminates in a graphically told sexual encounter between the pair, and considers the realities of what Susan would have had to face if she was the sole survivor of the Pevensie family, after the others had been killed in the British Railways crash (which Lewis dates to 1949 in his 'History of Narnia'.) Bookended by dream sequences, it sees a young journalist, Greta Campion, visit the aged Professor Hastings, who we are meant to believe is a possible future Susan; she certainly has had many of the same experiences as the older Pevensie girl. Greta is annoyed that Susan appears to have been abandoned by her God because she's 'too fond of lipsticks and nylons and invitations to parties'; however, Professor Hastings points out that Susan's life would have been changed irrevocably by the deaths in her family. Later that night, the professor dreams of Mary Poppins and Narnia before passing away in her sleep.

In his introduction to 'The Problem of Susan' in his collection *Fragile Things*, Neil Gaiman mentions that this was the first piece of fiction that he 'attempted' after suffering from meningitis, and there is a clear undertone in those comments that he is not attacking the Chronicles of Narnia as such. (Indeed in later interviews, he has been absolutely clear: 'I love them'.) However, he obviously thinks that, no matter what Walter Hooper may claim in *Past Watchful Dragons* – that Susan in a sense merely missed out on the chance of Heaven at the point that her brothers and sister died, rather than for ever – the way in which Lewis deals with Susan is 'intensely problematic and deeply irritating'. He therefore wrote a story that had the same attributes.

'The Problem of Susan' divides readers: Gaiman was amused by one female reader describing it as 'blasphemous' and he admits 'it just seems to be a story that people either love, or it pisses them off'. It's not Gaiman's finest work, but it does address a question that many people have about Susan's fate – even if it does open up some questions of its own – and is well worth seeking out.

There have been various fan-fiction responses to 'The Problem of Susan', one of the best coming from American teacher Katherine Heasley, who posts online as HonorH, in a story called 'The Queen's Return', which first appeared at Christmas 2005. This expands on Susan's move away from Narnia as a teenager, and her emotional hollowness after the train crash that destroys her family. But all is not lost, and she has another encounter with Aslan, as well as her sister, that reminds her of the aphorism 'Once a king or queen in Narnia, always a king or queen in Narnia.'

'It never occurred to me, when first reading *The Last Battle*, that Susan was for ever cast out of Narnia/Heaven,' she explained in an interview for this book. 'The redemptive themes of the series as a whole made it seem obvious, even to my very young self, that she still had a chance. She was still alive, after all; she wasn't mentioned as being on the train, and there was no reason to believe she was dead. Years later, it came as rather a shock to me that people were upset that Susan was "condemned to Hell" for liking "lipstick and pantyhose". It was a foreign point of view to me. Perhaps it was my optimistic nature, or my own Christianity, but I didn't see it that way. Couldn't, really, believe that was Lewis's intent.

'I'd always had my own private head canon about Susan – that the shock of losing her family led to her rediscovery of what was truly important – and it slowly gelled into this form. I used to read through the Chronicles once a year, and one Christmas, I was seized with the impulse to write down what became of Susan. I felt like the story needed to start earlier, though, and explore why she drew so far away from Narnia that she became convinced it was all a product of their imaginations. "Lipstick and pantyhose" are trappings of womanhood for girls. They're a sign you're no longer a child, a hint at burgeoning sexuality. It's a rough time for a lot of girls (it certainly was for me), and Susan showed in earlier stories a dislike for taking risks. So, in my mind, the sequence of events became clear: Susan was growing up, and fear of rejection by her peers ("Those Girls") led to her rejection of anything that could make her different, in their eyes. She pushed away her childhood in an effort to seem more sophisticated to them. She mistook the trappings of adulthood for maturity. It took the true maturity that only comes with pain and loss to open her eyes and heart to Aslan again.

'I also wanted to give Susan something to, if not make up for what she'd lost, at least add back meaning into her life. She was called not to die, but to live and to become Susan the Gentle again in her own world. Thus, she becomes a philanthropist, a caregiver, a wife, a mother and a grandmother. Sorrow is turned to joy, and the years the locusts ate are given back in full. It was, I felt, the best guess I could make at Lewis's intent.'

The story can be read at http://archiveofourown.org/works/635041.

18

TILL WE HAVE FACES

'A Myth Retold' is the subtitle of Jack Lewis's final published novel, which is firmly for an adult audience, as he once again returns to the world of allegorical storytelling, looking to ancient myth for the source of his tale. In a note preceding the text for the first American edition, Lewis recounts the story of Cupid and Psyche in its barest form, as it is related in Plato's *Metamorphoses*. He then explains the key difference that he makes in the story which allowed him to have insights into the characters (indicated below in the synopsis at the relevant place).

Till We Have Faces is told by Orual, Psyche's ugly older step-sister, who has a grievance against the gods for the way in which they have treated her. She is now an old woman and doesn't care what they do to her; she simply wants the record set straight.

Psyche's birth isn't welcomed by her father, the King of

Glome; he already has two daughters – Orual and Redival – and he'd hoped his new wife would produce a son. This leads to an argument with the priest of Ungit (their name for Aphrodite); further tensions are created as Psyche gets older and is very beautiful – the people of Glome want her to bless their children with her touch, and when a plague hits, she goes out touching the sick. However, she becomes known as 'The Accursed' when this fails to cure the pestilence, and the priest of Ungit tells the king that Psyche must be given as a sacrifice to the Great Brute, Ungit's son, the God of the Mountain – Cupid.

Orual offers to go in her place, but her father refuses: Orual is disfigured, and hardly the most beautiful in the land. Redival, however, is delighted by the news since she has always been jealous of her sister. Psyche herself seems fascinated by the idea of meeting the gods, and even attracted by the idea of death. (Orual admits when writing about the meeting that she felt bitterness at Psyche and grudged her any comfort, particularly as Psyche obviously doesn't reciprocate her love.)

The sacrifice appears to work: Glome is restored to normality, and Orual decides to go up the mountain to recover her sister's remains. Her friend Bardia, the captain of the troops, teaches her sword-fighting to try to distract her from her grieving, and agrees to accompany her. Orual deliberately keeps herself feeling depressed as she travels, despite the delights she sees, and becomes uneasy when they reach the tree to which Psyche had been bound. There's no sign of her, bar a ruby some distance away. They scout around and find a secret valley – and Psyche.

Psyche explains how she had been transported to the palace of the Mountain God by the west wind, and prepared by invisible servants for her night with him. When Orual asks to see the palace, Psyche is amazed: they're standing in it – but Orual can see nothing but meadow. (This is the key alteration that Lewis made to earlier retellings of the myth.) Orual tries to persuade Psyche of what she perceives is the truth, but

Psyche is adamant, and refuses to come back to Glome with her. She has a duty now to her husband, even if she has never seen him and he only ever comes to her in darkness. She sends Orual away.

That night Orual believes she catches sight of the palace just for a moment but then can't be sure what, if anything, she saw. She resolves to save Psyche from the monstrous god, even if that means killing her, despite the fact she's obviously happy. When they get back to Glome, she asks the Fox, an elderly Greek who has been her guide and tutor for many years, for his opinion, and he suggests that Psyche may be the victim of a crazed vagabond, and is now fantasizing. Bardia, though, believes they shouldn't meddle with the work of the gods. Orual decides she must show her love for Psyche by being stern and saving her from herself.

Orual returns to Psyche's valley and tries to turn her sister against her husband by pointing out that nothing beautiful hides its face. She stabs herself through the arm to show how serious she is: if Psyche won't look at her god that night when he comes to her, then Orual will kill her, and then herself. Shaken, Psyche agrees. When she does look at her husband, she is sent into exile, and the god comes to Orual telling her that she shares her sister's fate. Orual now sees the gods as enemies. When she returns to Glome, she decides to wear a veil at all times, hiding her ugliness from the world.

Some time later, the King falls ill, and Orual becomes his mouthpiece, coming to an accommodation with the new priest of Ungit, Arnom. She becomes ever more queenly, fighting as her own champion in a sword fight, and marrying Redival off in a politically astute match. She succeeds her father, but realizes how lonely she is when Bardia takes leave with his family. Over the coming years, she is a good queen, bringing Greek influence to her court, and eventually working out a succession to ensure stability.

On her travels, she is told about a new goddess, Istra – Psyche's name in her own language. Her priest explains that Istra was betrayed by her two sisters, who were jealous of her and plotted to destroy her happiness. Angered by this rewriting of history, Orual writes her own book.

She picks up the story a few days later, after being given a new perspective by two visitors. When she was young, Redival was courted by a soldier who was castrated by the King in consequence; Orual meets the man once more, who tells her he felt sorry for Redival, because Orual had given her love to the Fox and Psyche, and ignored Redival. Then after Bardia's death, his widow reveals she was jealous of her husband's loyalty to Orual; Orual removes her veil and the women reconcile. However, Orual realizes that her love for Bardia must have looked like the way she thought the Brute loved Psyche – a loving and a devouring.

She then has a vision of her father returning to her, taking her underground. When she's asked who Ungit is, she looks in a mirror and realizes that she herself is. She considers suicide, but the voice of a god tells her not to. She dreams of presenting her complaints to the gods, and realizes how absurd she is. Finally, with the ghost of the Fox and then Psyche herself guiding her, she glimpses in a reflection in the water the true nature of the redemption that awaits her.

Four days thereafter, mid-sentence, she falls asleep and dies.

The story of Cupid and Psyche had fascinated Jack Lewis for many years before he sat down to pen *Bareface* – the original title of *Till We Have Faces*. In the first British edition, he admitted that he first worked on it as an undergraduate, and his diary for 23 November 1922 corroborates this. At that stage he was thinking of a 'masque or play', and in September 1923 noted he had been contemplating a poem (some of which survives) on the subject. Even at that point, the twist of Orual not being jealous but simply 'unable to see anything but moors' had occurred to him. It was three decades more before he sat down to write, inspired by a conversation he had with Joy Gresham on the topic of what book to write next. Gresham, according to a letter she wrote to her husband, became 'indispensable' to Lewis during the writing: she was able, apparently, to 'tell him how to write more like himself'. The book was dedicated to her.

The key difference between the 1920s' versions and the 1950s' was Lewis's Christianity. In the published book, Orual is the one eventually shown the error of her ways; in Lewis's earlier attempts, as he told his friend Christian Hardie, 'she was to be in the right and the gods in the wrong'. The difference in perception between Psyche and Orual he likened to 'the story of every nice, affectionate agnostic whose dearest one suddenly "gets religion".' Orual has to cope with the object of her affection transferring her feelings onto someone (or something) else; her natural affections for her sister turn sour, and she becomes jealous of the god.

Lewis's publisher, Jocelyn Gibb, wasn't impressed with the idea of calling the book *Bareface* as she felt that it would make people think it was a Western. Lewis wasn't sure exactly why that might deter people from picking it up, and he has a point: his previously published novels were in genres that many looked down on – fantasy and science fiction. The eventual title derives from the final chapter, in which Orual wonders how the gods can meet men face-to-face 'till we have faces' and are speaking from the centre of their souls.

Till We Have Faces was published in September 1956 in the UK and four months later in America. It received great acclaim, even if all its reviewers didn't necessarily understand what Lewis was attempting with it. *Catholic World* hailed it as 'the most brilliant of Mr Lewis's four novels'. Lewis described it as his personal favourite, displacing *Perelandra*, which had previously held the honour.

It appeared only a year after the publication of *The Last Battle*, but Lewis's storytelling gifts are shown reaching new heights in *Till We Have Faces*. The narrator alternately irritates and enlightens, and there are insights into human nature, particularly in the first part of the story, which are as applicable in ancient civilization as they are today. In a way it's a shame that there's a condensation of the original myth and, especially, an explanation of how Lewis changed it at the start of the story – not so much because it spoils the surprise for those familiar with the Platonic version, but because it puts a background of conflict in the reader's mind before they reach that critical part.

Although he never completed it, Jack did start work on another novel, which told the story of Helen of Troy ('the face that launched a thousand ships' according to legend) and her husband Menelaus after the fall of Troy. The first chapters and a brief fragment of a later portion of *After Ten Years*, written in 1959, are reprinted in *The Dark Tower and other stories*. It begins with 'Yellowhead' Menelaus, whose wife Helen ran off with Paris causing the Trojan War, waiting inside the Trojan Horse for the coast to be clear so he and his fellow Greeks can sack the city. Once that has been achieved, Menelaus is not happy to learn that the Spartans he has led as king for the past decade only followed him because he was married to their legitimate queen, Helen – and if anything happens to her, his own position will be at risk.

There is also a fragment from a later chapter, set in Egypt, which picks up on another aspect of the legend of Helen: according to this, she stayed in Egypt and the gods sent an imitation of her to Troy. Lewis's friend Roger Lancelyn Green believed that Jack may have been considering giving Menelaus the choice between the real Helen – ten years older, and showing some of the ravages of time – and an imitation, who would resemble the woman that he lost.

After Joy's death, though, Jack lost interest in writing fiction, and all that remains of *Ten Years After* is this brief glimpse.

3. THE RELIGIOUS WRITINGS

I

THE AUTOBIOGRAPHICAL WORKS: *SURPRISED BY JOY* AND *A GRIEF OBSERVED*

Towards the end of his life, Jack Lewis produced two volumes of autobiography to add to the allegorical account of his journey towards Christianity that appeared in *The Pilgrim's Regress*. *Surprised by Joy*, which was published in 1955, covers quite a lot of the same ground, in terms of the time period it covers. However, while *Regress* dealt with the various schools of thought which Lewis encountered, and the problems that he found with them, *Surprised by Joy* is more of a conventional autobiography, albeit one that maintains a sharp focus solely on specific elements of the author's life.

Subtitled 'The Shape of My Early Life', the book derives its title from William Wordsworth's 1815 sonnet 'Surprised by Joy – Impatient as the Wind'. There is, of course, an odd coincidence in the choice of title, given that the year after this volume of autobiography was published, Jack Lewis married Joy Gresham. However, the concept of Joy was part of Lewis's make-up long before the human Joy became part of his life – the early chapters make reference to some of those earliest experiences, some time before he was able to find a name for them.

Lewis is coy about referring to many of those he met in his school days by their real names, and even the places to which he was sent are given codenames. This gives a slightly fantastical air to the early chapters, although Lewis's detestation and hatred of the place he called Belsen – obviously not a name that he could have ascribed to it at the time, since the German concentration camp was a part of the Second World War – is the darker side of the many public-school 'jolly japes' accounts of the period, such as readers at the time would be used to from the work of Billy Bunter creator Frank Richards.

The book does not pretend to be a comprehensive account of everything that happened to Jack Lewis growing up, and, as with all autobiographies, spotting the material that is omitted is as indicative of the author's state of mind, as is the priority given to items within. Indeed, Theodore A. Gill commented about it that, 'If a good book is one that says more than the author wrote, this one is right up in there.' Researching the biography of Lewis which forms the first portion of this volume meant cross-checking Lewis's own accounts with those of his contemporaries, as related to biographers who were able to speak to them, and it is clear that Lewis exaggerated certain elements for effect – or perhaps because the passage of time had added extra dimensions to his memory – particularly when discussing Malvern College. He plays down the stories he wrote as a child, although it should be remembered that he could not have dreamed that his tales of Boxen would one day be given the lavish attention afforded to the Chronicles of Narnia.

The period around Lewis's war service is another case in point. We are given impressions of his time in the trenches, but he explains that these events aren't germane to the topic that he's writing about – how he came to Christianity. Some biographers perhaps read more into the way he glosses over this than it justifies: many of those who served or suffered in the World Wars were not willing, or indeed often able, to discuss what they experienced with others who didn't have the same frames of reference. However, Lewis teases the reader by making clear that he deliberately omits reference to a key part of his life, which other evidence would suggest is his relationship with Mrs Moore, which grew stronger following his invaliding back to England from the front line.

The book is at its strongest when Lewis is talking about the crisis of faith, and his journey through theism to Christianity. He admitted that part of his reason for writing was to exorcise some of the obsessions that he had maintained since his school days, and once that cathartic element is dealt with, the more considered writer emerges.

This wasn't the first attempt that Jack Lewis had made at an autobiography – sixty-two pages of a notebook have been found, dating from 1930, which relate how the experience of Joy led him to become a theist, and how he 'arrived at God by induction'. However, his conversion to Christianity the following year would have removed some of the pillars of his argument, and the book was abandoned for nearly two decades.

Lewis had been working on *Surprised by Joy* for seven years by the time it was published – the same period as he was writing the Narnia books. It wasn't well received across the board at the time: it was neither a conventional autobiography, nor a book written to guide the worldly towards Christianity – although it could be argued that much of Jack Lewis's other writing, notably *Screwtape* and the Narnia stories, already achieved that. Those who enjoyed it included Dorothy L. Sayers, who commented that 'Professor Lewis writes with delightful and humorous candour', while *The Times Literary Supplement* noted that it contained 'one of the oddest and most decisive end-games He [God] has ever played'.

The death of his wife Joy, however, was the catalyst for the second autobiographical work, *A Grief Observed*, although this was never published under his name during Jack Lewis's lifetime. Lewis wrote the book following Joy's death from cancer on 13 July 1960, cataloguing and examining his own reactions to the terrible event. If *Surprised by Joy* was prompted by questions from outside about Lewis's conversion to Christianity, *A Grief Observed* came about because Lewis the writer needed to ask and answer questions of himself.

The book is divided into four sections, which Walter Hooper in his catalogue of Lewis's work subtitles 'The trough of despair', 'Beginning the climb', 'A slow ascent' and 'And into the dawn'. In raw detail, it charts the writer's progress as he plumbs the depths following the death of his beloved wife H. In the first part, he rails at God, wondering where He has gone, and why He is silent, not reassuring him that H's existence is continuing elsewhere. His self-pity is almost all-consuming.

This is a point he accepts at the start of the second part, but he is concerned that he will replace real memories of H with imagined ones. He also contemplates the idea of an evil God, although he realizes this is nonsense.

The third portion sees the writer begin to see that God is still there, although he worries about what H may be going through. He starts to accept her loss and realizes that he has to carry on with his life – a thought that makes him feel guilty about not still prolonging his own unhappiness. But grief doesn't simply disappear: like a bomber on a raid, it comes round again and again.

The final and shortest part finds the writer focusing on grief being a process – not one he can ever hope to fully understand, but he has achieved a spring-cleaning in his mind. H is still present in his life, but in a different way from before.

A Grief Observed was shown to Roger Lancelyn Green at the start of September, shortly after Jack Lewis had finished writing in the four notebooks that he had found around the house. Lewis didn't want it published under his own name, and his agent submitted it to Faber and Faber, where it was read by a company director, poet T. S. Eliot. He guessed immediately that Lewis was the author and suggested that Jack should adopt a proper English penname, rather than the Latin title 'Dimidius' ('halved') that Lewis had proposed. It was therefore written as by N. W. (standing for Nat Whilk, the Anglo-Saxon for 'I know not whom') Clerk.

Few other people realized that Lewis was the author – to the extent that some well-meaning friends suggested that he should read the book, as its insights might be helpful to him. Those who did guess were asked to keep it secret. It was only published under Lewis's name after his trustees carefully considered Faber's request to do so following Jack's death. Owen Barfield and Cecil Harwood knew that Lewis was more concerned about the writing than the writer, and they ran a risk of making a spectacle of him. However, publication under Jack's name would mean that a book that otherwise would have disappeared into the well of such volumes after a short time could continue to help others.

Both Lewis's autobiographical works are thought-provoking. *Surprised by Joy* has aspects of a thriller to it, as Lewis is apparently stalked by a God whom he really does not want to believe in, but to whom he eventually submits. *A Grief Observed* sees him once more query many of those same tenets that he has accepted for three decades, as he queries a Cosmic Sadist and Vivisectionist. *Surprised by Joy* hints at the raw emotions beneath the surface as Lewis grew up; in *A Grief Observed*, they are on the surface, and once more Jack has to work his way through emotional reactions to a deeper understanding of his faith.

2

THE PROBLEM OF PAIN

While *Out of the Silent Planet* and *The Pilgrim's Regress* were Christian in their outlook and bases (albeit in both cases, elements of these were kept obscured from some of their readers by the depth of the allegories and analogies that the author used), Jack Lewis's first major seller was unashamedly a defence of Christianity.

The Problem of Pain deals with one of the most widely raised accusations levelled at Christianity: if God is good, why does He allow so much suffering in the world? At the time Lewis was writing this, the Second World War was imminent – the declaration came on 3 September 1939, by which time some of the qualities of the Nazi regime were already apparent – and it was only twenty years since a generation of young men was virtually wiped out by the Great War.

Lewis sums up the problem as: 'If God were good, He would wish to make His creatures perfectly happy, and if God were almighty He would be able to do what He wished.

But the creatures are not happy. Therefore God lacks either goodness, or power, or both.' The basis of his argument is simple: we misunderstand the meaning of the terms 'good', 'perfectly happy' and 'almighty'. Until we sort those out, then it's impossible to answer the question.

The first few chapters provide the explanation. It's a matter of perspective. 'Almighty' doesn't mean that God can do anything whatsoever – He can't give man free will, and then withhold it at the same time, since that would be nonsensical, like the idea of a square circle. If there is free will, then the possibility of evil is inherent.

God is 'good', Lewis argues, because He wants what is best for mankind, and that is God, since man is made by God for God, and 'perfect happiness' comes only when man is in harmony with God. Happiness is relevant only in the heavenly sense, so God seeks to improve man – He truly loves man, not in a disinterested way but in an all-embracing way. Lewis points out that man doesn't necessarily understand just how far he has fallen. If man could understand how wicked he seems in God's eyes, then His actions, which seem severe, may not be as bad as man considers them to be. In other words, God has to correct man.

Having established the parameters, Lewis moves on in chapter 6 to pain, which is defined as natural evil – i.e. evil not caused by human agency. Pain helps man towards God: it tells mankind that everything is not right with his life. It's God's 'megaphone to rouse a deaf world'. It reminds man that what we have isn't sufficient: it's human nature to turn thoughts to God when things are bad, not when things are going well. God knows man needs Him to be happy, but watches man look everywhere else for happiness before turning to Him. Pain is also vital for man to learn to surrender his will to God; if man's actions are what God wants him to do, but that isn't why he's doing them, then it's 'a happy coincidence'. Only if they are painful are they definitely God's will. Tribulation is a necessary part of the redemption that God offers. Pain is there to bring man to God – the question isn't 'Why is this being allowed to happen?' but 'What are we being directed to do through this pain?'

Lewis doesn't suggest that pain doesn't hurt. 'That is what the word means,' he notes. He is arguing that the old Christian doctrine of being made 'perfect through suffering' is not incredible; however, he doesn't try to make it palatable. That 'is beyond my design'. Pain is designed to prevent man from going to Hell: God will go to any lengths to stop man from experiencing that, and spending eternity without God. However, there are some people who will never turn to God, and since God has given man free will, they have the ability to do so. Hell is the by-product of that choice.

After a section on animal pain, about which Lewis admits he is speculating but notes that animals lack consciousness so can't suffer in the ways that humans do, Lewis turns his attention to Heaven, the prize for those who follow God's will. The prize that man receives there will make all the pain on Earth worthwhile, and each person's prize will be individual to them, and show different things about God. It's a transcendent joy that people can't describe, but simply are aware that they yearn for. It's what people are nostalgic for without fully realizing it, because that is the true home for mankind.

The *Problem of Pain* was written at the request of Ashley Sampson for his 'Christian Challenge' series of popular theological books, designed to introduce Christianity to people who weren't regular churchgoers. These were published by the Centenary Press, the publishing firm Sampson had founded but which had been bought out by Geoffrey Bles. Sampson had read and enjoyed both *The Pilgrim's Regress* and *Out of the Silent Planet*, and felt that Lewis was the right person to address the thorny topic of pain in a way that would be comprehensible by those who weren't as steeped in the great Christian writers as scholars who had written about it before. As he explained in the preface to the book, Lewis himself was uncertain that he was an appropriate choice, since he wasn't a clergyman, and he initially requested Sampson to publish it anonymously. Sampson refused and the book was printed as by C. S. Lewis MA. (It occasionally has been listed as a medical textbook, and on one occasion some subeditor presumed to correct what was clearly an error in the original, and changed the author's qualification to MD for an advert in *The Church Times*!)

Jack admitted himself that writing such a book in the vernacular was 'the real test. If you can't turn your faith into it, then either you don't understand, it or you don't believe it.' Writing in the preface to the French translation of *The Problem of Pain* in 1950, he explained that since his conversion, 'it has seemed my particular task to tell the outside world what all Christians believe'. He wasn't dealing with doctrinal issues that separated Protestant from Catholic, but with the most fundamental elements of faith – those things that he was convinced should be at the heart of the faith of all those who professed to be Christian.

Lewis wrote the book across the autumn and winter of 1939–40, reading sections to the Inklings, to whom it is dedicated, for their comments and approval. It appeared in October 1940, and went through regular reprintings. It was clear that reviewers felt that Lewis had been the right man for the job: '[I]t will help many people, I think, to revise what they have taken for granted and face possibilities which had not occurred to them,' wrote Edwyn Bevan in *The Spectator*, while the *Church Times* described it as 'a book that no thoughtful person can afford to miss, a really constructive message for the times'.

While the general argument found favour with many (save perhaps those on the liberal side of the Church, whom Lewis would pillory in one of the more biting letters from Screwtape to Wormwood the following year), Lewis's thoughts on the subject of animal pain were more controversial with some. His claim that 'There is no such thing as a sum of suffering, for no one suffers it. When we have reached the maximum that a single person can suffer, we have, no doubt, reached something very horrible, but we have reached all the suffering there ever can be in the universe. The addition of a million fellow sufferers adds no more pain' has also surprised many – it would seem to imply that the pain of the six million Jews in the Holocaust, or other victims of genocide, is no more than the pain felt by any one of them.

These objections haven't prevented *The Problem of Pain* from becoming one of the most widely read books that Jack Lewis wrote. It doesn't talk down to its audience, nor is it compromising: these aren't opinions that Lewis is stating – except in the chapter about animal pain, where he admits he is theorizing; it might have been better if that had been excised. To him, what is set out in the first few chapters are the core beliefs of Christianity, and from those he extrapolates the rest.

Of course, although Lewis had suffered during his life, he freely admitted that the book was highly theoretical, and there were no guarantees that he would react in the way that he expects Christians to when facing pain himself. As his book *A Grief Observed* recorded, though, Lewis was able to deal with the realities of severe pain through his faith, even if it did take some time to get there.

One of the readers of *The Problem of Pain* was Dr James W. Welch, who had been appointed as Director of Religious Broadcasting for the BBC in 1939. Thanks to him, Jack Lewis's work would reach a considerably wider audience.

3

MERE CHRISTIANITY

The first of Jack Lewis's books to be based on his radio scripts, *Mere Christianity* continues to be popular as a guide to the basics of the faith, and is often used within the Alpha Course (the back-to-basics outreach mission used by many churches around the world) as a starting point for discussion. *Mere Christianity* is in fact the title given in 1952 to the omnibus edition of three separate books, but since this is the only version now available – and Lewis made a number of alterations and additions, as well as providing a preface that draws elements together – it's treated as a single volume here.

The 'mere' in the title isn't meant to be disparaging: it refers to the central parts of the Christian faith accepted by all those who call themselves Christians. Lewis didn't make assumptions about this: the texts of the original radio script for what became book II of *Mere Christianity* ('What Christians Believe') were sent to Roman Catholic, Presbyterian, Methodist and Church of England theologians, all of whom agreed with the points he made (the Catholic and the Methodist had minor comments on the balance but not to any major extent). In his usual manner, Lewis apologized for other faults that people might find in the book, it 'did at least succeed in presenting an agreed, or common, or central, or "mere" Christianity'. Indeed it provided 'an H.C.F.' – a highest common factor – which showed that the differences between the various different denominations aren't as fundamental as nonbelievers expected.

As with *The Problem of Pain*, Lewis first explains why there is a need for the concept that he is discussing. Before talking about what it means to be a Christian – the purpose of the talks, and the book – he establishes that there is a Moral Law, and a Power behind that; once people accept that, and realize that they 'have broken that law and put [themselves] wrong with that Power – it is after all this, and not a moment sooner, that Christianity begins to talk'.

Book I, 'Right And Wrong As A Clue To The Meaning Of The Universe', deals with the proof for the existence of God. Lewis talks about the laws of nature as they used to be understood – not scientific laws, such as gravity, but the moral law. This is similar to the Deep Magic to which Aslan refers in *The Lion, the Witch and the Wardrobe*, the ingrained sense of right and wrong that people refer to when they complain something isn't 'fair' or that the enemy in a war is 'wrong'. Cultures across time have been fundamentally similar in their approach to this law, even if there are surface differences. That concept of right and wrong isn't based on personal experience, nor is it just 'instinct' – in one of the many analogies in the book, Lewis suggests our instincts are like the keys on a piano; the moral law is the tune being played by them. And that moral law isn't something that we can be taught, otherwise why would we think that 'civilized' behaviour is better than the 'savage' behaviour exhibited by the Nazis?

But why does that mean there is a God? Lewis argues that the materialist answer (nature is all that there is) doesn't explain why we feel that fundamental sense of right and wrong. Someone out there must be guiding man, and if it has set up this moral law, then it must be Someone who is as hard as nails. Why should Someone who sets up this strict moral law put up with mankind failing to follow it? Christianity teaches that man must repent of breaking this moral law and then will be forgiven: you don't go to the doctor for medicine to cure you unless you feel sick.

Book II, 'What Christians Believe', sets out the stall. Christianity isn't a simple religion that says 'there is a good God in Heaven and everything is all right – leaving out all the difficult and terrible doctrines about sin and hell and the devil, and the redemption'. Lewis makes the analogy of enemy-occupied territory. 'Christianity is the story of how the rightful king has landed, you might say landed in disguise, and is calling us all to take part in a great campaign of sabotage.' The enemy is the devil, but man has been given free will so can choose to be part of the fight. The enemy tries to persuade man that he can be like gods, but Lewis argues that man was made by God to run on Him, as a car is designed to run on petrol. A car with water in the fuel tank won't run. Happiness without God is impossible.

Lewis then runs through human history: God provided the moral law initially, and gave men 'good dreams', about a God who dies and is resurrected (the various stories across mythology). He then worked with one group, the Jews, to hammer home what sort of God He was. And then Jesus said that he was God, and he could forgive sins.

This last is the crux of Lewis's argument: Jesus cannot just be a great moral teacher. If he was simply a man who made these claims, he was either a lunatic ('on the level with a man who says he is a poached egg') or the Devil of Hell. If he was neither of these things, then his claim to be the Son of God must be true. The central tenet of Christianity is that He was killed for mankind, His death washed out man's sins and by dying He disabled death. Lewis then gives various explanations for why God took human form, and then explains that when people become Christians, they become the body of Christ, which grows within them and with them.

Book III, 'Christian Behaviour', deals with more day-to-day situations, but comes from three central ideas of morality: the relationship between man and man; the way things are inside each person; and the relationship between each man and the power that made him. Lewis sets out what a society operating by totally Christian rules might be like, but accepts that this isn't what everyone wants – but equally, if everyone was fully Christian, they would want it. He discusses the relative merits of psychoanalysis, criticizing Freud particularly, pointing out that psychoanalysis can help deal with specific problems, but not the underlying morality of people.

In a section on sexual behaviour, he notes that the old rule of chastity – sex purely inside marriage – is the correct mode. According to him, there is an obsession with the sexual act (with a comic analogy about food and the striptease of a mutton chop) but it must be fought. However, it's by no means the worst of sins: 'the pleasures of power, hatred' are worse, so a 'cold self-righteous prig who goes regularly to Church' may be closer to Hell than a prostitute.

Discussing Christian marriage, he explains how that differs from civil marriage; he also defends the man as the head of the marriage. A Christian must forgive his enemy, and not feel superior to others, since that leads to the sin of pride. Christians hope for Heaven – not playing the harp for ever: the instruments are just a symbol to indicate an eternity of something pleasurable. They show faith: holding on to beliefs even when they are challenged by events in day-to-day living and staying devoted to God despite the temptation not to, and eventually reaching a stage where they place all decisions in His hands.

The final book, 'Beyond Personality: Or First Steps In The Doctrine Of The Trinity', starts to delve into theological matters and shows how man can become more like God. Lewis deals with questions of prayer and God being able to deal with them because he is outside time; the nature of the Trinity; and how man can be *a* son of God, but will never be *the* Son of God. He discusses the difficulties of being a Christian, but points out the rewards. He also explains the position of those who act in a Christian way, yet don't believe. In summary, Christians must forget their old ways and submit 'with every fibre of your being, and you will find eternal life'.

Jack Lewis was asked to give the original broadcasts because he was a layman, not a clergyman, and because he was a recent enough convert to Christianity (just over a decade) that he could clearly remember how the religion looked from the outside. He felt that he had to go 'like a bull at the gate' to get his points across in the ten or fifteen minutes assigned to each broadcast.

Coming to *Mere Christianity* after reading the Chronicles of Narnia sometimes feels as if you're getting the annotated version of the stories – many of the underlying principles about how to live life, as shown by the various denizens of Narnia, are laid out clearly, and sometimes very bluntly here. The sections which are taken purely from the radio talks are easy to follow, even if you don't agree with Lewis's arguments; those chapters, which are clearly marked and have been added to deal with criticisms raised of the talks, or to expand points which Lewis felt were unclear, ironically tend to be heavier in terms of readability. There are elements where science has overtaken Lewis's description of events (notably his talk about the development of the foetus within the womb), and he is uncompromising about what is and is not perverted, particularly when talking about sexual behaviour.

The first two sections were published as *Broadcast Talks* in 1942, and acclaimed by the Catholic weekly *The Tablet* among many others: 'We have never read . . . any book more useful to the Christian.' The third was published separately, and comprised the original fifteen-minute versions of the talks. (Lewis had been asked to cut them back by a third for broadcast.) The final part was enlarged when Lewis collected the four as *Mere Christianity*, but like its predecessors it was well received. However, audience research for the BBC was clear that Lewis was dividing the audience, and Jack declined to produce further talks.

4

THE ABOLITION OF MAN

Based on the lectures he delivered at Durham University's Riddell Memorial Lectures in February 1943, *The Abolition of Man* deals with a subject very close to Lewis's heart – the perceived wrong direction in which education was heading.

Lewis's ire was provoked by the publication of what he called *The Green Book* in 1939 by 'Gaius' and 'Titus', which he compared to a work by 'Orbilius'; to preserve the blushes of the writers that he was pillorying, Lewis gave them Latin pseudonyms and referred to their work by alternate titles. *The Green Book* was in fact *The Control of Language: A Critical Approach to Reading and Writing* by Alex King and Martin Ketley; Orbilius was E. G. Biaggini, whose *The Reading and Writing of English*, published in 1936, was criticized by Lewis. Both of these were textbooks, intended for students in the upper forms of schools (currently equating approximately to British Year 11 and the American 10th grade), which he felt removed key parts of learning.

The first part of the book, 'Men Without Chests', starts from a comment by Gaius and Titus which appears, to Lewis's mind, to tell students that statements about the value of something are really about the emotions of the speaker, and that such statements are unimportant. This runs contrary to natural law, which Lewis describes as the 'Tao': 'the doctrine of objective value, the belief that certain attitudes are really true, and others really false, to the kind of thing the universe is and the kind of things we are'. While Lewis accepts that Gaius and Titus are teaching their students to be able to debunk advertisements or political appeals, if *The Green Book*'s philosophy is taken to its logical conclusion, children will see all statements of value as simply statements of preference or dislike, and disbelieve in the Tao. Lewis finds it astounding that people espousing such educational views are regarded as 'intellectuals', and that people are being called to show drive and creativity when those derive from the qualities that are being discouraged.

In 'The Way', Lewis goes on to explain that without belief in the Tao, society as it currently exists will not survive, unless other ethical modes of behaviour are found. Educators can try to build a system based on 'useful' behaviour, but will hit a problem when people ask why they should deny themselves for others (perhaps to die in a war) if there is no basis for that sort of action in the Tao. Alternately, they can try to use 'instinct' as a basis, but that seems doomed to failure too, since instincts are often contradictory, and there is no instinct to preserve a society by dying for it. Effectively, then, all ethical behaviour comes from moral absolutes, which cannot be proven because they are so basic. The Tao is the source of the value judgements, and pushing any ideology is simply preferring one part of the Tao over another.

Lewis doesn't suggest that the Tao is immutable: there can be advances, such as from the Confucian 'Do not do to others what you would not like them to do to you' to the Christian 'Do as you would be done by'. However, to remove all moral ground and replace it, as Nietzsche does, with a new set of principles is an innovation, not an advance. As Lewis notes: 'It is the difference between a man who says to us: "You like your vegetables moderately fresh; why not grow your own and have them perfectly fresh?" and a man who says, "Throw away that loaf and try eating bricks and centipedes instead." (Unusually for Lewis, he emphasises that he is not discussing the source of the Tao, simply that it is there and has been there throughout civilization.)

But what happens if the precepts of *The Green Book* are followed, and the Tao and its values removed? In 'The Abolition of Man', the final section of the book, Lewis looks at what sort of humans will be left. When men talk about 'the conquest of Nature', they really mean that some men will have control over others using Nature as an instrument. Those who have rejected the Tao will be able to remould humanity. There will be no moral check or balance on these Conditioners, so what they want will be the guiding force – making them as much slaves of irrational nature as the ordinary people will be slaves of the Conditioners. The quest for power, which began back in the Renaissance, will be achieved, and Man's final conquest 'has proved to be the abolition of Man'. Lewis does, though, end on a more hopeful note, wondering if modern science can work hand in hand with the precepts of the Tao.

Many of the themes that Lewis develops in *The Abolition of Man* (which must have been very powerful to hear delivered, given the force of the phrasing that he uses throughout) also appear in his novel *That Hideous Strength*, which he was writing at the same time. The horrendous situation that he posits in the final third of the non-fiction book is the set-up that he envisages at NICE (the National Institute of Coordinated Experiments), although there is more of a religious connotation to the battle in the fictional version (see part II, chapter 6, for more about that).

Perhaps because the references to Christianity are limited,

this has received wider critical acclaim than some of Lewis's religious apologetics. It has been ranked among some of the best non-fiction books of the twentieth century, and was nominated as one of the 'five books to read to save Western Civilization' by Professor Peter Kreeft, alongside Aldous Huxley's *Brave New World*. At the time, Lewis was delighted to receive a letter from his friend Owen Barfield calling it 'a real triumph' and praising its 'precision of thought, liveliness of expression and depth of meaning' – rarely for him, Jack kept the letter.

It's not an easy book to read, despite its short length (around a hundred pages). It was not aimed at a general audience, as *Screwtape* and the *Mere Christianity* lectures were, nor even at a wider Christian readership who might pick up *The Problem of Pain*. This is the scholarly Lewis, who still tempers his quotations from classical sources with analogies from everyday life, and builds much of the lectures around the concept of dying for one's country, which of course was high in everyone's thoughts at this stage of the Second World War. The core message is as applicable now as it was then: if we lose sight of the moral dimension, then mankind will lose its humanity.

5
MIRACLES

According to the accounts in the four Gospels, Jesus Christ performed miracles during his time on Earth – starting with turning water into wine at the wedding in Cana in Galilee, to raising Lazarus from the dead, and feeding five thousand people from a tiny amount of bread and fishes. Many explanations have been suggested for these over the years, from mass hallucination to simple lying on the part of the Gospel writers. However, when he came to tackle the subject, Jack Lewis responded in typical fashion: rather than simply examining history to see if the miracles happened, he took a step back and asked whether it was logically possible in principle that miracles can occur – a subject of particular interest to him, since his lack of belief in the possibility was one of his key objections to Christianity during his atheist years. After all, if you don't believe in the possibility of the supernatural, then no matter what you see, you're not going to believe it can be miraculous.

Miracles begins with Lewis defining miracles as 'an interference with Nature by supernatural powers', and calls those
who think that there is something beyond Nature 'Super-
naturalists'. Their debate is with 'Naturalists', who believe
that Nature covers everything that exists ('the whole show'),
which came out by chance (rather than from some divine
source). On their logic, even their thoughts are the working
of chance, and the by-product of atoms moving around their
brains – so why should one thought be more valid than another? From there he argues that rational thought is something
beyond Nature, and from there deduces the existence of God:
it is more reasonable that God created Nature rather than the
idea that Nature produced rational thought by chance. Moral
judgements and the 'natural law' (the Tao, discussed in *The
Abolition of Man*) equally cannot derive from Nature.

Just because we accept that there is a supernatural explanation for the creation of Nature, of course, it doesn't mean that
miracles can or must occur. But is Nature so all-encompass-
ing that the idea of supernatural interference is impossible? A
miracle isn't a bending of the rules of Nature, but something
new being 'fed into' it: it's something that Nature couldn't
do on its own, but requires the intervention of a supernatural
force.

Miracles are essential to Christianity: they follow a pattern
that we can't necessarily understand, but we should be certain that had they not happened, that would have been wrong.
The central Christian tenet, the incarnation of God as man,
is miraculous, and everything connected to life flows from
that – it explains what life is about, since it is the 'missing part
of the work' that pulls together all the disparate parts of life.
Christian doctrine holds that man was originally immune
to death, but then, when man gave in to temptation in the
Garden of Eden ('the Fall'), he lost that immunity. Through
Christ's resurrection, he is called into a new life in which he
will be immune once more.

The miracles that Jesus carried out are divided into two

sorts: 'the Old Creation' and 'the New Creation'. The former are ones where God, through Jesus, alters Nature, by extra fertility, healing or, in the case of the withering of the fig tree, destruction. The 'New Creation' are those which 'anticipate the Resurrection': walking on water, the raising of Lazarus and the Transfiguration (where Jesus takes his disciples to a mountain, he is flanked by the prophets Moses and Elijah, and a voice from Heaven describes Jesus as 'my Son'). They are glimpses of the altered life as a result of the defeat of death – a step into a new Nature, which, Lewis states, is supernatural to our own natural five-sense-driven world. Naturists believe the building has one floor – this is all there is; Christians are shown there is a skyscraper above – the new Nature is beyond what we can yet comprehend.

Lewis had been working on a study of miracles for over five years before *Miracles* was published. He had preached on the subject in London in the autumn of 1942, and written on certain aspects for the church newspaper *The Guardian* around the same time. He was prompted to make a complete study after receiving a letter from author Dorothy L. Sayers, who asked him why there weren't 'any up-to-date books about Miracles'. Was it, perhaps, because science had progressed to a level that no one could believe any more? Lewis informed her that he would start such a book straightaway, and within four months had completed six chapters. He realized that this was going to be a long endeavour – it eventually took him two full years to complete it to his satisfaction – and excerpts appeared in both *The Church of England Newspaper* and *The Guardian* before publication in 1947 (it's not known why there was a two-year delay between his finishing the book and its appearance).

Although Jack Lewis made occasional revisions to his work, the largest alteration that he made came in editions of *Miracles* that appeared after 1960. This was as a direct result of a challenge by Miss G. E. M. Anscombe, a Research Fellow of Somerville College, at the Socratic Society. She believed that the third chapter of the book, which dealt with Lewis's proposition that naturalism was self-refuting, was wrong; a debate followed in which both Lewis and Miss Anscombe told others that they believed they were victorious. Lewis felt she had misunderstood his argument, but accepted that he might have been unclear: although the initial paragraphs of the chapter remained in future editions, Jack rewrote the majority of the chapter, using a different analogy. Miss Anscombe, herself a professor for many years, was delighted that Lewis showed his dedication to the truth by being prepared to make the alteration.

Elsewhere, *Miracles*, which turned out to be Jack Lewis's last Christian apologetic, was greeted with delight by Christians of an orthodox frame of mind. The reviewer for *Theology* magazine noted that Lewis made theology readable: 'The rather rare combination of the gifts of poet, philosopher, and theologian is quite irresistible.' There are many, though, who do not agree with its arguments and maintain that Lewis simply provides examples of his propositions rather than a proper explanation.

Like *The Abolition of Man*, *Miracles* was not written for a general audience to read. Lewis had a gift for communication and use of the 'common touch' – some of the most striking images in *Miracles* involve an analogy with Euston Station in London, and a child regarding poisonous items as 'horrid red things' – but the arguments he presents are not by any stretch of the imagination simple. The book demonstrates the clarity of Lewis's faith, and presents a man determined to knock down any obstacles. But as with all of his arguments in favour of Christianity, much depends on the reader's willingness to engage in the debate.

6

REFLECTIONS ON THE PSALMS

Jack Lewis's first non-fiction book for over ten years was not, as he hastened to make clear in his introduction, another 'apologetic' on the lines of *Mere Christianity* or *Miracles*. 'I am nowhere trying to convince unbelievers that Christianity is true,' he points out. 'A man can't always be defending the truth; there must be a time to feed on it.'

The volume is a study guide for the Old Testament book of Psalms, traditionally, although inaccurately, known as the Songs of David. These were written by many different poets at different times (Lewis suggests that maybe only Psalm 18 was by King David himself) and accordingly reflect many different views of God and the chosen people's sufferings.

Lewis's book is divided into twelve chapters, dealing with such matters as 'Judgement in the Psalms', 'Connivance', 'Nature' and 'Second Meanings'. He also provides two appendices, one with the texts of some of the most frequently mentioned psalms, the other with a handy checklist of which psalms are discussed in the book. By no means do all of the 150 songs that are included in the Old Testament book come under his microscope – the ones that deal with historical events are notably bypassed – and Lewis is at pains to point out that there are elements of the psalms which conflict greatly with the teachings of Christ in the New Testament.

The first, and larger, part of the book covers topics from the perspective of the writers of the psalms, putting them in context and explaining how these have relevance to everyday twentieth-century life. There are digs at people who fawn over adulterous film stars, or who criticize a government body while still hoping for an introduction to someone within it so they can get a job there themselves. He starts by looking at the characteristics of the psalms which are 'at first most repellent', preferring to get the nasty stuff out of the way.

The first item discussed is the concept of judgement and compares the Jewish way of looking at it – as if it's a civil court – with the more profound version in Christianity. On cursing, he comments on the raw hatred on show, despite other portions of the Old Testament (notably Leviticus) ordering against such an attitude. As far as death is concerned, the psalm writers mostly did not believe in an afterlife, something Lewis suggests may be because God did not want the Jews to be like the Egyptians, who spent their time looking after the well-being of the dead.

Those less pleasant aspects out of the way, Jack moves on to the joy and delight in God, and the praise that the psalmists felt for the Laws of God, something he professes to find bewildering at first. He notes that they instinctively understood that the Lord was righteous.

Regarding 'Connivance', Lewis notes that Christians should avoid mixing with 'very bad' people, because of the temptation to be like the psalmist, and condone their evil. The psalmists' approach to Nature is unusual because at that time, a doctrine that a god created the heavens and the Earth was not common.

The latter part of Lewis's book is concerned with the second meanings that can be found in the Psalms – things that the psalmist couldn't have been aware of. Lewis mentions one of his regularly expressed theories, that stories in pagan mythology that could refer to Christ are deliberate, and were 'a likeness permitted by God to that truth on which all depends'. He explains his own views on scripture – which bits he believes are historical – and how the Bible 'carries the Word of God' that carries an 'overall message' rather than being 'an encyclopaedia or encyclical'.

He then goes through the psalms that have been appointed in the Book of Common Prayer for certain times of day and specific seasons, and discusses in some details why they are appropriate. He ends with a discussion of the quote from St Peter's second letter, 'one day is with the Lord as a thousand years, and a thousand years as one day', which he interprets alongside Psalm 84 to mean that man may be removed from the 'tyranny, the unilinear poverty' of time.

Jack Lewis wrote his *Reflections on the Psalms* in the autumn of 1957, not long after his marriage to Joy Gresham. It has sometimes been suggested that the reason he didn't write another 'apologetic' after *Miracles* was that he was upset by the reaction to it, and no longer felt on safe ground writing such works. Biographers close to Lewis tend to disagree, and note that he simply turned his attentions elsewhere: eight of Lewis's best pieces – the seven Chronicles of Narnia and *Till We Have Faces* – were written and published after *Miracles* was complete, which covered some of the same ground but in a different way.

One apparently direct consequence of the book's publication in September 1958 was an invitation the following month from the Archbishop of Canterbury for Jack to become a member of the 'Commission to Review the Psalter'. To involve someone who had recently commented on the occasional mistranslation of the psalms in the version used in the Book of Common Prayer would seem an obvious step.

Those used to reading the psalms, or hearing them in church, will find this book of great interest, perhaps even more so in the twenty-first century, when the psalms are more often to be heard in 'responsorial form' rather than the versions about which Lewis was writing. Similarly, Christians wondering if the psalms still have relevance to them will find much to consider – as the review in *The Times Literary Supplement* in September 1958 stated, 'This book may not tell the reader all he would like to know about the Psalms, but it will tell him a good deal he will not like to know about himself.' It has been said that the best autobiographies read as if you're sitting over a pint with the author discussing his or her life; this volume feels as if you've got the chance to catch Jack Lewis's opinions on some of the oldest literature in the world.

7

THE FOUR LOVES

The last book published under Jack Lewis's name during his lifetime was based on ten talks on the subject of the four loves, which he was commissioned to give by the Episcopal Radio-TV Foundation of Atlanta, Georgia. While there were objections to the frankness of some of these by Americans, resulting in their not receiving as wide an audience as they should have done, writing the book allowed Lewis the opportunity to examine all four variants equally.

The Four Loves are defined as Affection, Friendship, Eros and Charity, but Lewis begins the book by distinguishing between two other sorts of love: 'Gift-love' and 'Need-love'. The former is the sort that 'moves a man to work and plan and save for the future well-being of his family which he will die without sharing or seeing'. The latter is the sort 'which sends a lonely or frightened child into his mother's arms'. Human love is most like divine love when it is Giving, but Need-love isn't always purely selfish, as mankind needs others to survive healthily – and Need-love is how man reacts to God.

Lewis expands the definition of 'Affection': originally it was just the fondness between parents and children, but it covers all people of whom we feel fond – not necessarily our friends, since we actively choose them, but those with whom we come in contact, but may not have much in common. To illustrate this, Lewis mentions Don Quixote and Sancho Panza, and the quartet of animals in *The Wind in the Willows*. He also points out that we all expect to be the object of Affection, and dislike it when we are not, and emphasises that Affection can be abused, both by the person demonstrating it, if it's for the wrong reasons, and those receiving it.

Friendship, Lewis believes, is no longer as highly regarded as the other forms of love, although in ancient times, it was seen as the love that raised man 'almost to the level of gods or angels'. He starts with 'a very tiresome bit of demolition', removing the thought that such friendships between men are 'really homosexual', and notes that simply being with other people is 'the matrix of Friendship' rather than true Friendship. That occurs between two people who are the only ones to share a particular interest or insight. Lewis explains that there are potential problems with such a true Friendship, if the interest is in something bad, or if pride develops as a result of the Friendship. However, because that latter risk exists, it makes Friendship more valuable – only a high spiritual love can be something that can be attacked by pride.

Lewis is careful to separate Eros – 'that state which we call "being in love"; or, if you prefer, that kind of love which lovers are "in" ' – from what he describes as 'Venus', which is the 'carnal or animally sexual element within Eros'. Sexual acts can occur without our being 'in love'; Eros makes a man want a particular woman and need to be with her, whether or not he is happy with her. Venus is a transitory pleasure, but it is equally dangerous to make Eros a god in its own right because the sensation of being in love is so all-consuming – a sense of humour about it is essential.

The final love, Charity, is divine love, which is the source of

Affection, Friendship and Eros, and which stops them from fading. These 'natural loves' don't stop man from loving God, and Charity nurtures and strengthens them. Unlike the natural loves, though, Charity is all 'Gift-love' – there is nothing needy about it; we need it. It's the love that God has for man, and why He sent his Son into the world; if an individual is concerned with Charity as well as the natural loves, then he will not fall prey to the risks inherent in each.

Jack Lewis received an invitation early in 1958 from Bishop H. J. Loutit of South Florida, on behalf of the Episcopal Radio-TV Foundation, to give some talks to an American audience. He agreed, since he felt that he wanted to talk about the four loves, 'which seems to bring in nearly the whole of Christian ethics'. The scripts were written, and recorded in August 1958, although Caroline Rakestraw, the founder of the organization, who travelled to London for the sessions, antagonized both Jack and Joy Lewis with her requests for alterations. Mostly these were presentational but Jack wasn't willing to change his style.

The contents of the talk on Eros were to cause problems. The Episcopal bishops on the board of the Foundation considered that what Jack said about sex was 'too frank for the American people', and cancelled the broadcasts – which was more than a little unfortunate, since they had already been widely publicized. Instead, an article in *The Living Church* explained, they would be 'channelled into college and urban communities for a more sophisticated audience'.

Caroline Rakestraw arranged for the tapes to be made available, and in 1970 cassette recordings were released to the general public as *Four Talks on Love*. Jack ignored the comments of the American bishops, and re-edited the scripts into book form, amplifying aspects as he felt required. The book found favour with many readers and reviewers, one of the most notable being Pope John Paul II, who quoted from it regularly, and told Lewis's biographer, Walter Hooper, that it was one of his favourite books.

8

LETTERS TO MALCOLM: CHIEFLY ON PRAYER

The first of two books completed by Jack Lewis which were published under his name posthumously (the other being *A Grief Observed*, which was reprinted as by C. S. Lewis later in 1964), *Letters to Malcolm: Chiefly on Prayer* was finished about six months before he died. Lewis reverts to the epistolary form that was so successful in *The Screwtape Letters*, giving one side of a correspondence with an imaginary friend, Malcolm, as the two old colleagues discuss prayer.

The twenty-two letters to Malcolm cover many different elements of prayer, starting with the merits of 'home-made' against 'ready-made' prayers (some of the latter are appropriate at certain times), and the problems with praying at night and avoiding sleepiness. What should be included in prayers is covered, as are aspects of the Lord's Prayer. After debating whether 'religion' is just a department of life, like the social or the intellectual, Lewis then discusses the concept of petitionary prayer in the abstract.

This is thrown into sharp perspective by the news that Malcolm's son George is ill, and echoes of *A Grief Observed* can be heard in Jack's comments about the anguish of prayer in such a situation. This leads in the next letter to another of Lewis's regular observations, about God's nature outside Time, and how prayers are heard by God even before man was made.

Man's need for his prayers to be heard, perhaps more than to have them granted, is tackled next, while the passage in St Mark's Gospel about 'what we pray for with faith we shall receive' is interpreted to mean that most men pray with insufficient faith. The idea that all mystics, of whatever faith, will find the same things is dismissed – using the analogy of a voyage, it's not the journey and what is encountered on that, but the landfall at the end that differentiates the Christian.

Jack comments on the ease of praying for other people rather than himself, and suggests that praying for someone is easier than actually doing something, and that the burden of the spiritual work is on the person prayed for and God, rather than him. He then criticizes an 'anonymous' poem on prayer (actually one of Lewis's own), and comments that prayer could be described as God speaking to God, since prayer is only enabled by the Holy Spirit. He concludes this letter with a definition of the importance of the Incarnation, and how it separates Christianity from pantheism. The following letter deals with the constant presence of God.

Letter XV begins on a practical note: how does he begin to pray? His own way of approaching God in prayer is noted, and the next letter discusses the use of images as an aid. Prayers of worship and penitential prayers are then dissected.

In the majority of his works, Lewis doesn't talk much about Holy Communion, but this is rectified in Letter XIX, although he admits that he does not have great insights to share and that the concept of the body and blood at Communion is one that he still finds challenging. The next letter is about prayers for the dead, and Lewis notes that he still

believes in the concept of Purgatory – at least as he saw it in
The Great Divorce two decades earlier – and maintains that
the dead, unlike God, may still be within Time, particularly
given the resurrection of the body that is to come. The problem with prayer being irksome is the subject of the penultimate letter, while Lewis lets loose on the dangers of 'liberal'
Christianity in the final piece.

Letters to Malcolm wasn't Jack's first attempt at writing about
prayer – in a letter to Don Giovanni Calabria in January 1953,
he asks for prayer support for a book he was writing 'about
private prayers for the use of the laity, especially for those
who have been recently converted to the Christian faith'. He
had noticed that there were many useful books for those who
were strong in the faith, but not so many for those who were
novices. However, by February 1954, he had abandoned the
book; 'it was clearly not for me', he wrote at the time.

In Spring 1963, the idea of the *Letters* came to him, and
Jack wrote the entire book over the space of two months. It
was greeted with praise by his publisher, Jocelyn Gibb, who
acclaimed it as 'the best you've done since *The Problem of
Pain*'. It appeared as planned in January 1964, two months
after Jack's death.

Even Jack's friends who read it in manuscript form were
taken in by the picture of Malcolm, his wife Betty and their
son George painted in the stories. There are many lovely
asides which help bring them to life – such as Jack mildly
chiding Malcolm for forgetting a long conversation that they
once had in the Forest of Dean about a particular aspect of
prayer.

Letters to Malcolm was received, not surprisingly, with a
touch of sadness by the critics. 'A fine capstone to this side of
his literary career,' wrote Nathan A. Scott Jr in the *Saturday
Review*, while the *Times Literary Supplement* review concluded, 'That this should be the last book that we have from
C. S. Lewis is a matter for genuine regret.' The *Church Times*

review perhaps summed up both the book and Jack's career best: 'It is splendid, glorious stuff, the product of a luminous and original mind, tough and honest in facing the agonizing questions raised inevitably by any consideration of prayer, and yet endowed with an extraordinary sensitivity and tenderness for the fears and foibles of man.'

As with all his best work, Jack's final book is accessible to anyone who is prepared to think about what they're reading. He explains the basis for his thoughts, and uses analogies as appropriate. His genuine, heartfelt desire to pray comes across throughout – a proper epitaph for such a man.

4. THE ADAPTATIONS

I

NARNIA ON TELEVISION

'I am absolutely opposed – adamant isn't in it! – to a TV version. Anthropomorphic animals, when taken out of narrative into actual visibility, always turn into buffoonery or nightmare. At least, with photography. Cartoons (if only Disney did not combine so much vulgarity with his genius!) wld. be another matter. A human, pantomime, Aslan wld. be to me blasphemy.'

So wrote Jack Lewis on 18 December 1959 to BBC Radio producer Lance Sieveking, shortly after the first broadcast of a reading of the Chronicles over the airwaves. Unsurprisingly, therefore, there were no television adaptations of any of the Narnia stories during Lewis's lifetime.

However, after Jack's death in November 1963, the television landscape changed. The arrival of BBC2 on the new 625-line system, which improved picture quality, and the prospect of the start of colour transmissions meant that production values had to improve, and programmes like *Doctor Who*, which started the day after Jack died, pioneered advances in special effects.

One of the staples of BBC Television was the children's series *Jackanory*, in which a presenter would read a children's story in instalments. This was very popular, and in 1967, ABC, one of the production companies that made up the independent television network in the UK, decided to make its own equivalent version of *The Lion, The Witch & The Wardrobe*.

'It was meant to be a story told to camera,' adaptor Trevor Preston told a BBC documentary in 1988. 'Then the production team said they could illustrate it, and it grew and grew and grew.'

The producer was Pamela Lonsdale, who would go on to oversee many seminal children's programmes for the ITV network, including *Rainbow*, and other adaptations, such as *Stig of the Dump* and John Wyndham's *Chocky*. 'Originally it was on a very low budget because it was to be on a *Jackanory*-type presentation, with really only a small set and a few pictures,' she recalled. 'We increased the budget and we ended up with the princely sum of something like £1,000 or £1,200 per episode. That was quite a lot then.'

Preston divided the story into ten half-hour episodes (which included a commercial break), of which only the first ('What Lucy Found in the Wardrobe') and the eighth ('The Triumph of the Witch') remain today. The animals are all performed by people in costumes – Bernard Kay as Aslan stands upright throughout his appearance in the latter episode – and the story is narrated by Jack Woolgar as the Professor. He provides the context for the scenes; the picture then dissolves to the actors in studio; and then the camera goes back to Woolgar for the next piece of description. Liz Crowther played Lucy, with Zuleika Robson as Susan, Paul Waller as Peter and Edward McMurray as Edmund; Elizabeth Wallace made a chilling White Witch.

The series was broadcast on Tuesday afternoons, from 9 July 1967 to 10 September. One potentially demanding

critic was pleased: 'On Television last night I saw the opening instalment of J's *Lion, Witch and Wardrobe* by which I
was agreeably surprised,' Jack's brother Warnie confided to
his diary. 'It's very promising and I think J would have been
pleased with it – no hint so far of what he feared, a touch of
Disneyland.'

According to contemporary reports, the series was very
faithful to Lewis's text, with his references to other mytholo-
gies left intact (something that many adaptations were quick
to lose). The switch from narrator to live-action drama makes
it feel in places like a filmed radio version, but the lack of
money for effects meant that the production had to concentrate on the relationship between the characters, making it
in that sense, one of the truest versions of the Chronicles on
film.

A decade later came one of the most fondly remembered versions. If the ABC adaptation ran contrary to Jack's wishes by
using 'anthropomorphic animals', then the 1970s TV movie
was more in line with his thinking. The second television version of *The Lion, the Witch and the Wardrobe* was produced
by the American animation company Bill Melendez Productions in association with the Children's Television Workshop
(CTW), the people behind *Sesame Street*.

In early 1978, David A. Connell from CTW approached
Melendez, who was best known for creating the seasonal
television special *A Charlie Brown Christmas*, when he discovered CTW had a major problem. The studio with whom
CTW had been developing an animated version of the first
Narnia story for the previous two and a half years was now
unable to continue with the project (for reasons that are no
longer known). There was a set air date for the project on CBS
Television in the US: 1 and 2 April 1979, which at that point
gave a mere nine months to get everything sorted, and allow
time for promotion of the broadcast.

When Melendez learned what the project was, he was keen

to be involved, but told CTW that he didn't have sufficient troops or enough room at his headquarters in Los Angeles to make the film in the time available. CTW was after around a hundred minutes of animation, to be aired in two parts and transmitted on consecutive nights. It was a joint project with Kraft, who were sponsoring a programme to encourage youngsters to read – copies of a special edition of Macmillan Publishing Company's 'Collier Edition' of *The Lion, the Witch and the Wardrobe* were to be provided by the Episcopal Radio-TV Foundation to schools across America. Children would be encouraged to read the story, then watch the first part of the film, and then discuss it in school the next day: the books had a study guide appended to assist discussion.

Melendez agreed to take on the project if he could do it his way – by which he meant transferring responsibility over to his London office (Melendez Films), run by his son Steve. Father and son discussed the many potential problems, and Steve Melendez agreed to produce the film. However, they knew they would need more resources, so decided to adopt the approach that had worked for the Beatles film *Yellow Submarine* a decade earlier: farm out the work to various animation houses. In the end, TV Cartoons (TVC) in London came on board, as well as a studio in Barcelona, and the Melendez Productions office in Los Angeles. In those pre-fax or -email days, all the drawings had to be taken between the three countries by someone catching a plane; Steve Melendez often took on this responsibility himself.

Work began on recording the voices of the actors, and preparing character sheets, with renowned production designer Alan Shean masterminding the look of the piece. At that point, the project hit a snag: the Episcopal Foundation, overseeing the production on behalf of the Lewis Estate, didn't like the voices of the children. Melendez had found an American family with the requisite number of siblings from one of the American schools in London, but the word came back that they were 'too raw'. That meant that the entire soundtrack had to be rerecorded.

The Foundation also didn't like Shean's designs for the children (one of which, much nearer Pauline Baynes's style, is in the gallery on the DVD). Steve Melendez had personally overseen four minutes' worth of animation by this stage, all of which had to be redone. Additionally, the Foundation wanted more realistic backgrounds than Melendez was providing. They asked for the characters not to smoke, although they finally agreed that the Professor could still do so.

On a project that was tight for time, this loss of five weeks' work compounded the problems. However, it's very hard to tell from the finished product that there were so many difficulties. Victor Spinetti, who voiced Mr Tumnus, helped locate three new children (the boy from the original family who played Edmund wasn't recast), and a fresh soundtrack was laid down.

The project was split into three parts: the early section was done in the UK, overseen by Nick Spargo; from where the Pevensie children spot Mr Beaver through to the off-screen arrival of Father Christmas was handled by Bob Balser in Barcelona; George Dunning at the London studio picked up the story there, while TVC dealt with the crowd sequences. Balser had been animation director on *Yellow Submarine*, and was used to working on high-profile projects; for Narnia, he had to bring in a crew of thirty, many of whom had to be taught rudimentary English to carry out the job properly. All the backgrounds were done separately, while four 'cycles' of snow were prepared which could be used interchangeably. Composer Michael J. Lewis was signed up, and his score was recorded at CTS, with the professional musicians taking only two hours to lay down the climactic battle sequences.

As the team realized when they started work on the script, there isn't very much excess description in Jack Lewis's original story, and accordingly they were quickly aware that edits would need to be made in order to ensure the film was the correct length. Accordingly, some of the early parts of the tale are concertinaed: the film begins with Lucy tumbling out of the wardrobe after her first trip to Narnia, with no explanation as to why the children are in the Professor's house. The entire Second World War element is removed; the Pevensies are in modern dress. Once in Narnia, the robin is not seen, and the sequence where Father Christmas hands the three children the gifts was removed. Instead, the children meet the fox and his party, who have been given presents, and the children's own gifts are therefore awarded to them by Aslan later in the story. A sequence depicting the reign of the four kings and queens was storyboarded and the narration recorded, but this was eventually deleted (again, this is on the DVD).

Certain alterations were requested by the Foundation during the production process: the moment when the White Witch stabs Aslan with the knife isn't shown on screen – the picture cuts to lightning and thunder. The animators felt that this would be far more dramatic than seeing the knife entering the lion, and argued, successfully, for their way to be retained.

Two different versions of the soundtrack exist: the American DVD contains the original US performances, with Victor Spinetti, Don Parker, Beth Porter and Dick Vosburgh taking the lead roles. For the British premiere on Easter Sunday, 6 April 1980, a new cast was recorded, drawing from the ranks of veteran screen actors. Arthur Lowe, Leo McKern (*Rumpole of the Bailey*), Sheila Hancock, June Whitfield and Leslie Phillips added a touch of class to proceedings.

Some of the parts were left intact for both versions. Three of the Pevensie children weren't changed (a new Edmund was found) and the voice of Aslan was played by Stephen Thorne either side of the Atlantic. Thorne was known to British audiences for his roles in the science-fiction series *Doctor Who*, and would go on to appear in the BBC's epic radio adaptation of *The Lord of the Rings*. He returned to the part of Aslan in 1988 for the BBC Schools version of *The Magician's Nephew* and *The Lion, the Witch and the Wardrobe*, as well as the subsequent Radio 4 plays of the rest of the Chronicles.

The broadcast was a success: anecdotal evidence suggested that children enjoyed the synchronization of reading and watching the story, and it was awarded two Primetime Emmy Awards – for Outstanding Animated Program, shared by David D. Connell and Steve Melendez; and for Outstanding Individual Achievement: Animated Program for Connell and Bill Melendez. For some years, it was a seasonal staple, and its release on DVD brought one of the best Narnia adaptations to a new audience.

The most recent version was made nearly a quarter of a century ago. For many years Sunday teatimes on BBC1 would see an adaptation of a classic serial suitable for a family audience. Although by the late 1980s, the branding of the Classic Serial had pretty much disappeared, audiences were used to seeing dramas at this time, and in 1987, the BBC decided to produce *The Chronicles of Narnia*. By making it a co-production with BBC Enterprises (the name at the time for the sales arm of the corporation) and Wonderworks, a group of PBS stations in the US, the BBC were able to raise sufficient funds to go for a full live-action drama.

By this time, advances in technology meant that, even on a TV budget, flying and animation were feasible, and much was made in the publicity for the series about the state-of-the-art animatronic head that was created for Aslan. The lion took three months to sculpt and make, after the designers had spent time watching the real creatures at close quarters at Longleat, the house of the Marquess of Bath – although they elected to give their Aslan softer eyes than a real lion's.

Four stories were included in the series: *The Lion, the Witch and the Wardrobe* was given six half-hour instalments; *Prince Caspian* was condensed into two half-hours; *The Voyage of the Dawn Treader*, perhaps surprisingly, received only four; while *The Silver Chair* returned to the full six. There was

considerable continuity of actors and production personnel across the three series (*Caspian* and *Dawn Treader* were
broadcast as one series).

The scripts were written by Australian author Alan Seymour who relished the freedom of being able to put down
words on the page and 'conjure up the most difficult and
complicated effects', according to an interview he gave during
production of the first series. 'You know that you don't have
to solve that problem. You're setting a problem for the director, and the visual-effects department to cope with later on.'

Twelve-year-old Sophie Wilcox was one of the hundreds of
children who auditioned for the Pevensie siblings. The owner
of the drama club she attended also ran an agency for child
actors, and suggested her for the part of Lucy. She recalled
seeing the animated version on television, and one of her
memories of primary school was of sitting on the floor listening to her teacher read the story. 'I went for the first audition, then I got called back to the second,' she recalled in an
interview for this book. 'But for the third audition I had come
down with shingles, and had burned my hand on a smoke
machine in a school production. It was an all-day workshop
and I remember Mum asking if I was all right to go. I said I'd
go and if I wasn't having a nice time, I could just leave.'

To find a group of children who would portray a convinc-
ing family, director Marilyn Fox workshopped various different combinations during the day. 'There were probably
about sixty of us there,' said Wilcox, 'and they sent half home
at lunchtime – it was a bit like *Pop Idol* or *The X Factor*. I
was just a twelve-year-old girl having fun. I didn't have any
expectations on me to get it. I had no nerves, I was just enjoying saying the lines and meeting other kids that liked acting,
and that was probably why I got the part.'

Wilcox remembers that the final part cast was Jonathan R.
Scott. 'At the end, it got to the point where it was Richard
Dempsey, Sophie Cook and I, and they kept calling in two
boys, Jonathan and someone else for Edmund, and they kept

swapping them back and forth, playing out scenes. When I walked out of the rehearsal rooms at Acton that night, I knew I'd got it. The four of us looked really right. We fitted well, and could be related. But I looked nothing like the illustrated Lucy from the book and when the film came out, I was so flattered that Georgie Henley, who played Lucy, looked very similar to me.'

Because of the restrictions on the hours children could film, the production crew often deliberately left it until the last moment before bringing them on set. This minimized the time wasted, but also meant they could capture the children's natural response to the sets. The first scene filmed was the Pevensies' arrival in Narnia. 'We really were stepping into this world; it was so much fun,' Wilcox notes.

The first serial was filmed around Great Britain: the snow scenes were shot at Aviemore, in the Scottish Highlands, although the amount of snow wasn't sufficient, so extra fake snow had to be added – which made life very difficult for the actors playing the Beavers. Kerry Shale and Lesley Nicol often required the services of 'beaver retrievers' to get them upright if they overbalanced. The BBC's Scenic Department spent three weeks preparing the area, fulfilling the script's request for the ice near the Beavers' dam to be 'frozen into foamy, wavy shapes'. The children's departure from London and arrival at the Professor's local station were both filmed on the West Somerset Railway, while Manorbier Castle in Wales stood in for Cair Paravel.

For the combined version of *Prince Caspian* and *The Voyage of the Dawn Treader*, a lot of the on-board action was filmed at Milford Haven, in Wales, where a full-size *Dawn Treader* was built (the various Narnian adornments were placed on top of a working ship). The top half of the ship was recreated in the studio for the scenes involving practical effects, such as the sea serpent. The water filming was one of Sophie Wilcox's favourite times. 'Even if I was cold, to me it felt like part of the adventure. I probably didn't savour it as much as I should have done. It's that wonderful youthful thing of throwing your-self in completely.' Goldney Hall at Bristol University and Hawkstone Park in Shropshire provided other locations, and many of the island scenes were filmed on the Isles of Scilly, a small collection of islands off the west coast of Cornwall.

A quarter of a century later, the filming remains one of Wilcox's fondest memories. 'It's amazing that something I did twenty-five years ago is still known and cherished by lots of people,' she said. 'I was really lucky: I was playing a part that was loved. If I was recognized, then it was incredibly positive. Jonathan, who played Edmund, was met with real malice because people, even adults, think you are who you're playing.'

Wilcox wasn't part of the final story, *The Silver Chair*, for which the Peak District National Park provided plenty of open spaces for the quest, while the underground caves at Castleton were ideal for the sequences towards the end of the story.

Alan Seymour didn't emphasize the religious links in the stories, but nor did he remove them altogether – speaking while promoting the first series, Barbara Kellerman, who played the White Witch and then returned as the Green Lady for *The Silver Chair*, noted that the allegories were there for those who wanted to find them.

That's not to say that he didn't make changes: whereas many versions of *The Lion, the Witch and the Wardrobe* tend to gloss over the wartime setting, or the relationship between the Professor, the children and his staff, the first episode of Seymour's script actually adds more than Lewis gave us, with Michael Aldridge's Professor established firmly. Some of the details regarding Lucy and Edmund's first visit are altered, meaning that there's a discussion over borrowing boots, rather than coats, from the wardrobe, and Edmund isn't wrapped into the Witch's cloak.

To Lewis purists, some of the later changes are more sig-nificant: the Witch has more obvious magical powers – she creates a tent out of nothing, and the Turkish Delight unwraps itself when she meets Edmund – and Aslan seems to have acquired some flying powers when he returns the children to the battle. The death of the Witch is also altered: she falls off a ledge, rather than being dealt with directly by Aslan.

Other alterations were a necessity of the production. The animatronic Aslan, voiced by Ronald Pickup, and performed by Alisa Berk and William Todd-Jones, simply couldn't knight someone with a sword or place a crown on their head, so the former was achieved by Aslan inclining his head on the characters' shoulders, and the latter through video effects.

Allowing only an hour for *Prince Caspian* meant omissions were necessary, and while Seymour's version hits the key points of Lewis's tale of the return to Narnia, much of the detail is missing. (Many, though, found that preferable to the wholesale rewriting of the plot that occurred for the second Walden Media movie.) *The Voyage of the Dawn Treader* and *The Silver Chair* are relatively faithful to the original text, although the references to the deeper kingdom are lost (and a dragon makes an appearance!).

For *Dawn Treader* and *The Silver Chair*, Eustace was played by David Thwaites, with Puddleglum, the marsh-wiggle, portrayed by former *Doctor Who* star Tom Baker, whose lugubrious interpretation of the character more than makes up for any shortcomings in the production values. Other key cast across the serials included Warwick Davis as Reepicheep and Glimfeather (he would return to Narnia playing Nikabrik in the movie of *Prince Caspian*); Samuel West as the adult Caspian; *Catweazle* lead Geoffrey Bayldon as Ramandu, and *Burn Notice*'s Gabrielle Anwar in a very early role as his daughter.

The Silver Chair provided star Camilla Power, who played Jill Pole, with 'one of the best summers of my life', as she recalled in an interview for this book. 'It's amazing looking back at it: it was real epic stuff that hadn't been done in that way before. Nowadays, on BBC budgets, you're lucky if you get five extras in a scene; but we had amazing costumes and loads of extras. Aslan, with Ailsa and Todd inside, was extraordinarily expensive. It was a huge undertaking for the BBC. At the time you just do it, and you're having fun, but when you look back, you realize it was something extraordinary.

'I remember feeling really wrapped up in that world,' Power added. 'In the caves in Derbyshire, they built these amazing slides we could go down, and we were in some quite narrow, dark places. I had a huge costume, with petticoats and pixie boots, and one lovely night we were in a disused quarry in Wales with all the Underworlders who were dressed in horrible latex. Bill Wallis [the Warden], myself, David and Tom were in a boat, and you couldn't quite take on board that you weren't really in it.' Baker himself recently described the filming as a 'marvellous time'.

With a haunting theme written by Geoffrey Burgon, the BBC *Chronicles of Narnia* enthralled audiences both sides of the Atlantic. *The Lion, the Witch and the Wardrobe* was nominated for a Primetime Emmy in the Outstanding Children's Program category, as well as four BAFTA Awards, winning Best Video Lighting, and a Royal Television Society nomination for Best Production Design. The second series garnered six BAFTA nominations, while *The Silver Chair* was nominated for five BAFTAs, although neither series won any.

For many years the only version available on DVD was through BBC America, although a four-disc edition, including some short interviews and contemporary reportage, is now on sale worldwide. The mix of two-dimensional effects and live action does occasionally make the stories resemble Disney's *Bedknobs and Broomsticks*, but without a budget to spend on computer graphics, these four chronicles provided a visual interpretation of Narnia that remains in the memory alongside the Pauline Baynes illustrations.

2

NARNIA ON AUDIO

There are many recordings of the Chronicles of Narnia, the majority of which are straight renditions of the text. In the days of gramophone records, the stories needed to be abridged to fit the available time, and one-hour versions were released between 1978 and 1981 by Caedmon of New York (and later reissued by HarperAudio). These featured Ian Richardson reading *The Lion, the Witch and the Wardrobe* and *The Silver Chair* (Richardson maintained a link with Narnia: one of his last recordings was of Brian Sibley's book about Lewis, *Shadowlands*); Claire Bloom covering *The Magician's Nephew* and *Prince Caspian*; Anthony Quayle reading *The Horse and His Boy* and *The Voyage of the Dawn Treader*; and Michael York, who went on to read unedited versions of some of Lewis's non-fiction work, performing *The Last Battle*. Two-hour editions of all the stories, read by Sir Michael Hordern, were first released in 1980, abridged by Harvey Usill, with music by Marisa Robles.

With the advent of CDs, unedited versions became possible,

and there are a number of different recordings now to choose from. The most commonly available see Sir Kenneth Branagh tackling *The Magician's Nephew*; Michael York with *The Lion, the Witch and the Wardrobe*; Alex Jennings reading *The Horse and His Boy*; Lynn Redgrave performing *Prince Caspian*; Sir Derek Jacobi taking *The Voyage of the Dawn Treader*; Jeremy Northam in *The Silver Chair*; and Sir Patrick Stewart going beyond another final frontier in *The Last Battle*. (The cassette version of Andrew Sachs reading this is also worth seeking out.)

The first dramatization of the Chronicles was authorized by Jack Lewis himself. He had been in correspondence with BBC Radio producer Lance Sieveking for many years – they had discussed a radio version of *The Screwtape Letters* (see chapter 5 of this section) – and after Sieveking retired from the BBC in 1956, they met to discuss a possible adaptation of *The Lion, the Witch and the Wardrobe*. This initial discussion on 5 September 1957 led, two years later, to a six-part serial, penned by Sieveking, which was broadcast in forty-minute episodes during *Children's Hour* on the BBC Home Service (the forerunner of Radio 4) between 18 September and 23 October 1959. Glyn Dearman (Tiny Tim in the Alastair Sim version of *Scrooge*) played Peter; Carol Marsh (Rose from the Richard Attenborough *Brighton Rock* movie) was Susan; Jean England was Edmund; and Ann Totten, Lucy. Daniel Day-Lewis's mother Jill Balcon was the White Witch, and *Children's Hour* regular Preston Lockwood was Mr Tumnus. Perhaps the most intriguing casting, looked at from a modern perspective, was Deryck Guyler – now best known for his comedy roles in *Please Sir!* and *Sykes* – as Aslan.

The reception to this was clearly warm enough that Sieveking considered working on a second story, *The Magician's Nephew*, and scribbled Jack's phone number on the congratulatory letter he received from the author about the first serial. However, this never came to fruition.

* * *

The next version took nine years to complete, although there was a six-year gap between the first two stories and the rest of the Chronicles. Veteran radio scripter Brian Sibley, who had turned J. R. R. Tolkien's *The Lord of the Rings* trilogy into an epic twenty-six-part audio adventure for BBC Radio 4 in 1981, was assigned the job of adapting the books.

'I had been writing quite a lot for Schools Radio, mainly for the Religious Broadcasting department,' Sibley recalled in an interview for this book. 'Partly because of the success of *The Lord of the Rings*, Geoffrey Marshall-Taylor approached me and asked if I'd be interested in doing the Chronicles. I said yes because I'd always been a devotee of the books since I was a kid.'

Sibley had written a screenplay and subsequent book about Jack and Joy Lewis's relationship (see chapter 5 of this section), so was steeped in Lewis by that point. He was delighted to work on the stories, and began with *The Magician's Nephew* before adapting *The Lion, the Witch and the Wardrobe*. 'I was much criticized for doing that,' he noted, 'but I did *Magician's Nephew* first because Lewis had said the chronological order was the correct order.'

The stories were broadcast in a twenty-minute slot mid-morning between 14 January and 24 March 1988, using the format familiar to Schools Radio at the time: a narrator and actors. Veteran British actor Maurice Denham played the Professor, Digory Kirke, who then narrated the tales. 'He had a wonderful avuncular tone,' Sibley explained. 'I wanted very much to have Stephen Thorne play Aslan – he played Jesus and had done the voice of God for me in other plays, and of course he was Treebeard in *The Lord of the Rings*. He had a kind of authority, a gravitas, a humanity.' Thorne had already played the part once before in the 1979 Bill Melendez animated film (see page 211). Polly March had also played her character before, appearing as Mrs Beaver in the Westminster Theatre production a few years earlier; she was recommended to the producer by Sibley, who had worked with her on a play at Edinburgh about Edward Lear. She would go on to make regular appearances in the Focus on the Family versions a decade later, including a third voicing of Mrs Beaver.

Lucy was played by Camilla Power, who, coincidentally, would play Jill Pole in the BBC TV production of *The Silver Chair* a couple of years later. 'There weren't that many children around whose parents were mad enough to allow them to be involved with show business, and who had "RP" voices,' Power recalled, referring to the 'received pronunciation' speech that characterized 'BBC English'. 'I had an RP old-fashioned-sounding voice, so I used to get quite a lot of things like Victorian children when I was young. It was my first radio, and such fun – radio always is, because you don't have to get dressed up. It was like having a big play, and we had these great actors coming in.' Some footage that was filmed at the recording at BBC Radio's base at Langham Place in London featured in the documentary *Past Watchful Dragons*, which preceded the BBC TV *Chronicles of Narnia*.

Although Sibley and Marshall-Taylor were ready to continue with *The Horse and His Boy*, Schools Radio didn't order any more. There may have been concern that the radio productions were clashing with the bigger-budget TV versions that began broadcasting later in 1988; Sibley was not made aware of the reason why no further dramatizations were commissioned. However, six years later, John Taylor, another radio drama producer, decided to return to the Chronicles. He and Sibley had worked on various projects together, including a version of J. R. R. Tolkien's *Tales of the Perilous Realm* in 1992, and they wanted to start again from scratch with a new recording of *The Magician's Nephew*.

However, Sibley recalled, 'the BBC were a bit parsimonious – they said that they'd got the other two already.' This was a bit of a problem since the earlier serials were not of the same production quality. Although more had been spent on them than on the average Schools Radio drama, the budgets were not as great as ordinary Radio 4 productions, and the text had been abbreviated in places to fit into the slots available. Sibley had also wanted to 'have the same kids as the kids throughout' but that wouldn't be possible after such a gap.

'We did try to persuade the BBC to do them again, but they weren't having it,' Sibley explained. 'The first two were re-edited into half-hour episodes to fit the Radio 4 format, and then we started on *The Horse and His Boy*.'

Rather than be narrated by the Professor (who couldn't feasibly have known what was going on, if he were to remain in character), the story of *The Horse and His Boy* was related by the Narnian talking horses, played by Martin Jarvis (who played King Lune in the Focus on the Family version of this story a few years later) and Fiona Shaw. Sibley moved away from Lewis's structure for this story, counterpointing the ongoing storylines, rather than following one through to a cliffhanger and then returning to bring the other characters to the same point. He also faced a problem with the portrayal of the Calormenes in the story:

'We were very conscious of not wanting to give the people in Tashbaan a comic Arabian Nights-type accent, not making them too ethnic. I think the people were just characters, they weren't cast in anything that might be representative of the Muslim religion. We were making it a time when we could be accused of making racial stereotypes, so we were very careful to keep it on the level of "good guys and bad guys" rather than "good guys and bad black guys". I played that element down, and cut down a lot of the high language to try and make it seem less a parody of another religion.'

For the Chronicles from *Prince Caspian* onwards, Sibley had to tell the story without the benefit of a narrator. 'John pressed me very heavily to abandon the narrator format, because he thought it was passé and old style,' Sibley noted. 'But this was a huge challenge for me as a dramatist at the time, because you always had the narrator as the Voice of Authority to tell you where you were and what was happening.

Descriptions are hellishly difficult if you don't have a narrator, and you always lose something of the authorial voice. But that was John's remit.'

Taylor was a great believer in bringing in 'star names' for the cast. Robin Bailey took on a small role in *The Voyage of the Dawn Treader*; former *Doctor Who* Sylvester McCoy played Reepicheep, and happily came in to record his short scene for *The Last Battle* to ensure the continuity of the casting. Shift and Puzzle, the two key characters from the last book, were portrayed by John Sessions and Timothy Spall, while Bernard Cribbins, beloved by British audiences as Mr Perks in *The Railway Children*, 'was fantastic as Puddleglum in *The Silver Chair*. He had that wonderful downtrodden attitude, but with just a bit of hope. He was really engaging.'

There was a noticeable shift in quality between the first two and the remaining five Chronicles – as heard in the Schools' versions, Aslan's roar isn't exactly the most inspiring thing ever heard, for example – but Sibley was faithful to the details in Lewis's text. He might abbreviate in places, but characters such as the robin in *The Lion, the Witch and the Wardrobe* whom the children follow were retained.

His few additions were mainly there to deal with the absence of a narrator: 'In *Prince Caspian*, I created a prologue where the children go to visit the Professor, talking about trying to get back into Narnia. I was able to re-establish the Professor, and did one or two things like that to put things into context.' One addition, though, might make a listener query what's going on: at the start of *The Silver Chair*, Sibley counterpoints events in Narnia during Caspian's reign (mentioned by Lewis throughout the story) with a conversation between Lucy, Edmund and Eustace wondering what happened to Caspian after the *Dawn Treader* returned home. This included the Pevensies explaining how time moves differently in Narnia. However, when Eustace arrives in Narnia and meets the older Caspian, he comments that he hasn't thought about the time difference.

Occasional omissions were noted by Lewis scholars – only one vision for instance in the Book of Spells that Lucy looks at in *Dawn Treader*, or a shortened conversation between Aslan and Jill on the cliff at the start of *The Silver Chair* – but these don't disturb the flow of the piece.

The Horse and His Boy premiered 4–25 September 1994; *Prince Caspian* followed 18 June to 9 July 1995; *The Voyage of the Dawn Treader* was broadcast 4–25 September the same year. *The Silver Chair* debuted from 15 September to 6 October 1996, and the series concluded with *The Last Battle* from 2–23 March 1997. All were released singly, as well as in a box set; two special editions of the collection were available at different times, one with artwork by Andrew Skilleter, and the other in a 'wardrobe' edition that included a booklet by Sibley explaining the genesis of the productions.

Inevitably, homogenizing the stories to a two-hour length meant that some of them work better than others. Their synthesizer music scores also date them. However, they are still highly enjoyable and are well worth seeking out.

Rather surprisingly, though, if you hear *The Chronicles of Narnia* advertised on BBC Radio 4 Extra (the BBC's digital archive channel), it's not their own production that is being broadcast, since the BBC acquired the rights to other audio versions of the Chronicles. These were produced between 1998 and 2004 by the American Focus on the Family Theatre.

The adaptations are considerably longer than the BBC versions: most of them run to three hours or more, which allows for more detail. They were also given a bigger budget, so they have full orchestral scores and larger casts. Unlike the later BBC adaptations, these retain a narration throughout, read by distinguished British character actor Paul Schofield, although, ironically, this does sometimes slow the pace of the story down.

The Focus on the Family Theatre editions are worth listening to for the introductions to the stories provided by

Jack Lewis's stepson, Douglas Gresham, which in places are highly personal. There was close cooperation between the estate and the Focus on the Family group: following the success of the Chronicles of Narnia, Focus was authorized to do the first dramatization of *The Screwtape Letters*. The productions are broadcast on a network of radio stations as well as the internet – the Theatre took advantage of the release of the *Voyage of the Dawn Treader* movie to rerun their own version, cheekily pointing out that audiences could hear the 'more accurate' account of the story before they went to see the Michael Apted film. They are also available on CD.

The serials were recorded in London, with a cast of mainly British actors: David Suchet, best known for playing Agatha Christie's detective Hercule Poirot, voices Aslan throughout, giving a very different interpretation of the lion. Suchet adopts a very pronounced enunciating style, which the plays' producer explained would be consistent with the facial gymnastics that would be necessary for a lion to speak English understandably.

Many other veterans of BBC radio drama were involved. Wendy Craig appeared as Hwin in *The Horse and His Boy*, Bernard Cribbins played the Chief Duffer in *The Voyage of the Dawn Treader*, while Ron Moody took on the role of Puddleglum that Cribbins had portrayed for the BBC. Derek Nimmo was Glimfeather in *The Silver Chair*, while the key pair of Shift and Puzzle in *The Last Battle* were played by Victor Spinetti (who had been heavily involved with the 1979 animated TV version), and Andrew Sachs. Suchet's daughter Katherine was Susan, and his son Richard played Caspian.

The scripts were written by Paul McCusker, who also directed the plays. 'Adapting a book can be a thankless job,' McCusker explained in a 2010 interview. 'You're up against the expectations of those who have read the original work and expect you to represent it well. But you also have to deliver an engaging experience in a different medium that has its own expectations.'

The Lion, the Witch and the Wardrobe uses audio in an effective way that visuals simply couldn't to depict the return of the Pevensies from Narnia at the end, and there are various alterations to the original stories. In *The Voyage of the Dawn Treader*, a new character is added as the governor of the Lone Islands, Gumpas, gains a secretary, Rynelf Dilber (fans of American comics may recognize a possible derivation of the name). In *The Silver Chair*, Eustace and Jill use Christian names throughout, rather than address each other by surname, as they mostly do in the book. In *The Horse and His Boy*, the Narnian council in Tashbaan is reduced in size, and the lines redistributed; McCusker deals with a minor plot hole in the book, as King Lune explains to Bree what talking horses like to do. *The Magician's Nephew* is embellished with an extra scene between Digory and his mother.

Working with a large cast did cause the producers some problems. The standard recording method was to have half-a-dozen microphones in the studio, erected in a semi-circle, with an actor standing at each. For the death of Aslan, though, they needed a crowd, and it was easier to have more people in at once than multi-track. 'The entire studio was filled with people – twenty-five or thirty people,' McCusker recalled. 'Everything was miked just right, Paul directed the performance, and it was magic – and all of a sudden we looked over at the machine that was recording and it had stopped. We didn't know where it had stopped. In a take like this where everyone is overlapping you can't just cut in. You have to get everything in one take.'

The extended running time certainly allows these productions to go into detail that was not possible in the earlier versions. Occasionally, though, the listener might wonder if maybe a few more judicious cuts might have been made to the narration, but these present an equally valid dramatization of the stories.

3

NARNIA ON STAGE

'C. S. Lewis is one of the most amazing storytellers that has ever been and theatre is all about storytelling. His stories translate so well to stage – I think they adapt way better to stage than to film. Theatre is an ancient art, and Lewis had such an incredible ear for dialogue, he created such wonderful characters and really understands humour. He's a visual writer, so when you put his stories into plays, they're even warmer and funnier than when read.'

So says New Zealand dramatist and teacher Erina Caradus, who, a few years ago, wrote and directed her own versions of *The Lion, the Witch and the Wardrobe*, *The Magician's Nephew*, *Prince Caspian* and *The Voyage of the Dawn Treader*. These were staged to great acclaim in Dunedin, New Zealand.

She's one of the many writers who have adapted the Chronicles into a theatrical format. One of the earliest was Don Quinn, whose short, forty-minute production of *The Lion*, *the Witch and the Wardrobe* continues to be revived in the United States. Described by distributers Dramatic Publishing as 'a charming play about courage and the love of freedom', it doesn't tie the story to its original Second World War setting, noting that the time is 'the present'. It begins with the Professor addressing the audience, and explaining that his old house is haunted, and 'by persuasion of a charitable group which provides country vacations for city children', he has taken in four children as house guests. From there, the story progresses with Lucy entering the wardrobe and meeting Mr Tumnus, although they don't return to his home. The notes suggest that only four sets are needed – the Spare Room, the edge of the forest, the Beavers' cottage and the White Witch's castle – and a cast of fifteen.

The next non-musical version was also short, and is unusual in that it's written as a two-hander for a male and a female actor. Le Clanché du Rand's 1984 adaptation, which had an off-Broadway run during 2012 and 2013, is based on Peter and Lucy, who try to tell the story between them. The benefit of a lack of props and scenery is that the story isn't as limited as other stage productions, but it all gets a bit convoluted. As a review of a Winnipeg production noted in 2011, 'No matter how appealing the narrators are, it becomes hard to stay focused on someone simply reciting a story for an entire hour, even if they do attempt to physically re-enact some of the events. The complicated tale of fantastical Narnia begs for some more props and visuals. Things became particularly confusing when the pair attempted to portray four siblings amongst all the other characters.'

One of the most commonly performed versions was written by Glyn Robbins and first produced by Aldersgate Productions, Vanessa Ford Productions and the Westminster Theatre, which is where it was first staged in November 1984 before going on tours for four successive Christmas holidays. Like the Quinn version, this is set in contemporary times (one of the house rules established in the opening scene is that the children may watch television in the library only when the Professor is not working in there), and it's suggested that the Pevensies are in the country on holiday.

To indicate the odd movement of time in Narnia, the play begins by showing the events of the game of hide and seek as experienced by Peter and Susan, rather than by those who enter the wardrobe – so Lucy enters for the game, and comes out almost immediately. The same happens with Edmund and Lucy's trip. When they all decide to enter (to avoid Mrs Macready, an element often overlooked in adaptations), the story jumps back to Lucy's first visit and her encounter with Mr Tumnus. There are some nice touches throughout, particularly the very last scene, where the Pevensies realize that the Professor might know more about Narnia than he's let on. A cast of thirteen, with some doubling up, is required for this, which features a number of scene changes and lamp posts and wardrobes flown on and off the stage.

The other regularly performed version, particularly in the United States, is by Joseph Robinette, which was first produced in 1989. A sound-effects CD is made available to accompany performances in which 'all the memorable episodes from the story are represented' – and quite a bit is added. After an optional prologue set in the Professor's house, introducing the children (and neatly avoiding the need to involve the Professor as a speaking character), the action shifts to Narnia, and Robinette provides a long scene of exposition between Mrs Beaver, a centaur and a unicorn, followed by Fenris Ulf (the name used in the American editions for Maugrim, captain of the White Witch's wolf guard) reminding Mr Tumnus of his duties. Only after all that does Lucy tumble into Narnia, and when she returns to our world, we see Fenris Ulf arrest Tumnus before Edmund arrives. Such alterations continue throughout, as Robinette respects Lewis's text without restricting himself to the scenes that are shown in the book.

Erina Caradus decided to write her own version of *The Lion, the Witch and the Wardrobe* in 2003 because, 'There were too many things I wanted to change in the existing adaptations – I wanted a play which would bring the original story alive,' as she noted during an interview for this book. (Less seriously, she also commented that an advantage of writing the script herself was that, as the director, 'I can print the scripts out big and I can scribble all over them'!) Her adaptation of *The Lion, the Witch and the Wardrobe* follows the plot line as Lewis delineated it mainly because the story has a classic plot structure, unlike most of the succeeding Chronicles. 'Act One sees Narnia and the four children getting deeper and deeper into trouble and ends in the Beavers' home with Lucy's desperate statement, "Oh, can no one help us?" And Mr Beaver replies, "Only Aslan. We must go on and meet him. He's our only chance now." In Act Two, there are signs of hope that are all dashed when we reach the climax of the play and Aslan, on whom we pinned our hopes, is brutally murdered. But redemption does come, the Witch is vanquished and Narnia is renewed.' Caradus retains the Second World War setting, drawing more of her dialogue from Lewis's original than the majority of adapters. She wrote on the basis that 'nothing is impossible' and that she would solve any practical problems of the staging as she scripted and adjust these in rehearsal.

Caradus is one of the few writers to tackle the other Narnia stories. Glyn Robbins wrote a version of *The Magician's Nephew* that opened at the Ashcroft Theatre in Croydon, England, in September 1988. In keeping with his contemporary setting for *The Lion, the Witch and the Wardrobe*, Robbins sets this play in the 1940s. He also adapted *The Horse and His Boy* in 1990, which formed part of a tour of Narnia plays that went on for about five years. His first sequel, though, was *The Voyage of the Dawn Treader*, which opened at the Theatre Royal, Bath, in September 1986. Robbins provides a prologue for this, explaining why the seven Lords disappeared and underlining Miraz's treachery, but otherwise follows Lewis's text closely – although there are quite a few scenes where events happen off stage and are recounted to the audience (such as Aslan appearing to Eustace when he's a dragon).

In America, a version of *The Magician's Nephew* was written by Aurand Harris in 1984, with a touring version following ten years later. In his notes, Harris points out: 'This is a play with a serious theme, but the production should also be directed to highlight the dramatic climaxes, the scenes of physical and lyrical beauty and the humorous moments of comedy.' Harris's version removes the flying horse from proceedings, and Digory is taken by magic to fetch the apple Aslan requires rather than on horseback. This was done to tighten up the plot – Harris focuses firmly on Digory's quest to cure his mother – and to prevent practical problems on stage.

Erina Caradus was determined to create a version that told the full story. 'Told well,' she noted, 'I believed this could be a powerful play.' She also set about solving some of the problems that were simply avoided in the earlier play. During Act Two, the cabby's horse Strawberry disappears behind a curtain, and a shadow image is used to show his wings growing. And while she too focused on 'the story of the choices of Digory and their consequences', far more of Lewis's original story is retained. She added Digory's mother into the play: 'I decided that Mother was a key character even though we don't meet her until the end of the story, so I set two scenes in her bedroom – the inert figure in the bed makes a poignant backdrop and makes Digory's grief more tangible.'

For her version of *Prince Caspian*, Caradus had to solve the problem of the book's odd structure: in Lewis's original, four chapters are devoted to a flashback related to the Pevensie children by the dwarf Trumpkin. 'I went with the book structure,' she explained, 'but I tried to converge the stories more. Once Trumpkin started telling his story, it blacked out. His voice continued, then the lights came up on the nurse with Caspian, a scene which Lewis didn't write.' Much of the first act featured new scenes which showed rather than told the story of Caspian's upbringing – Lewis presents a scene between Miraz and Caspian as a boy, but nothing more until he leaves the castle.

Caradus also reworked one of the oddities of the story: towards the end of the tale Miraz is betrayed by Lord Glozelle and Lord Sopespian, who are introduced only a few pages previously. 'You can't do that in a play without establishing them earlier,' Caradus noted, 'so I used them to partly fill out the earlier story.'

All stage versions need to have approval from the C. S. Lewis estate, and Caradus had few problems with them – even the extensive additions to *Prince Caspian* – until she reached her most recent production, *The Voyage of the Dawn Treader*. Douglas Gresham was keen that a lot of the dialogue with the Dufflepuds was used, particularly as it had been retained in the radio adaptation, but, as Caradus pointed out, that was for a different medium. After some discussion, the scene was pared back. Clever design of the *Dawn Treader* got round a number of staging problems: the ship, replete with huge purple sail and upper deck, was easily moved into different positions by the ship's crew, acting as stage hands. For the island scenes, the ship separated, sliding neatly into the wings, and new sets took its place. Unlike Robbins, she dramatized the curing of Eustace's dragon condition by Aslan, with his transformation into the beast forming the end of Act One.

The scripts for Aurand Harris's version of *The Magician's Nephew* and all of Caradus's adaptations make mention of the importance of underlying music – the notes to producers emphasize that officially sanctioned scores are available for hire. 'Theatre is an auditory experience,' Caradus said. 'Music conveys a mood: fear, sadness, despair, delight, tension. If it is used well, it won't be noticed, but the mood will be set for the audience and the actors. For instance, in *The Lion, the Witch and the Wardrobe*, not much is said before Aslan is killed, little is said when the girls cry over Aslan's body, nothing is said in the battle, or when the Witch walks with Aslan. But with music I can do justice to these scenes rather than skip over them.' Some adapters have chosen to take this one stage further, and create musical versions of the Chronicles.

The first was by British writer and composer Irita Kutchmy in 1982. First presented as *The Magic Land Beyond the Wardrobe Door* by Wimbledon High School in July 1983, it was published by Josef Weinberger, and is a very music-filled take on the book. Reviewing different musicals for schools in 1997 in *The Times Educational Supplement*, Tom Deveson wrote, 'The musical idiom derives essentially from jazz. It might seem surprising to hear a bluesy White Witch tempting Edmund with Turkish Delight or a funky Aslan warning against the sway of evil things, but it makes an effective change from more pious or even unctuous versions of the story.' Kutchmy doesn't miss an opportunity to provide a song for the various characters (there's even one teasing Lucy, which delays the main entrance into Narnia for perhaps a bit too long), and keeps the Second World War setting. It's more faithful to the book than some adaptations – the children are even hiding from Mrs Macready giving a tour of the Professor's house when they all hide in the wardrobe, an aspect hardly retained elsewhere, and they follow the robin to meet the Beavers. It's not been to everyone's taste (Michael Gray, reviewing a 2010 performance, called it a 'trite travesty [which] has little sense of style either in its words or its music') but for those looking for a version of the show suitable for younger children to perform, this may fit the bill.

A few years later, Jules Tasca (book), Thomas Tierney (music) and Ted Drachman (lyrics) teamed up to write their musical, simply entitled *Narnia*. First staged in Santa Maria, California, in 1985, *Narnia* is set during the Second World War, and moves the plot forward with various songs in time-honoured fashion. Tasca foreshadows Edmund's love of Turkish Delight in the pre-Narnia establishing scenes and sends Edmund and Lucy into the wardrobe for the first time together. This concertinaing of the story continues throughout, allowing time for the songs, which reflect the period of their composition, with what appears to be an homage to *Mary Poppins* in the number 'Wot a Bit a Spring Can Do'.

In 2002 a production began that was hailed by Douglas Gresham as one of the best versions of the Chronicles he had seen. The Philippines-based Trumpets Playshop production featured book and lyrics by Jaime del Mundo and Luna Inocian, and music composed by Lito Villareal. They too retained the Second World War setting, and sent Lucy and Edmund through the wardrobe together.

The show was praised by B. J. David, in a revival a few years later for 'the words of songs like "Open Doors" (the opening song) and "Beloved Narnia" [which] are just pure poetry. The non-musical lines also deserve attention, as they were packed with wit that has the audience giggling and chuckling.' The songs are described as 'a pleasurable blend of classical music, 1950s show tunes, and Christmas carols'.

The all-Filipino production had a very distinctive look: 'The two factions that are battling for Narnia are distinguished by what they wear: the minions of the White Witch have garments that are inspired by Japanese kabuki, giving them an exotic oriental air. On the other hand, Aslan and his fellow resistance fighters were clad in medieval costumes, evoking the ideals of chivalry.' Short excerpts can be viewed on YouTube and it appears to be one of the most joyful productions of the story.

Adrian Mitchell's adaptation for the Royal Shakespeare Company in 1998 also captures the joy of Jack Lewis's story. It establishes the Second World War setting, and there's a nice touch even before the children enter Narnia (which they do per the original book, in increasing numbers): the Professor has a painting of Polly and Digory on the back of Fledge – i.e. the Pauline Baynes cover for *The Magician's Nephew* – on the wall of his manor house. In his introduction aimed at children, Mitchell notes, 'I promise that I've been very faithful to the book and its characters. I've had to invent one short scene, cut a few speeches and replace some descriptions with songs or dialogue.' The resulting show is very recognizably Lewis – Douglas Gresham is credited as 'Narnia consultant', which partly explains its fidelity – although the songs, with music by Shaun Davey, are not the show's strongest part ('a pleasantly forgettable collection of medieval-influenced melodies', said the *What's On Stage* reviewer in 1999). In the first run, Richard Dempsey returned to the role of Peter Pevensie, which he had played in the BBC productions a decade earlier.

Two productions of *The Lion, the Witch and the Wardrobe* opened in the summer of 2012 on opposite sides of the Atlantic, both taking a similar approach to the creation of the inhabitants of Narnia. In Washington, DC, Washington Ballet teamed up with Inspiration Stage for a show in which each character was represented both by a dancer and an actor, while in London's Kensington Gardens, threesixty° presented a production that used every inch of a huge circular tent to portray the action.

The concept behind the American show came from Kathryn Chase Bryer, David Palmer, Janet Stanford and Septime Webre; Stanford directed and wrote the libretto, with some additional lyrics by Bari Biern, and the music was by Matthew Pierce. Although the idea of a ballet based on *The Lion, the Witch and the Wardrobe* wasn't new, Stanford brought an extra dimension to it. She was inspired by seeing the British National Theatre's production of Michael Morpurgo's *War Horse*, in which the titular equine is played by a giant puppet. 'I just thought, every child should get to see this giant puppet,' she told the *Washington Post*. 'I didn't want to see a guy in tights trying to be Aslan.'

Stanford contacted puppet designer Eric Van Wyk, who built a nine-foot-long, eight-foot-tall lion, which had thirty moving parts controlled by three puppeteers, based on observations of real lions as well as paintings by Peter Paul Rubens and drawings by Arthur Rankin. Design and construction took 180 hours with the build only completed shortly before the show opened in June. It was described as 'an eight-foot-high, flame-coloured kitten romping majestically through zero gravity'.

Portraying elements with ballet and puppets gave the production more scope: earlier sequences featured puppet Luftwaffe planes, and dancers mimicking a locomotive alongside the song 'Goodbye' to set the Second World War scene. The friendship between Tumnus and Lucy was shown as a pas de deux between the pair while an elf was used to demonstrate the glee that all Narnians felt as the Witch's power recedes.

A series of videos showing rehearsals were posted on YouTube, and reviewing the performance, Celia Wren wrote, 'Theater, as an art form, is a lot like Lucy's wardrobe. As an audience member, you enter a confined space, only to discover – if you're lucky, as you are here – a world of emotion and vivid excitement.'

David Suchet, who played Aslan in the Focus on the Family Theatre radio versions of the Chronicles, returned to the role for the threesixty° show in London. This was adapted for the stage by Rupert Goold, and directed by Goold and Michael Fentiman with music, lyrics and sound score by Adam Cork. The threesixty° company puts on its performances in a specially created circus tent that allows scenes to be portrayed on the 'walls' as well as on the twelve-foot-square central stage.

Like the Washington production, the show took its visual cue from *War Horse*, with giant puppets representing many of the creatures, and the 'circus' roots of the venue gave the producers latitude to include such things as bungee jumping and trapeze work. The whole show had a feel of a mixed heritage: Goold noted that the Lewis estate didn't want it to be a 'specifically Christian show', and production designer Tom Scutt included elements of Inuit, Maori and Philippines culture in the look of the show. Visual effects projected onto the roof of the tent were very useful in widening the scope of the production, and instruments played live on stage (accompanied by a pre-recorded orchestral score) helped to bring Narnia alive.

Unlike with many versions, Goold and his team didn't use child actors to portray the Pevensies, partly because of the restricted hours children are allowed to work, and also because the show depicts them growing up. They chose young adults 'because they sit either side of childhood and maturity. I'm not sure twelve- or thirteen-year-olds could deliver that sort of quality,' he commented in one of the production videos.

Goold commented wryly that the estate queried any changes that they made to Lewis's storyline, and it is comparatively faithful – the reasons for entering the wardrobe are altered (the final time is after Lucy has had a nightmare about Mr Tumnus being arrested, and believes she can hear sounds from it). In its own way, this was Narnia portrayed on as wide a canvas as the Walden Media movies.

In addition to various musical interpretations of the Chronicles, including the pieces composed to accompany the different ballets, and songs from Christian rock groups such as Second Chapter of Acts' 1980 album *Roar of Love* (subtitled 'A Musical Journey into the Wonder of C. S. Lewis's Narnia'), which takes the story into rock-opera territory, there has also been an opera. The libretto was by Gerald Larner, with music by John McCabe, and it was first produced in Manchester Cathedral as part of the 1969 Cathedral Arts Festival. McCabe later arranged movements from it into an orchestral suite.

The seventy-five-minute work condenses the story, getting into Narnia quickly, and depicting the destruction of Mr Tumnus's cave. Edmund's lies about visiting Narnia are removed (since there are no scenes outside Narnia), and to fit the operatic structure, with repetitive phraseology and counterpointing words and music, Larner has expanded Lewis's dialogue. It concludes with the children returning through the wardrobe by choice straight after the conquest of the Witch rather than growing older in Narnia and then following the white stag.

The other Chronicles haven't been as inspirational to composers: one version given a one-off performance licence by the Lewis estate was penned by American composer Kevin Norberg. His adaptation of *The Voyage of the Dawn Treader* grew from a college production that was originally intended as a straight stage play.

Looking back thirty years, Norberg recalled that composing the piece was a 'great introduction to Narnia. Eustace as a character begs for great stuff – I composed more for him than for Lucy. Lucy to me was an Everyman, us inserted into the story. I tried to take her point of view from the separation from Aslan, not connecting with him. I composed a piece called "Lucy's Prayer" – her prayer to Aslan. That was a good metaphor for what it's like for a believer to pray and not have your prayers heard, and then break through.'

Norberg adapted the original script into a stage musical, adding seventeen songs throughout, which were contemporary Broadway style 'with a little Gilbert and Sullivan in there', notably in a song between Eustace and Caspian called 'Break the Rules'. His song for Eustace when he's turned into a dragon, 'I Can Fly', formed the lead into the act break.

Rupert Goold's view of working on Narnia seems to sum up the situation for an adapter best: 'I wanted to make an adaptation and a stage presentation that was faithful to what I remembered, but perhaps more importantly to create a production that would be faithful to as many other people as possible's ideas of Narnia.'

4

NARNIA ON FILM

'I just went to the estate and said, "Let us do this faithful and let us do this right." Thankfully they entrusted us to do it.' Producer Perry Moore may have telescoped a considerable period of negotiation in that comment to journalists shortly before the first of the Narnia cinema films opened in 2005, but he summed up the ethos that finally persuaded the C. S. Lewis estate to grant cinema rights. Although it's often claimed that the movies were only agreed because of the success of the *Harry Potter* and *Lord of the Rings* film franchises, Moore was already in talks before the first of those reached cinemas.

Moore wasn't the first person to go after them. Frank Marshall and Kathleen Kennedy, who worked with George Lucas and Steven Spielberg on some of the epic movies of the 1980s and 1990s, tried to gain the rights, but their intention to make the scenes in our world set in contemporary times, rather than during the Second World War, fell foul of the estate's desires. Douglas Gresham was more enamoured with the approach made by Moore on behalf of Walden Media, and in 2001 a joint press release from the C. S. Lewis company and Walden announced that a live-action movie of *The Lion, the Witch and the Wardrobe* was on the way. A rolling option on all seven books was agreed: if both sides were happy, then all the Chronicles could appear over the space of a few years.

'It has been our dream for many years not simply to make a live-action version of *The Lion, the Witch and the Wardrobe*, but to do so while remaining faithful to the novel,' Gresham said. 'We are delighted to make this film with Walden Media, which we are confident will create the adaptation that my stepfather would have wanted.'

Moore prepared a mission statement for anyone working on the movie who might be concerned about its potentially limited appeal. 'It's a wonderful, great messiah story, not unlike *Star Wars*, not unlike *The Matrix*. If you want to see something more in it, we're doing a movie that's a faithful adaptation of the book, that's there for the people who want to see it. But we're making a movie for everyone, because that book and that story is for everyone. It's not for one group, it's for everyone.'

New Zealander Andrew Adamson, who had turned *Shrek* into a cinematic giant for Dreamworks, was approached to helm the adaptation. Like many others who have reworked Lewis's story into new media, Adamson 'set out not to make the book so much as my memory of the book. I realized in reading the book as an adult that it was kind of like the house that you grew up in, much smaller than I remembered. I wanted to catch the more epic story that I remembered, which I think was expanded by my experiences over thirty years, by the fact that I had read all seven books, and that the world had actually been expanded by C. S. Lewis when writing all seven books.' This desire to create an epic was to lead to some of the more controversial changes to the second book filmed, *Prince Caspian*.

Moore and Adamson were aware that certain elements

would need tackling. The director got into some serious discussions with Douglas Gresham over what he perceived as a sexist attitude displayed by Father Christmas, when he gives weapons to Lucy and Susan but doesn't want the girls to use them because 'battles are ugly when women fight'. He pointed out to Gresham that Jack's female characters became stronger after Lewis met Gresham's mother (the early Narnia tales were written before Joy had penned her first letter to Jack) and they compromised on a line about battles being ugly affairs. The battle scene was also magnified considerably from the 'flashback' scene in the book (the focus of the novel is on Aslan and the two girls, rather than the fight) with Adamson taking advantage of the menagerie of creatures that would be involved, with birds, griffins, centaurs and phoenixes all caught up in the melee.

Four British children were cast as the Pevensies: William Moseley as Peter; Anna Popplewell was Susan; Skandar Keynes played Edmund; and Georgie Henley beat off competition from 2,000 other young girls to portray Lucy. The decision was taken to film as much of the movie in chronological order as possible partly for a very practical reason: the four children cast as the Pevensies were still growing. 'There was nothing I could do about that even though we joked about getting Skandar to start smoking,' Adamson recalled. 'He grew six inches from when I cast him to when we finished the film. But also within the story, Narnia does make you more mature. It does make you grow emotionally, and I wanted to portray that physically so even at the beginning I sort of planned in particular with William, keeping him out of the sun, letting him be a sort of soft British schoolboy and then as we got into the production, getting him out training with the stunt guys, getting him out horse riding, getting him out in the sun, and letting him actually physically mature on screen. So shooting chronologically allowed me to get the benefit of both those things.'

Pre-visualization – preparing storyboards and animating

sequences to test how they will look – and preparation of weaponry by Weta Studios got under way in March 2002, more than two years before the live-action filming began on 28 June 2004. Scenes were filmed in New Zealand, England and the Czech Republic for eight months across seventy-five different sets, under the codenames 'Hundred Year Winter' and 'Paravel' to try to prevent too much disruption from visiting members of the public. Filming concluded in February 2005 before the major post-production work started, with the film set to open that December.

Little links to the rest of the Chronicles were included in the set design – the carvings on the wardrobe through which the children enter depict the story of *The Magician's Nephew*. Brian Cox was originally cast as the voice of Aslan opposite Tilda Swinton as the White Witch, but, according to Adamson, Cox graciously bowed out of the project when they both realized it wasn't working – the director believed that Cox was struggling with Aslan's 'lack of humanity'. Liam Neeson took over and found a vulnerability and accessibility that Adamson was seeking. Douglas Gresham can be heard as a radio announcer at the start of the film.

As well as expansions of existing scenes, the screenwriters – Ann Peacock; Adamson; and Christopher Markus and Stephen McFeely – added new material to Lewis's story. The film begins with a depiction of an air raid in London (which was also added into the stage versions created around the turn of the millennium), which the director felt was important both to set the Pevensies' trip to the countryside in context, and to help explain why Edmund was behaving as he did. Peter is also less commanding in the earlier scenes in the film, compared with the book. In common with many adaptations, the reasons for all the children entering the wardrobe are altered: rather than avoiding Mrs Macready taking a tour around the house, they are escaping her anger after Edmund destroys a window with a cricket ball.

Once they are in Narnia, stakes are magnified on more

than one occasion. The chase sequence, while very exciting, is rewritten; the wolves never get that near to the children and the Beavers in the book, nor is there a scene where they all end up in the water. Meanwhile, Edmund and Tumnus are imprisoned together, although they don't meet in the original until the end of the story, and Edmund's actions on arriving at the Witch's castle differ considerably. The character of the Fox (voiced by Rupert Everett) is also amplified. On the children's return to England, the Professor is there in the room when they tumble out of the wardrobe, holding the cricket ball, a scene that doesn't occur in the book, but which emphasizes how little time has passed. Markus recalled that most of the changes were made because the film 'needed more character than, frankly, the book had'.

Further changes were made for the extended edition on DVD, which ran just under seven minutes longer. These mostly consisted of slightly longer establishing scenes, and a reordering of other shots to compensate, particularly during the trek to join Aslan and the Battle of Beruna.

The film was deemed a financial and critical success, earning over $750 million before DVD sales were taken into account. It won an Academy Award for Best Make-Up, as well as two Saturn Awards (given to key films in the science-fiction-and-fantasy genre), and a BAFTA Film Award, receiving nominations for many others. Prestigious American critic Roger Ebert gave it three stars out of four, commenting that Aslan 'is neither as frankly animated as the Lion King or as real as the cheetah in *Duma*, but halfway in between, as if an animal were inhabited by an archbishop'. Peter Bradshaw, in the *Guardian*, felt it was a five-star movie: he couldn't 'see how it could have been done better.' He wouldn't feel the same about its sequel – an opinion shared by many, fans of both Jack Lewis's original writing and the first movie.

Interviewed during the promotional tour for *The Lion, the Witch and the Wardrobe*, Andrew Adamson wasn't sure if he would jump back in for the second film in the series, but after a break, he agreed to continue working with the four children for the Pevensies' last movie as a quartet. The script for *Prince Caspian* was already in the process of being written: if the same children were going to be used, then it would have to be done swiftly or they would have aged considerably more than their cinematic counterparts.

Although the production team had considered moving straight on to *The Voyage of the Dawn Treader*, the decision was taken to continue the Pevensies' adventures chronologically, even if that produced some problems with the scripting because of the nature of the original story. 'This film is probably a little darker and grittier than the last one,' Andrew Adamson admitted, referring to the considerable additions that were made to the story and the development of the background. 'I think the second story has a lot of what the first film had, but now complemented with some great action.'

Douglas Gresham – who seemed to become very defensive in interviews about the movie, even before it premiered – described *Prince Caspian* as being 'about a return to truth and justice after centuries of corruption. *Prince Caspian* started with a poorer story than *Lion/Witch*, but has worked out probably to be a better movie . . . The book doesn't have the power of the story of *The Lion, the Witch, and the Wardrobe*, which is based on the greatest story ever told. You can't really top that. *Prince Caspian*, when you look at it from a filmmaker's viewpoint, is a story basically about a long walk in the woods with a battle at the end. As a movie that doesn't really work.'

Returning screenwriters Chris Markus and Steve McFeely felt that removing the Pevensies from the action for long periods of time wasn't what a movie audience would want or tolerate. Accordingly, the children meet Caspian considerably earlier in the film than they do in the book, and an entire new subplot creating a triangle between Susan, Peter and Caspian was added. The writers felt that they had remained true to the spirit of Lewis's story, and were simply telling that tale 'in a way that allows you to sit in a theatre and watch it'.

Comparisons can be drawn between the book and film of *Prince Caspian* with the first Daniel Craig 007 film, *Casino Royale*, which was based on the book by Ian Fleming. A minor incident in the original spy story where a bomber blows himself up thanks to some sleight of hand by Bond, became a huge chase in the movie, culminating in the near-destruction of an airliner – and the bomber blowing himself up after similar legerdemain by 007. In Lewis's *Prince Caspian*, a raid on Miraz's castle is considered, and rejected; in the film, it becomes a huge action set piece, but the end result – nothing major is achieved – is the same. This love of spectacle haunts the whole movie ('we have to start epic and then get more epic', Adamson claimed).

Codenamed 'Toastie', *Prince Caspian* was filmed between February and September 2007 in New Zealand, the Czech Republic, Poland and Slovenia, with considerably more shot in the northern hemisphere than for the first film. The castle of Pierrefonds – which was just about to become transformed into Camelot for the BBC's twenty-first-century version of *Merlin* – was considered for Castle Miraz, but filming costs proved too expensive. Accordingly, the idea that the Telmarines, the race who have conquered Narnia in the 1,300 years between the two films, would look French was abandoned, and a more Spanish look adopted.

The four children returned, joined by Ben Barnes as Caspian, and Sergio Castellito as Miraz, who has a much larger role in the film than in the book. The animated Reepicheep, the Talking Mouse, was voiced by Eddie Izzard, with Aslan once again brought to life by Liam Neeson. Warwick Davis, the BBC's Reepicheep, played Nikabrik, while Trumpkin, the key dwarf, was played by Peter Dinklage, who would go on to great fame in the adaptation of George R. R. Martin's *Game of Thrones* sequence.

Prince Caspian didn't perform anywhere near as well at the box office as its predecessor, taking around $420 million against a budget of $220 million. It didn't receive the same acclaim either: while Roger Ebert again awarded it three stars, he queried a lot of the moral decisions behind the film. 'What responsibilities do the Sons of Adam and Daughters of Eve (how does that work?) bear for their own decisions, and the consequences of their actions, if everything can eventually be set right by some *deus ex machina* – the healing properties of supernatural potions, or the corrective powers of magic lion's breath? What becomes of free will, of *meaning* itself?' Peter Bradshaw in the *Guardian* made a comment that was repeated around the world in reviews: 'in my view some of the magic has gone'. Perhaps indicative of the market at which it ended up being aimed, it won a Teen Choice award, and composer Harry Gregson-Williams was honoured by his peers with a BMI award, but no other awards came, from considerably fewer nominations.

Andrew Adamson had already decided that he would not return to the series for the third instalment, opting to remain as a producer, and Michael Apted had signed on to direct *The Voyage of the Dawn Treader*, based on a script revised by Steven Knight. Pre-production began in October 2008 with a view to a May 2010 release. But just before Christmas 2008, a bigger obstacle to future productions appeared: the Walt Disney company, which had partnered with Walden Media to distribute the films, decided to exercise its option not to continue for 'budgetary and logistical reasons'. According to reports, Disney had indicated in March 2008 that it wouldn't continue past the original trilogy, unless *Prince Caspian* did particularly well at the box office. Disney denied these stories at the time, although producer Mark Johnson commented the following month that Disney had 'no plans' to be involved with a fourth movie.

As soon as the news broke, it was suggested that 20th Century Fox might step in to provide the necessary financing, and so it was to prove. In late January 2009, a $140 million production was given the green light.

If *The Voyage of the Dawn Treader* had continued as a Disney-distributed movie, then filming would have taken place in Malta, Iceland and the Czech Republic starting in early 2009. However, the change in company, and the allotted budget, meant that shooting did not start until 27 July 2009, and the company was based in Queensland, Australia.

Steven Knight had completed a draft script, building on a version by *Prince Caspian* writers Markus and McFeely. A new version of that was written by Richard LaGravanese, which was then reworked by Michael Petroni. This made some changes to Lewis's story, but nowhere near as many as had been eventually approved on *Prince Caspian*. After running times for the first two movies of over two hours twenty minutes, the emphasis was on maintaining the pacing and the audience interest; the final movie ran for 112 minutes.

'When I read the book I was alarmed,' Michael Apted admitted in December 2010 at the launch of the film. 'I liked very much the story and the tone of it and the colour of it and the imagination of it. [But] it was pretty clear to me that there was no drive to it whatsoever. It felt very episodic. That's catastrophic in a movie. You've got to have a reason in a movie to go from A to B to C, especially in a commercial movie. So that was a big problem.

'It took us nearly two years to figure it out. The way we did it was to look at the next book and see where that began and where *Dawn Treader* ended and to realize there was a complete chunk of the story missing. *The Silver Chair* is about Eustace going down underground to where captured Narnians have been preparing to attack Narnia and the Witch was down there organizing all this and Caspian was an old man.

'So what we decided to do was to take that piece of narrative, i.e. that Narnians had been kidnapped and taken somewhere no one knows, and use that as the driving force . . .

In fairness, Lewis had never written about it but had talked about the outcome of it. That helped us.' From comments that Apted made later in the press conference, it was clear that he knew there was no guarantee that *The Silver Chair*, or any other Narnia stories, would ever be filmed, and so he felt a certain justification in using these elements.

Eustace's transformation into a dragon and subsequent healing by Aslan were also modified. In the book, this is an incident on one of the islands, Eustace learns from his errors, and becomes a more useful part of the crew. In the film, he remains a dragon for considerably longer. A quest to find seven lost swords apparently vital to Narnia's safety was added.

All of the Pevensie children returned for the film – Peter and Susan are seen in cameos – and Ben Barnes reprised his role as Caspian. Will Poulter was cast as Eustace Scrubb, with Simon Pegg replacing Eddie Izzard as Reepicheep. Although there were plans to shoot part of the film in Baja, Mexico, concerns over safety led to the decision to base the production at Village Roadshow Studios in Australia. The *Dawn Treader* herself was built on a gimbal, which could be moved to simulate the movement on the seas, with a few exterior shots filmed along the Gold Coast. After shooting ended, Fox announced that *The Voyage of the Dawn Treader* would be released in 3-D, following the success of James Cameron's *Avatar*, and the process was applied during post-production.

After Disney hadn't made specific provision for publicity to faith-based groups on *Prince Caspian* (although they had done so on *The Lion, the Witch and the Wardrobe*), Walden Media were keen not to make the same mistake again, and in February 2010, they invited a hundred Christian leaders to a 'faith summit' in Los Angeles. Clips from the movie were shown, and the script analysed.

Producer Mark Johnson was humble about the situation: 'We made some mistakes with *Prince Caspian*, and I don't want to make them again,' he said, singling out the 'boys' action movie' sensibility which made it 'a little bit too rough' for families. It was imperative to 'regain the magic' that had been present in the first film.

Unfortunately, the box office didn't match the expectations. Although it took $415 million, its opening weekend was weak. It didn't trouble the major award ceremonies, apart from a People's Choice Award for Best 3D Live Action Movie. Roger Ebert maintained his tradition of giving it three stars, but noted that, despite Apted's efforts to impose a story onto the episodic structure, 'mostly what you have is a series of opportunities for special effects. The characters have characteristics rather than personalities, and little self-consciousness. They spring to the service of the plot, which, not particularly coherent, boils down to one damn thing after another.' Peter Bradshaw in the *Guardian* was even less impressed, awarding only two stars of a possible five. The film was 'a bit of a damp squib' which 'can't quite live up to its opening scene'. Certainly, it is the least memorable of the trio.

Michael Apted had said that he would be willing to return for a second film, and there were various reports during 2011 that the series would go back to the prequel book, *The Magician's Nephew*. 'We are starting to talk to Fox and talk to the C. S. Lewis estate now about *The Magician's Nephew* being our next film,' Michael Flaherty, co-founder and president of Walden Media, told the *Christian Post* in March. 'If we can all agree to move forward, then what we would do is find someone to write the script. So, it could still be a couple of years.'

However, the contract between Walden Media and the estate had expired by October that year, as Douglas Gresham confirmed in an interview with Middle-earth Radio: 'That leaves us in a situation for a variety of different reasons. We can't immediately produce another Narnian Chronicle movie. But it is my hope that the Lord will spare me and keep me fit and healthy enough so that in three or four years' time we can start production on the next one. We will, I hope, be able to start production and find another budget.'

In May 2012, Gresham gave a talk in Oxford in which he addressed the future of the franchise. According to him, there is a seven-year moratorium on any other producer than Walden Media making a movie, and that he hoped to see *The Silver Chair* next before the cameras, possibly with Andrew Adamson back in the director's chair.

Seven months later, in December 2012, Flaherty was interviewed by *World Media* magazine and he acknowledged that the Lewis estate, Walden Media and 'the studio' (Fox) were 'not all of one mind. I would love to find a way where the economics work, acknowledging the decline. I'd like to do *The Magician's Nephew*. Other people want to do *The Silver Chair*, and there's disagreement about the economics and the overall vision of where the franchise should go next. My hope is that we may all become of one mind, but unless something providential happens there, I'm focusing on a number of other stories.'

Whether a new production company would want to 'reboot' the series with a sure-fire success, and redo *The Lion, the Witch and the Wardrobe*, or continue the Walden Media Chronicles remains to be seen. What is pretty certain, though, is that the lion has not roared for the last time on the big screen – there just may be a rather longer gap than anyone had anticipated.

5

OTHER ADAPTATIONS

Although the Chronicles of Narnia have attracted the greater share of attention from those looking to mount productions of Jack Lewis's work, both the Cosmic Trilogy and *The Screwtape Letters* have been adapted over the years.

The first Ransom story, *Out of the Silent Planet*, has inspired various songs over the years, including an album by hard-rock group King's X in 1988 and a song by heavy-metal band Iron Maiden. Apart from a talking-book reading by Steven Pacey, broadcast by the BBC in twelve half-hour episodes, there haven't been any audio versions, and a proposed film, to be made by the team that created the animated *Watership Down*, never went beyond the discussion stage.

Perelandra, on the other hand, formed the basis for one of the more unusual versions of any of Jack Lewis's work, and one that he himself approved shortly before he died. This was an opera written by David Marsh with music by Donald Swann (who also set some of J. R. R. Tolkien's poems to music in the song cycle *The Road Goes Ever On*). In his autobiography, Swann talks of the pleasure he had working on the opera, 'which, symbolically, changed my career more than anything else'.

Marsh and Swann shared a love of the book, and in 1960 gained the go-ahead from Lewis's agents to write a setting. Swann wrote most of the music at his cottage in Suffolk, occasionally travelling to meetings with Lewis and Marsh in Oxford, where they would discuss the intricate details of the world that Lewis had created. Not all of the adapters' ideas made the final version: Marsh wanted to include a line about spiders eating their prey, but Lewis didn't think that was right for the world before the Fall. Lewis had his own suggestions for some lyrics for a duet between the King and Queen of Perelandra, but Swann was unable to make them work, so they weren't included – unfortunately, he didn't reprint them in his autobiography. One of their meetings early on was at The Kilns, from which Jack excused himself after an hour, explaining that his wife had died the previous night. Swann felt 'quite overcome' by Lewis's graciousness in such difficult circumstances.

Whereas normally adaptors try their hardest to retain as much of the original as possible, it became a 'point of honour' that none of the lines be lifted directly from the novel, according to Swann's official archivist, Leon Berger. Some of the structure of the novel was changed as well: it opens in Ransom's cottage after Lewis and Havard have been summoned to meet him on his return from Perelandra. While they wait, they come under attack from the dark eldila – the scene is inspired by Lewis's walk to the cottage at the start of the book, although he's on his own during that – before Ransom arrives back from Perelandra, and begins to explain, in flashback, what has happened to him on Venus. Marsh and Swann also added a scene with Weston in his space capsule on the way to Perelandra.

The completed opera was three hours long, and Jack attended a concert performance in Circencester in the summer of 1963, along with his friend Dr Havard, which, the author noted, moved him to tears. It was one of Swann's regrets that Lewis died shortly afterwards, and wasn't able to pass his ideas on to directors and producers.

Three concert performances of *Perelandra* were given in the summer of 1964 but received a mixed reception. The opera was described as 'largely pastiche with a strong whiff from the nineteenth century' by the *Times* critic, although the Cambridge Press praised its 'passages of stunning beauty'. Swann and Marsh revised the score, bringing it down to just under two hours, losing the first two scenes, and converting some musical sections into dialogue. This two-act version was premiered in America in 1969, with the *New Yorker* writing, 'It is unashamedly old-fashioned. It represents the Handel-Mendelssohn tradition, which is the tradition of most unselfconscious British music. A few dissonances appear from time to time to designate evil. But most of it is as innocent and sincere as Perelandra itself.' Swann recalled that two all-in wrestlers were cast as Ransom and Weston for one of the performances, which gave a verisimilitude to the fight between the two men.

To Swann's great disappointment, no further performances followed, after the rights were sold to Hollywood, although Marsh and Swann created a choral suite from the score in 1977, with assistance from conductor Jonathan Butcher. Towards the end of Swann's life, Butcher and Leon Berger worked with the composer on a third revision, reinstating some of the cut scenes. Concert performances of that were given in 2009 in Oxford, under the auspices of the Oxford C. S. Lewis Society, with two of the original cast reprising their roles from forty-five years earlier.

The scale of the story of *Perelandra* doesn't necessarily lend itself to operatic treatment: the planet's seas are covered in floating islands, and the Green Lady is naked when Ransom first meets her. Although it would seem more logical to approach it as an oratorio (i.e. a purely sung, rather than acted, piece, with narrative recitative), Swann produced a very varied score, much of which will come as a great surprise to anyone who knows him only as half of the musical comic duo, Flanders and Swann.

The movie version never materialized. An unabridged audio edition is available, also read by Steven Pacey.

Ransom's final battle is told in *That Hideous Strength*, which would seem ripe for adaptation. Although no television or film version has yet appeared (the idea of it was mooted with Jack as early as 1949), the book was serialized as part of the Classic Serial on BBC Radio 4 in 1990.

Adapted by Stephen Mallatratt into four one-hour episodes, it is remarkably faithful to Lewis's original text, incorporating chunks of the descriptive passages (which are credited to Lewis himself talking) into the narrative. Jane's nightmares are suitably horrific, and the Merlinian elements retained. Kathryn Hurlbutt played Jane Studdock, with Andrew Wincott as Mark, and Steve Hodson as Feverstone and Fisher-King/Ransom; the play was produced by Nigel Bryant, with music by Vic Gammon. If it should ever get repeated, or released on CD, it makes for enjoyable listening.

The Screwtape Letters have proved a rich source for other media. The first planned version came as early as 1949, when BBC Radio producer Lance Sieveking wrote to Jack to inform him that Revd Leonard John Bowyer was working on a radio version of the *Letters*. It seems from the correspondence that Bowyer's play would be set in a similar world to *Screwtape* (what Jack described as the 'Lowerarchy') and be the story of a man ruined by self-pity by the activities of the devils. However, it would not actually feature Wormwood and Screwtape, except possibly as a reference in passing. Jack specifically prohibited Sieveking from using the final letter within the play. No further reference is made to the play, which, if it did proceed, may have changed so considerably that Lewis's name was no longer connected with it. (Lewis points Sieveking in the direction of his publisher, who may also have had concerns about such a version.)

There are various audiobook readings of the entire *Letters* – the ones by John Cleese and Joss Ackland are both particularly enjoyable – but the first produced adaptation was James Forsyth's three-act play *Dear Wormwood*, written in 1961, which was later retitled simply *Screwtape*. The wartime setting is retained, and Wormwood's various temptations of the Patient (called Michael Average in the play) are dramatized. Forsyth altered the ending: rather than the Patient dying and being received into Heaven, Wormwood tries to beg forgiveness when it seems that his mission has failed. However, the play closes as he is being offered a fresh mission by Screwtape in his new position as head of Ad Vice advertising advisers.

A comic-book version of the *Letters* was published by Marvel Comics in conjunction with religious books publisher Thomas Nelson as part of their Christian Classics Collection in 1994. The script and layouts were by Charles E. Hall with inks and calligraphy by Pat Redding and colours by John Kalisz. This wasn't in standard comic-book format: it was more of a graphic-novel treatment, with the letters taking up roughly half of each page, with an appropriate illustration (either of the devils, or of the Patient) alongside. Lewis's own epigraphs for the book and his cautionary note appear on the back cover.

Actor Anthony Lawton adapted *The Screwtape Letters* for his Mirror Theatre Company in 2000. The company's motto is 'Spiritual Theatre for a Secular Audience' and their productions deal with spiritual life, but in a way that will entertain. His version of *Screwtape* is a ninety-minute two-person play, with Screwtape dictating the letters to his secretary Toadpipe. Between each comes a dance in varied styles including tap, Latin ballroom, jazz, martial arts, and rock, and featuring extras such as bullwhips and fire-eating ('the squeamish should avoid the front row', counsels one reviewer). Lawton has updated contemporary references with each production: in 2008, Dick Cheney was Screwtape's pin-up, replaced by Sarah Palin for a 2010 show.

Also regularly performed around the United States is Jeff Fiske and Max McLean's interpretation of the book for the Fellowship for the Performing Arts, described as 'devilishly good' by *Christianity Today*. Written in 2006, and expanded before its off-Broadway run in 2010, the play is set in a stylish office in Hell, with Screwtape dictating to Toadpipe – but in this version, Toadpipe 'transforms her elastic body into the paragons of vices and characters Screwtape requires to keep his patient away from the "Enemy",' according to the show's official website.

Focus on the Family Theatre, the producers of a complete set of dramatized Chronicles of Narnia, have also tackled *Screwtape*, but rather than simply using Lewis's text, they created a full-cast drama, with *Lord of the Rings* star Andy Serkis as the devil. Bertie Carvel co-stars as Wormwood, with Geoffrey Palmer as C. S. Lewis and Roger Hammond as Toadpipe. Philip Bird and Laura Michelle Kelly play John Hamilton and Dorothy, whose lives are led into temptation. The four-CD audio encompasses the story as set out in the *Letters*, but presents some very different perspectives: the book is told purely from Screwtape's side, but the drama, by its nature, is more inclusive. Douglas Gresham 'hosts' the drama and it would certainly make the basis of a very good movie version.

Rumours of such a movie have been prevalent for some years; at one stage, it was mooted that it would be produced as part of the deal encompassing the Chronicles of Narnia by Walden Media. However, since their option lapsed, it seems that Screwtape's devilish ways are still avoiding the big screen.

Anthony Lawton hasn't only adapted *Screwtape*. In 2006, he presented a one-man show based on Lewis's novel *The Great Divorce*, 'on a grey stage, wearing grey clothes, with a grey face'. He plays Clive, the narrator, as well as all the other characters whom he meets during his vacation from Hell to Heaven. Described as 'a feast of rich language, profound psychological insight, and humour', Lawton's drama has received wide acclaim. The Fellowship for the Performing Arts also acquired permission from the Lewis estate to prepare a version, expected to open in 2013.

According to reports in the Hollywood trade press in 2010, rights to *The Great Divorce* have been optioned by Mpower Pictures and Beloved Pictures, with Stephen McEveety attached to the production team, and N. D. Wilson adapting the book for the screen. The movie was meant to be released in 2013, and a first draft was completed by April 2011 – Wilson commented at the time, 'I'm as dog-loyal to Lewis and his vision as any writer could be. Where I'm adding and expanding and shaping, I am constantly trying to check myself against Lewis's broader imagination as represented in his collected works – not simply this little volume.' However no further updates have been posted. (An amateur Christian group did film the story and uploaded their version to YouTube.)

According to interviews from 1999, Lawton was considering adapting Lewis's last novel *Till We Have Faces*, but for unknown reasons didn't continue. An unabridged audiobook is available, read by Nadia May, but, like Jack's first fiction work, *The Pilgrim's Regress* (which can be heard read by Simon Vance), it has yet to appear in other media.

Although not written by Jack Lewis, one other story should be mentioned: *Shadowlands*, the account of his and Joy Gresham's relationship. The 1993 feature-film version, starring Anthony Hopkins, is the best known, but unfortunately the most fictional. The stage play from which that was drawn remains closer to the truth, but even the original TV play by William Nicholson, on which all the later versions were based, fictionalized elements of the story. The concept was derived by producer Norman Stone and dramatist Brian Sibley, and their version, which hued closer to the true relationship, was bought by the BBC and rewritten by Nicholson.

AFTERWORD: THE SEARCH FOR JOY

Throughout his life, Jack Lewis sought further instances of the elusive Joy that he felt when he was young. His journey from atheism through theism to Christianity was fuelled by this, and in the second half of his life, he used his literary skills to communicate this, both to those who had already joined him as a Christian, and to the vast majority who didn't have his understanding. It's impossible to read any of his work – fiction or non-fiction – and not glimpse the Joy hiding within their pages, sometimes laid out clearly, and at other times tantalizingly close but not quite within grasp.

Lewis has had a great effect on many people: not simply those, like Walter Hooper and Douglas Gresham, who have devoted their lives to promoting Jack's work, but people who have become involved professionally with the books. Carrying out the interviews for this book, I received the overriding impression that people have enjoyed reliving those times – in many cases twenty-five to thirty years ago – and more people than one have described it as the happiest time of their lives.

There has been a 'ripple effect' as well: although the idea of a 'magic door to another kingdom' wasn't new when Jack used it in *The Lion, the Witch and the Wardrobe*, it has become indelibly associated with him. The comparison is often made with the TV series *Doctor Who*, which began the day after Jack died; the doors of the Doctor's Police Box-shaped TARDIS are an entry into a world that, like the wardrobe, is much bigger on the inside than the outside. (The show has paid tribute to Jack both with a Christmas special which incorporated elements of Narnia in 2011, and an excellent comic strip, 'The Professor, the Queen and the Bookshop' by Jonathan Morris and Rob Davis.)

Of course, there are those to whom Lewis is anathema – not simply people who share Tolkien's opinion of the Narnia stories, but those who feel positively betrayed by the Chronicles. They feel that they have somehow fallen for Christian propaganda, and part of their childhood pleasures were retrospectively removed when they realized the sense behind the tales. Some, such as Philip Pullman, the writer of the *Dark Materials* trilogy, which culminates in a vision of a Republic of Heaven, go further. While noting that as a critic, Jack was 'very acute and full of sense and full of intelligent and sometimes subtle judgements', Pullman described the Chronicles as detestable, partly because of the exclusion of Susan in *The Last Battle*, but also because 'Lewis kills the children at the end. Now here are these children who have gone through great adventures and learned wonderful things and would therefore be in a position to do great things to help other people. But they're taken away. He doesn't let them. For the sake of taking them off to a perpetual school holiday or something, he kills them all in a train crash. I think that's ghastly. It's a horrible message.' Around the time of Jack's centenary, Pullman described himself as one of 'those . . . who detest the supernaturalism, the reactionary sneering, the misogyny, the racism, and the sheer dishonesty of his narrative method'.

Maybe the Chronicles don't stand up to scrutiny when looked at through the prism of a twenty-first-century society that doesn't always seem to be based on some of the precepts that Jack saw as essential (the Tao to which he refers in *The Abolition of Man*). But that Joy about which Jack was so fervent continues to draw people into the stories. 'I am almost inclined to set it up as a canon that a children's story which is enjoyed only by children is a bad children's story,' Jack wrote. 'The good ones last.' Long may they continue to do so.

ACKNOWLEDGEMENTS

Thanks to the usual suspects for their help with the preparation of this book, and to those who for various reasons were happy to assist, but didn't want credit.

Special thanks to:

Duncan Proudfoot and Becca Allen at Constable & Robinson for commissioning this third book from me – from spies to prison breaks to Narnia in a year has made for a fascinating time. Next stop, Oz!

Gabriella Nemeth, my copy-editor, who once again spotted where my mind was racing ahead of my typing and saved me from some avoidable errors.

Ian Howden-Simpson, my father, for the loan of books from his collection of Jack Lewis's work which he thought would be useful (and indeed proved to be).

Karen Davies, Nick Joy, Penny Locke, Una McCormack, Nancy Miles, Lucia Pallaris, Camilla Power, David Richardson, Adina Mihaela Roman and Paul Spragg for their help tracking people down around the globe

Tom Baker, Leon Berger, Jonathan Butcher, Erina Caradus,

Katherine Heasley, Kevin Norberg, Hiawyn Oram, Camilla Power again, Sophie Wilcox, and especially Brian Sibley for their time discussing their involvement with different versions of Lewis's text, where appropriate within the parameters of the confidentiality agreements that they have signed.

Revd Canon Rebecca Swyer for assistance on the apologetics.

Carol Matthews for stepping in to relieve some of the pressure of other commitments and Brian J. Robb, not only for reading through the non-apologetic sections of this book, but also for jumping on board another Inkling project to ensure it could proceed smoothly.

Lee Harris, Scott Pearson, Catlin Fultz, Clare Hey, Patricia Hyde and Iain Coupar for helping keep the normal work flow moving.

The members of All the Right Notes choir, ASCAT church choir and the Hurstpierpoint Singers for providing musical outlets.

New York Times best-selling author David Mack for agreement to use his quote for the epigraph, and John Van Citters and CBS Consumer Products for permission to do so.

As always, the staff at the Hassocks branch of the West Sussex public library, who helped track down some obscure items and were so apologetic when it became clear that a few had inexplicably vanished from the archives. The internet is a fantastic tool, but libraries are an essential service that we cannot afford to lose.

And last, but by no means least, my partner Barbara and my daughter Sophie. More than usual on this book, I've had to spend time in the office which would normally be spent with them, and I am grateful for their love and support. And of course, our two terriers, Rani and Rodo, who haven't been quite so understanding that playtime has been curtailed, but have still cooperated the majority of the time!

BIBLIOGRAPHY

20th Century Fox HomeE'ntertamment Blu-ray, *The Voyage of the Dawn Treader*.

AV Club, Neil Gaiman interview quoted at http://rollick.livejournal. com/423627.html.

BBC DVD, *The Chronicles of Narnia: The Complete Four-Disc Collector's Edition*.

BBC TV, *Past Watchful Dragons: C. S. Lewis & The Lion, the Witch and the Wardrobe* (1988).

Brodie, Ian, *Cameras in Narnia* (London: HarperCollins, 2005).

Christianity Today, 'A Narnia Without Lewis or Aslan' (6 December 2005).

Christianity Today, 'A Poorer Story, but a Better Movie' (8 April 2008).

Christianity Today, 'The War for Narnia Continues' (1 June 2001).

Christianity Today, 'The Weight of Story' (6 May 2008).

CHUD.com, 'The Coverage of Narnia part 1' (11 August 2005). Raw transcript of press conference with Andrew Adamson.

Daily Telegraph, 'Lion the Witch and the Wardrobe: Narnia in the park' (29 May 2012).

Gaiman, Neil, 'The Problem of Susan', in Sarrantonio, Al (ed.),

Flights: Extreme Visions of Fantasy (Roc, 2004), and *Fragile Things* (London: Headline, 2006).

Gospel Coalition, 'An Interview with N. D. Wilson on Screenwriting *The Great Divorce*', at thegospelcoalition.org/blogs/justintaylor/2011/04/28/an-interview-with-n-d-wilson-onscreenwriting-the-great-divorce (28 April 2011).

Green, Roger Lancelyn, and Walter Hooper, *C. S. Lewis: A Biography* (London: HarperCollins, updated edition 2011). Recommended.

Hooper, Walter, *C. S. Lewis: A Companion & Guide* (London: Fount, 1997). An incredibly useful source book for quotations from and about Lewis, although Hooper's accuracy on many of the adaptations is questionable. Where this book contradicts Hooper, it is from source documentation or interviews.

Hooper, Walter, *Past Watchful Dragons* (London: Fount, 1985).

Lewis, C. S., *The Abolition of Man*.

Lewis, C. S., *The Dark Tower and other stories*.

Lewis, C. S., *A Grief Observed*.

Lewis, C. S., *The Horse and His Boy*.

Lewis, C. S., *The Lion, the Witch and the Wardrobe*.

Lewis, C. S., *The Last Battle*.

Lewis, C. S., *The Magician's Nephew*.

Lewis, C. S., *Miracles*.

Lewis, C. S., *Out of the Silent Planet*.

Lewis, C. S., *Perelandra*.

Lewis, C. S., *Prince Caspian*.

Lewis, C. S., *The Screwtape Letters* (expanded edition via iTunes).

Lewis, C. S., *Selected Books* (including *The Pilgrim's Regress*; *Till We Have Faces*; *Letters to Malcolm*).

Lewis, C. S., *The Silver Chair*.

Lewis, C. S., *Surprised by Joy*. Quite rightly described as a thriller, this focuses on Jack's early life with some interesting lacunae.

Lewis, C. S., *That Hideous Strength*.

Lewis, C. S., *The Voyage of the Dawn Treader*.

Lewis, C. S., and W. H. Lewis, *Boxen: Childhood Chronicles Before Narnia*.

Longfellow, Henry Wadsworth, *Tales of a Wayside Inn*.

MacDonald, George, *Phantastes: A Faerie Romance* (Milton Keynes: Paternoster Publishing, 2008). One-hundred-and-fiftieth-anniversary annotated edition.

MacDonald, George, *The Wise Woman* (London: Strahan & Co., 1875; new edition, Whitefish, MT: Kessinger, 2004).

Malik, Ernie, *Prince Caspian: The Official Illustrated Movie Companion* (London: HarperCollins, 2008).

Narniaweb.com, ' "The Giant Surprise" Next Narnia Film?' (1 April 2011).

Optimum Releasing, *The Lion, The Witch & The Wardrobe* (2006 edition).

Oram, Hiawyn, *The Giant Surprise, A Narnia Story* (London: HarperCollins, 2005).

Patheos, ' "C. S. Lewis" – not a person but a brand' (30 October 2005).

Pullman, Philip, 'The Darkside of Narnia' (*Guardian*, 1 October 1998).

Sayer, George, *Jack: C. S. Lewis and His Times* (Hodder & Stoughton, 2nd edition 2005). Recommended for a view of Jack by someone who knew him.

Sibley, Brian, *Shadowlands: The True Story of C. S. Lewis and Joy Davidman* (Hodder & Stoughton Centenary Edition, 1998). A highly readable short biography.

Surefish, 'A dark agenda?' (November 2002)

Swann, Donald. *The Space Between the Bars* (London: Hodder and Stoughton, 1968).

Swann, Donald, *Swann's Way. A Life in Song* (Heinemann, 1991).

Bob Smithouser, 'A Return to Narnia' (*Thriving Family*, November/December 2010).

Time, 'Religion: Don v. Devil' (8 September 1947).

Wagner, Richard, *C. S. Lewis & Narnia for Dummies* (New York: John Wiley & Sons, 2005). Despite its title, this is a very good introduction to the philosophical and religious themes discussed in the Chronicles of Narnia, as well as Lewis's other work.

Walt Disney Studios Home Entertainment Blu-ray, *The Lion, the Witch and the Wardrobe*.

Walt Disney Studios Home Entertainment Blu-ray, *Prince Caspian*.

Washington Post, 'Imagination Stage and Washington Ballet's "The Lion, the Witch and the Wardrobe" ' (1 July 2012).

Washington Post, ' "The Lion, the Witch and the Wardrobe" production features majestic Aslan puppet' (14 June 2012).

Wilson, A. N., *C. S. Lewis: A Biography* (London: Harper Perennial, updated edition 2005). There seem to be numerous factual errors in this book, and unsupported assertions. Some of these are set out at http://cslewis.drzeus.net/papers/anwilsonerrata. html, although the author of this article herself is the subject of some controversy.

INDEX